100 GREAT CYCLE RIDES AROUND BRITAIN

100 GREAT CYCLE RIDES AROUND BRITAIN

RIDES FOR FRIENDS AND FAMILY FROM PLEASURE TRIPS TO CHALLENGING ROUTES AND SCENIC WONDERS

Contents

Introduction

We've had great fun at *Cycling Active* over the past few years finding good places to get out on our bikes all over the country. From pootling along the Blackpool seafront to challenging cobbled climbs in Yorkshire, we've done them all and this is a collection of the best.

The routes use cyclepaths, roads and lanes, bridleways, old railway lines and there's even a couple of trail centres for the off-road enthusiast. The regional terrains are reflected in the routes with some hilly routes in the north and in Wales, some flat ones in the East and some interesting urban routes in London and the South East. They're all rated for degree of challenge with the mileage and an idea of how many hills you're going to have to climb.

The maps detail the routes and point out some of the things to look out for on the way but make sure you plan your ride in advance and go well prepared with a more detailed map, particularly when there are lots of changes of path to negotiate.

I'm grateful to all contributors who have travelled up and down the country in the last few years to ride these routes. The information on refreshment stops and bike shops has been checked and updated for publication but with seasonal opening times in some areas and recession-challenged businesses in most, it would always be wise to check ahead before setting out.

There's nothing like getting out on your bike and these routes will help you enjoy Britain at its best, very often, off the beaten track and at a pace that allows you to take in the scenery and stop off to enjoy a diversion along the way.

Robert Garbutt, Editor
Cycling Weekly **and** *Cycling Active*

The Crab and Winkle Way, Kent

Distance: 15 miles (24km)
Big hills: none
Challenge: ●●☆☆☆

A mostly traffic-free, family-friendly ride from the cathedral city of Canterbury to Whitstable

Forming part of Sustrans National Cycle Route 1, The Crab and Winkle Way offers about 7.5 miles of mostly traffic-free cycling on dedicated paths between Canterbury, the historic home of the Anglican church, and the popular seaside town of Whitstable in Kent.

The route opened in 2000 and follows the original Crab and Winkle railway route and uses one third of the original track bed. In 1830 it became the first regular passenger rail service in the world and furthermore the line and the original locomotive, the *Invicta*, were engineered by the pioneers of steam railways, George and Robert Stephenson.

The route is well-signed throughout with the familiar blue Sustrans cycle route signs (Route 1). The Crab and Winkle Way starts at West Canterbury Station but this route starts at nearby Westgate Grove. Cycle through the alley at the end to Whitehall Bridge Road. At the end of Whitehall Bridge Road go left then right into Queen's Avenue. Bear left onto London Road past the front of the Queen's Hotel. Use the path to reach Fisher Avenue at the corner of St Dunstan's Park. Turn left along Westgate Court Avenue enter Duke's Meadow and climb up the path on right-hand side.

Enter Neal's Place Road then turn left on a path that runs alongside the main

---

Useful refreshment stops

Whitstable Fish Bar, 47–49 High Street, Whitstable CT5 1AP. 01227 771 411

Whitstable Oyster Company, Royal Native Oyster Stores, Horsebridge Rd, Whitstable CT5 1BU. 01227 276 856 www.whitstableoystercompany.com

Bike shops

Cycles UK Canterbury (hire available), Whitefriars Development, St George Lane, Canterbury, CT1 2SY. 01227 457956

Whitstable Cycle Hire (hire available), 56 Harbour St, Whitstable CT5 1AQ. 01227 388058 www.whitstablecyclehire.com

Downland Cycles, The Malthouse, St Stephens Road, Canterbury, CT2 7JA. 01227 479 643 www.downlandcycles.co.uk

Canterbury Cycle Centre, Stour Street, Canterbury CT1 2NZ. 01227 787 880

Herberts Cycles, 103–105 High St, Whitstable CT5 1AY. 01227 272 072 www.herbertscycles.co.uk

---

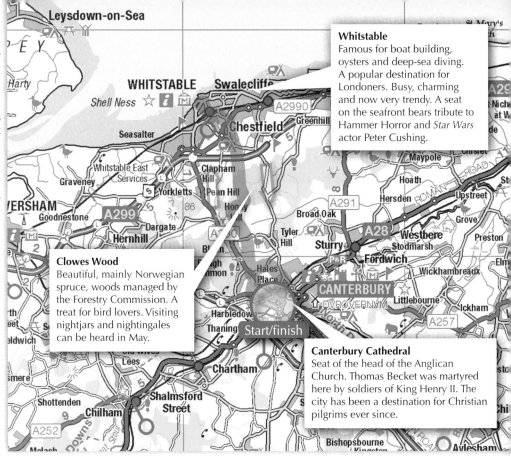

Whitstable
Famous for boat building, oysters and deep-sea diving. A popular destination for Londoners. Busy, charming and now very trendy. A seat on the seafront bears tribute to Hammer Horror and *Star Wars* actor Peter Cushing.

Clowes Wood
Beautiful, mainly Norwegian spruce, woods managed by the Forestry Commission. A treat for bird lovers. Visiting nightjars and nightingales can be heard in May.

Canterbury Cathedral
Seat of the head of the Anglican Church. Thomas Becket was martyred here by soldiers of King Henry II. The city has been a destination for Christian pilgrims ever since.

Whitstable Road until the beginning of the Crab and Winkle Way on the right. Follow the traffic-free path. After you have crossed the bridge over the New Thanet Way the path will end then begin again on the left-hand side after a short ride down South Street.

At Whitstable the path emerges into All Saints' Close. Ride down the close, turn right into Seymour Avenue then cross Old Bridge Road to Whitstable Station.

To continue to the coast, walk along the front of the station then down the steps on the right. Cycle along stream walk into Albert Street then Harbour Street to the beach at Sea Street.

Reverse the route for the way back. Take care crossing back to the cycle path from South Street as visibility is restricted.

For a different route, turn left at the end of the Crab and Winkle Way down Park Wood Road, across the top of the University of Kent campus. Turn right down Giles Lane through the campus, turn left then go straight across the roundabout onto the track/footpath alongside the playing fields. Emerge into Leycroft Close turn right into Beaconsfield Road then Forty Acres Road. At junction turn left and make your way down St Dunstan's Road and back to the West Gate.

Essex countryside

Distance: 34 miles (56km)
Big hills: 1
Challenge: ●●☆☆☆

Discovering the hidden
gems of the Essex
countryside: converted
barn houses, windmills,
16th century pubs
and picturesque
cricket greens

Once past the dense sprawl of North-East
London, the countryside changes
from urban parks and warehouses to
rolling countryside and farms. A bike ride

through these parts is very pleasurable
as the route wends its way up and down
quiet lanes, and the rider gets to see
country life at its best.

The route starts in the 16th-century
town of Saffron Walden – home of the
wealthy Gibson family, who conceived the
intricately decorated Bridge End Gardens
with its unique Turf Maze and the nearby
Fry Art Gallery. Along the main street
with its independent shops and boutiques,
there is a distinctly traditional feel.

Turn left out of the Eight Bells Café
and go up the high street. Turn left to
go through Purton End to Debden.
Follow the road through Debden Green
and Cutlers Green to Thaxted. At the
T-junction with the Swan Hotel turn
right and pass the Guildhall. Turn right
at the lights onto the B1051 towards
Broxted. Take the first left onto a single
carriageway road to Stanbrook. Follow the
single carriageway road to Tilty.

At Tilty Abbey turn right and follow
the road to Broxted Church End. To
approach the church gardens take the
small cut-through path on the right of the
T-junction. Otherwise turn left to reach
Broxted Brick End.

At the T-junction with the pub follow
the road towards Takeley and then turn

Useful refreshment stops
The Eight Bells, 18 Bridge Street, Saffron
  Walden CB10 1BU. 01799 522790
  www.8bells-pub.co.uk
The Cricketers, Clavering, nr Saffron
  Walden CB11 4QT. 01799 550442
  www.thecricketers.co.uk
The Swan Hotel, Bull Ring, Thaxted
  CM6 2PL. 01371 830321
The Cock Inn, Church End, Henham
  CM22 6AL. 01279 850347
The Axe and Compasses, Arkesden
  CB11 4EX. 01799 550272
  www.axeandcompass.co.uk

Bike shops
Newdales, 7 Market Walk, Saffron Walden
  CB10 1JZ. 01799 513980.
  www.newdales.co.uk

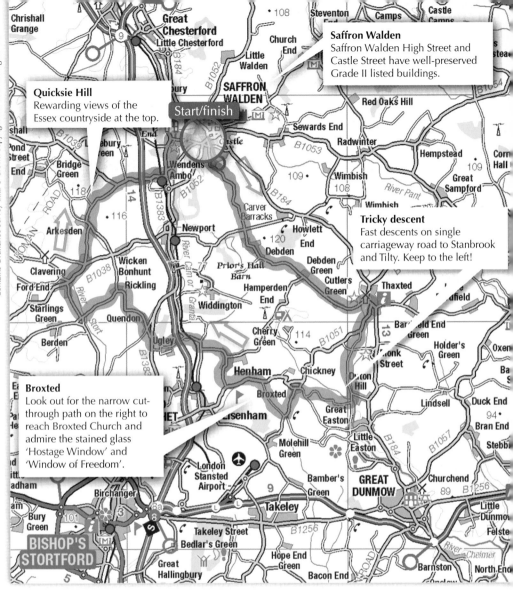

Saffron Walden
Saffron Walden High Street and Castle Street have well-preserved Grade II listed buildings.

Quicksie Hill
Rewarding views of the Essex countryside at the top.

Tricky descent
Fast descents on single carriageway road to Stanbrook and Tilty. Keep to the left!

Broxted
Look out for the narrow cut-through path on the right to reach Broxted Church and admire the stained glass 'Hostage Window' and 'Window of Freedom'.

Start/finish

right to head north to Henham, then follow the signs to Ugley. Go under the motorway to Ugley.

Turn right at the T-junction and ride briefly on the B1383. Take the first left to Rickling. After the village turn right to Wicken Bonhunt and at the T-junction take the B1038 to Clavering.

Turn sharp right at The Cricketers onto Clatterbury Lane to reach Arkesden. Turn right towards Saffron Walden and climb up the hill past the church. After the descent turn right into Wendens Ambo. Turn left briefly onto the B1383 and then first right onto Wenden Road back to Saffron Walden.

Chiltern hills

Distance: 18.9 miles (30km)
Big hills: 1
Challenge: ●●☆☆☆

An easy ride mixing the beauty of the Chiltern Hills with flat, traffic-free paths, bridleways and country lanes

From the Chilterns gateway town of Princes Risborough, access is gained to some of the most beautiful trails and lanes in the country. The heights of Whiteleaf Hill and Kop Hill both providing breathtaking vistas over the Vale of Aylesbury. This may be the Chilterns but a ride in this area need not involve hills, since a few routes can be done without challenging your gears or your thighs.

From the market square follow the sign for Thame. Follow Stratton Road to reach Manor Park Road. At the T-junction turn right and then left at the next T-junction. Go up the hill slightly and turn right into Picts Lane. Pass a few industrial buildings and at the T-junction turn right and go over the railway bridge, then right again. Go through the woods and then out into open fields. After crossing a single-gauge railway track, take the right-hand fork going up to reach the Phoenix Trail.

After five miles turn right onto a path signposted to Thame Town Centre. Go

down Moreton Lane passing a playing field. At the mini roundabout take the third exit and then turn left into Nelson Road. At the end of the road turn right. Go over a mini-roundabout and then take the left fork towards Chinnor. Take the second left into Queens Road, then turn right into Towersey Road (signposted to Lord Williams Lower School). It is a cul-de-sac but accessible by bicycle.

Useful refreshment stops

Anton Hazelle Chocolaterie Café, 40 High Street, Princes Risborough, Buckinghamshire, HP27 0AX. 01844 273993 www.antonhazell.com

Lashlake Nurseries Coffee Shop Chinnor Road, Thame, Oxfordshire, OX9 3QZ. 01844 212392

Time Out, 12 High Street, Thame, Oxfordshire, OX9 2BZ. 01844 260840

Red Lion, Whiteleaf, Princes Risborough, Buckinghamshire, HP27 0LL. 01844 344476 www.theredlionwhiteleaf.co.uk

The Birdcage, 4 Cornmarket, Thame, Oxfordshire OX9 3DX. 01844 260381 www.birdcagepub.co.uk

Bike shops

2 Wheels Thame, 99b High Street, Thame OX9 3EH. 01844 212455 www.2wheelsthame.co.uk

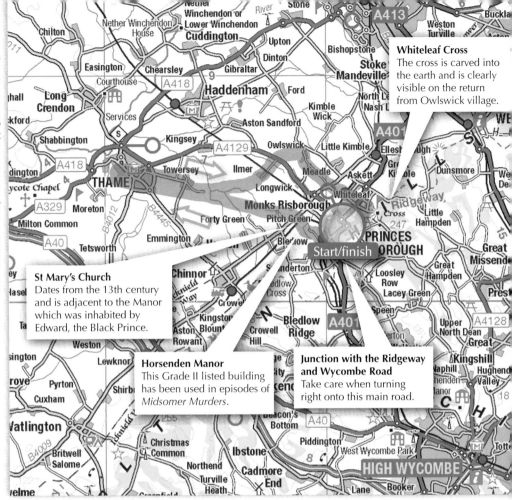

Whiteleaf Cross
The cross is carved into the earth and is clearly visible on the return from Owlswick village.

St Mary's Church
Dates from the 13th century and is adjacent to the Manor which was inhabited by Edward, the Black Prince.

Horsenden Manor
This Grade II listed building has been used in episodes of *Midsomer Murders*.

Junction with the Ridgeway and Wycombe Road
Take care when turning right onto this main road.

Continue straight over the main road to reach Towersey. When the road swings to the right and becomes Chinnor Road continue straight on along Manor Road which becomes a bridleway. Go through the woods and over a bridge. On reaching the field travel towards the church in Ilmer village. Go past the church and under a railway bridge, then cross the main road and follow the bridleway opposite until you reach the road in Owlswick and turn right. At the fork in the road bear left to Monks Risborough.

At the T-junction turn left and then immediately right into Mill Lane. Go down the hill through Monks Risborough. At the T-junction turn right and immediately left up the hill. As the road levels off at Whiteleaf Village turn right and follow the byway right to the end to reach the main road. Turn right onto the main road, and bear left after 50m (signposted for the railway station). At the crossroads go straight on and then right into Manor Park Road to retrace the route back to Princes Risborough market square.

Gatwick to Greenwich

Distance: 41 miles (66km)
Big hills: lots of ups and downs
Challenge: ●●●☆☆

A hugely varied day ride on off-road trails, cycle paths and quiet urban roads, from Gatwick to Greenwich

It's a long old route, this one, but there's one simple instruction: look out for the National Cycle Network Route 21 'Gatwick to Greenwich' or 'Waterlink Way' blue signs. That can be easier said than done, but with a bit of patience and preparation, it is perfectly achievable.

There are two particular points to take care at though: the first is when you cross the road after emerging from the first brief off-road section following Woldingham School. It's a blind bend and a reasonably fast road. The second place for caution comes at the top of the hill out of Addington Village. Again you have to cross the road on a blind bend.

Start at Evans Cycles' corporate headquarters, within the sight of the runway at Gatwick Airport. The NCR 21 soon takes you off the main road and onto a cycle track and a mixture of paths and road sections takes you to Horley.

Through housing estate cycle paths and countryside tracks you come to the urban expanses of Redhill. Then it's back onto a delightful bridleway and a chance to enjoy the fresh air of Mercer Country Park. The route takes you up the North Downs' muddy, forested slopes under trees and culminates in a viewing point looking out towards Kent, Surrey, the Sussexes and – on a good day – even the South Downs.

Another road section followed by a tree-lined track and then a smooth path through the rolling hills that hide Woldingham girls' school. Soon after a

---

Useful refreshment stops
The White Bear, Fairchildes Lane, Warlingham, Surrey CR6 9PH. 01959 573166 (pub well placed for a lunch stop on the route)
The Big Red Pizzeria, 30 Deptford Church Street, Deptford SE8 4RZ. 020 3490 8346 (convenient for a meal at the finish)

Bike shops
Evans Gatwick, Camino Park, James Watt Way, Crawley, West Sussex RH10 9TZ. 01293 574999
Mellow Miles Cycles (hire available), 67 Victoria Road, Horley, Surrey RH6 7QH. 01293 774486

---

gentle track runs adjacent to the fairways of Woldingham Golf Course and then cuts left, past the clubhouse and up a steep, rock-strewn climb.

Then it's the rabbit warren of roads that is New Addington where the NCN signs can be hard to find. From Addington Village, climbing up and inwards towards London, the route's former abundance of tracks through forest and field lose out to urban thoroughfares, and you zigzag between domestic streets. A green respite comes in the shape of South Norwood's pleasant country park, but then it's back to the asphalt.

The run-in to Greenwich though is largely on the Waterlink Way, a delightful course that steers from one park to the next, taking in a grand tour of South-East London's open spaces.

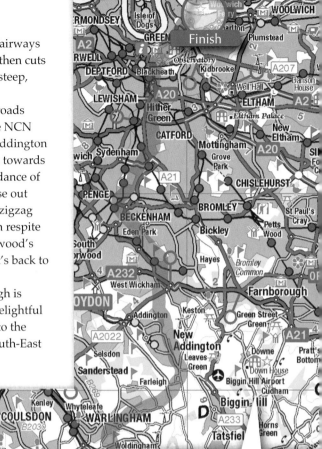

Biggin Hill Airport

In case you didn't get your fill of aviation back at Gatwick, this route passes within a whisker of probably the most famous WWII airfield: Biggin Hill. Now a hub for business travel, there are still some vestiges of its former life such as the unique RAF chapel, which is open all year round and features full-size replicas of the Hurricane and Spitfire outside its front door.

Mercer Country Park and Lake

Swapping pedals for paddles, there's no end of watersport options at Mercer Country Park and Lake, with canoeing, windsurfing and sailing all happening on the open water. For people with less active tastes, the park is also a haven for wild birds and other assorted wildlife.

Richmond and Hampton Court

Distance: 20 miles (32km)
Big hills: one steep, short hill
Challenge: ◑☆☆☆☆

A gentle meander along a historic section of the Thames and through London's largest parks

Hampton Court and Richmond are the crown jewels in a riverside route that's steeped in cultural history and has fired the imaginations of artists and writers for hundreds of years.

From Teddington Lock, take the Thames Path all the way to Barnes. Turn up Barnes High Street before turning right up Station Road. Continue past Barnes Green then turn right up Vine Road and straight on at the crossroads down Priory Road, entering Richmond Park via Roehampton Gate.

Turn left and ride the perimeter path clockwise until Richmond Gate. Ride past the Star and Garter to Richmond Hill Terrace and descend into Richmond via Nightingale lane. Cross Richmond Bridge and join the towpath to Twickenham.

Ride past Eel Pie Island and up Wharf Lane onto Twickenham High Street. Take the immediate left onto the A310 then turn right up Waldegrave Road until a T-junction with Teddington High Street.

Useful refreshment stops
Tide Tables Café, Richmond Bridge Riverside, Richmond TW9 1TH. 0208 9488285 www.tidetablescafé.com

Osteria Pulcinella, 36 Church Street, Twickenham TW1 3NR. 0208 8925854 www.osteriapulcinella.co.uk

Gelateria Danieli (Italian ice cream shop in a narrow street leading to Richmond Green) 16 Brewers Lane, Richmond, TW9 1HH. 0208 439 9807 www.gelateriadanieli.com

The White Swan, Riverside, Twickenham, TW1 3DN. 0208 7442951 www.whiteswantwickenham.com

The Anglers, 3 Broom Road, Teddington, TW11 9NR. 0208 9777475 www.anglers-teddington.co.uk

The Cricketers, The Green, Richmond TW9 1LX. 020 8940 4372

Bike shops
Putney Cycles (hire available), 337 Putney Bridge Road, London SW15 2PG. 0208 785 3147 www.putneycycles.com

Turn right over the railway bridge then immediately left down Park Road until Teddington gate of Bushy Park. Cross the park on Chestnut

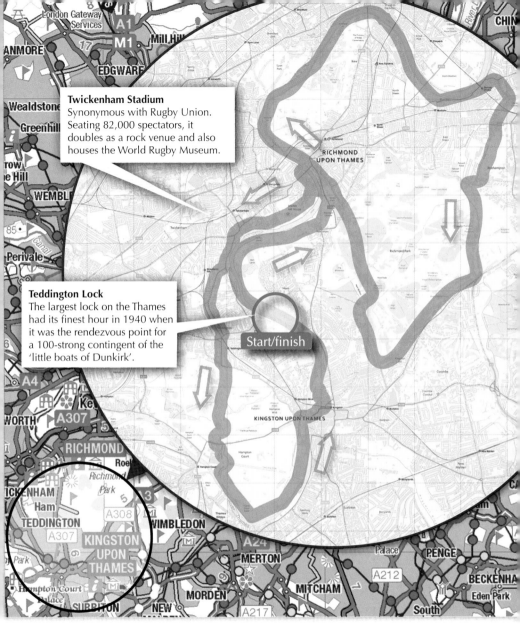

Twickenham Stadium
Synonymous with Rugby Union. Seating 82,000 spectators, it doubles as a rock venue and also houses the World Rugby Museum.

Teddington Lock
The largest lock on the Thames had its finest hour in 1940 when it was the rendezvous point for a 100-strong contingent of the 'little boats of Dunkirk'.

Start/finish

Avenue then cut through the palace grounds to pick up the towpath until Kingston Bridge.

Cross the bridge, following the A308 through a tunnel. Take Skerne road under the railway bridge by TGI Fridays then left down Down Hall Road. Turn right through Canbury Gardens until Lower Ham Road and take the towpath back to Teddington Lock.

Whitchurch and North Hampshire

Distance: 21 miles (34km)
Big hills: 1
Challenge: ✪✪☆☆☆

A pleasant ride through quiet Hampshire lanes and some of the prettiest scenery in the South

Before you know it on this ride, you have left urban sprawl behind and been transported to some of the most idyllic cycling country you'll find in the UK. It's a 21-mile loop to the south of Whitchurch. In the main the route is fast and easy pedalling. It bounds along next to rivers and past mills, dissects panoramic agricultural expanses, and there are few hills of any note. One major exception comes at the very end of the ride, with the climb up to the finish (and start) at Whitchurch station.

Turn left out of the station and left again. In 100m at the crossroads turn right down the hill into town. Take the first exit off a small roundabout in the town centre onto Winchester Street. After 1000m or so, the road forks – follow it round to the right, go under the bridge and turn immediately right. In another 1000m, at a junction on a right-hand bend, carry on straight ahead up the hill. In 1000m or so turn right at the crossroads (signposted 'unsuitable for heavy goods vehicles').

Go straight through Mill House yard and turn left at the T-junction. Pass through Longparish and turn left (signed to Barton Stacey). Turn left at the T-junction, up the hill and turn left opposite the church in Barton Stacey.

Go through Bullington and under a viaduct to turn right at a T-junction, then immediately left. Go straight over the crossroads then on the approach to Wonston village turn left (signed to Hunton). Turn left in Stoke Charity to

Micheldever Village then left in Micheldever Village to Micheldever Station. At the crossroads in Micheldever Station turn left over the railway, follow the road round past the railway station.

At the T-junction turn left then immediately right, down under the A303 then up the hill. After a couple of miles of open road take a little left-hand turn and climb up past Brickkiln Wood before descending back into Whitchurch. Turn right at the T-junction to take you along the road you started on and up the hill to the station.

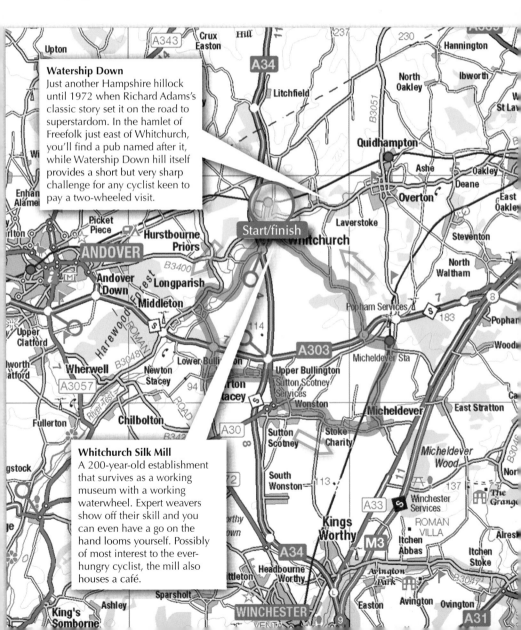

Watership Down
Just another Hampshire hillock until 1972 when Richard Adams's classic story set it on the road to superstardom. In the hamlet of Freefolk just east of Whitchurch, you'll find a pub named after it, while Watership Down hill itself provides a short but very sharp challenge for any cyclist keen to pay a two-wheeled visit.

Whitchurch Silk Mill
A 200-year-old establishment that survives as a working museum with a working waterwheel. Expert weavers show off their skill and you can even have a go on the hand looms yourself. Possibly of most interest to the ever-hungry cyclist, the mill also houses a café.

Wimbledon Common

Distance: 20 miles (32km)
Big hills: 1
Challenge: ●●☆☆☆

Escape London's pothole-riddled roads and head to leafy Wimbledon Common and beyond for some semi-urban riding

From the north-east corner of Wimbledon Common, follow the cycle path posts and signs into the centre. At the T-junction, turn left and ride to the Windmill. Pass the Windmill on your right; where the path splits, bear right and descend.

Continue to a clearing and several pathways. Follow the cycle path signs turning right and running alongside the Beverley Brook. Continue until the end of the path passes football pitches on the right. Turn left over the narrow bridge. Continue straight through an open field following the tracks.

Cross straight over at the pedestrian crossing. Enter the park at Robin Hood Gate. Before the roundabout, turn left onto the cyclepath marked Tamsin Trail. Follow clockwise, passing Kingston Gate on your left, crossing the tarmac road. At Ham Gate Avenue, turn right and ascend a small climb. Staying on the path, turn left at the top. Continue straight until Richmond Gate. Exit the park and cross

the mini roundabout to exit onto Richmond Hill.

After 100 metres, turn left at the small pathway into Petersham Common Woods. Descend, taking the first right turn on the trail. Exit the woods at the bottom and turn right on Petersham Road. At the pedestrian crossing, leave the road and turn left into Buccleuch Gardens joining the Thames Path, to the right. Continue for nine miles, going straight at the bridge crossing the Beverley Brook towards the Putney Embankment route. Turn right at the

Useful refreshment stops
Windmill Tea Rooms Windmill Road, Wimbledon Common, London SW19 5NQ. 0208 788 2910 www.windmilltearooms.com

Pembroke Lodge Tea Rooms, Richmond Park. 020 8940 8207

The Rose and Crown 79 Kew Green, Richmond TW9 3AH. 0208 940 2078

Bike shops
Putney Cycles (hire available), 337 Putney Bridge Road, London SW15 2PG. 0208 785 3147 www.putneycycles.com

Sigma Sport, St Johns Place, 37–43 High Street, Hampton Wick, Surrey KT1 4DA. 0208 614 9777 www.sigmasport.co.uk

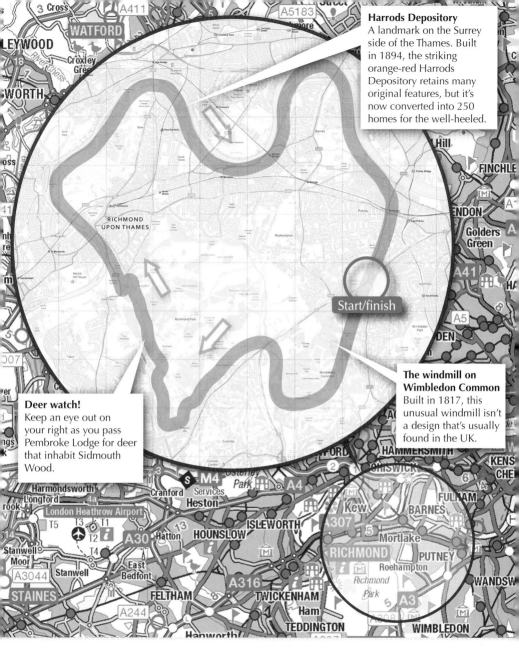

Harrods Depository
A landmark on the Surrey side of the Thames. Built in 1894, the striking orange-red Harrods Depository retains many original features, but it's now converted into 250 homes for the well-heeled.

The windmill on Wimbledon Common
Built in 1817, this unusual windmill isn't a design that's usually found in the UK.

Start/finish

Deer watch!
Keep an eye out on your right as you pass Pembroke Lodge for deer that inhabit Sidmouth Wood.

Duke's Head Pub then left onto Lower Richmond Road.

At the Putney Bridge T-junction, turn right onto Putney High Street. Continue straight at the Putney Hill junction climbing up Putney Hill towards Tibbets Corner. Follow the National Cycle Path Route 3 to re-enter the Common.

East London

Distance: 14.4 miles (23.2km)
Big hills: 1
Challenge: ✪☆☆☆☆

A leisurely urban ride taking in London parks, docks and part of the Thames Path

Along the Thames, beyond mighty Big Ben and the Palace of Westminster, lie a few more giants of the East London skyline. Canary Wharf and the Docklands complex stand proud above the river, reflecting the industrial heritage that was pivotal in London's development.

From Blackheath railway station, turn left up Tranquil Vale and bear right onto Royal Parade. Take the first left into All Saints' Drive. As the road curves to the right, go straight onto the cycle path signposted to Greenwich Park and follow it through the heath to Greenwich Park. At the mini-roundabout, turn left to go down the hill. At the bottom of the hill, exit the park and go to the end of the road. Turn left, then immediately bear right to reach the *Cutty Sark*.

Walk through the Greenwich Foot Tunnel. Turn left and then turn right onto Ferry Street. Turn right again onto Manchester Road and take the first left to enter Millwall Park. Follow the cycle path then turn right onto East Ferry Road.

Just after Mudchute DLR station, turn left onto the cycle path, signposted

'Route 1', towards South Quay. Go along Pepper Street and over Glengale Bridge. At the T-junction turn right onto Millharbour and take the third left into Lighterman's Road.

Follow the road then turn left into Byng Street. At the T-junction turn right onto West Ferry Road. At the roundabout take the third exit signposted Canary Wharf.

Useful refreshment stops

Hand Made Food Café, 40 Tranquil Vale, Blackheath, London SE3 0BD. 0208 297 9966

Honest Sausage, Greenwich Park, Greenwich, London SE10 9XJ

Pavilion Tea House, Greenwich Park, Charlton Way, London SE10 8QY. 020 8856 9695

Island Gardens Café, Saunders Ness Road, London E14 3EB. 020 7515 2802

The Crown, Blackheath, 49 Tranquil Vale, Blackheath, London SE3 0BS. 020 8852 0326 www.crownblackheath.co.uk

Bike shops

Cycle King Greenwich, 228–232 Trafalgar Road, London SE10 9ER. 020 8293 9180 www.cycleking.co.uk

Evans, Canary Wharf, 30 South Colonnade, London E14 5EZ. 020 7516 0094 www.evanscycles.com

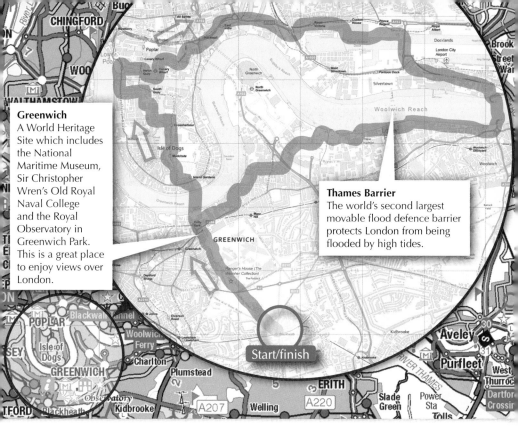

Greenwich
A World Heritage Site which includes the National Maritime Museum, Sir Christopher Wren's Old Royal Naval College and the Royal Observatory in Greenwich Park. This is a great place to enjoy views over London.

Thames Barrier
The world's second largest movable flood defence barrier protects London from being flooded by high tides.

Follow Bank Street and at the second set of traffic lights after Canary Wharf underground station, turn right and go through Churchill Place.

At the roundabout turn left and go along Trafalgar Way. Cross West India Dock and follow the cycle path route signposted to East India Dock. At Blackwall DLR station cross Pestons Road and immediately take Baffin Way next to the Ibis Hotel. At the mini-roundabout go left onto Blackwall Way and follow this road which directs you onto a cycle path which runs parallel to the main A13 road.

Follow the cycle path east. At the Excel Centre follow the cycle path signs for the Royal Docks and go along the Western Gateway. Follow the road right up to the Excel Centre. At the cul de sac turn right to go down the side of the Excel building and ride along the dockland path. Cross the car park and leave the Excel complex.

At the roundabout take the third exit into Festoon Way. At the T-junction turn right and cross the Connaught foot bridge. Then turn left and turn right (crossing the road) at the cycle signpost to North Woolwich and Leamouth. Double back on yourself to go round the Travel Lodge, following the path towards North Woolwich. Turn left into Factory Road and then, near the end of the road, right into Store Road to reach the Woolwich Ferry.

On leaving the Woolwich Ferry turn right at the first traffic island to pick up the Thames path. Follow the Thames Path back to Greenwich then retrace the route through the park to reach Blackheath.

The heart of London

Distance: 8.5 miles (14km)
Big hills: none
Challenge: ❶☆☆☆☆

A short, mainly traffic-free urban ride, taking in Royal Parks and tourist attractions

This ride starts from the very centre of London, next to the Charles I statue at Charing Cross.

From Charing Cross, ride through Admiralty Arch and down The Mall. Take the first right (or use pedestrian crossing) to join the cycle path along the right of the carriageway. Follow the path and go round the ornate wall to reach the cycle path along Constitution Hill. At Duke of Wellington Place, cross the road and go through Wellington Arch.

At Hyde Park Corner, cross Knightsbridge to enter Hyde Park. Cross South Carriage Drive and turn right, then immediately left onto Serpentine Road and turn right again to ride up the Broad Walk. Bear round to the left and follow the path to join North Carriage Drive. At the T-junction, turn left onto West Carriage Drive. Just after the Serpentine Gallery, turn left into Rotten Row West cycle path. Shortly after the Serpentine Café, turn right past the cycle hire docking station and leave Hyde Park via Albert Gate.

Cross Knightsbridge to enter William Street via the cycle lane. Continue down

Lowndes Square and at the junction turn right along Lowndes Street. Take the first left into Cadogan Place and continue to the end. At the T-junction, turn right and at the next junction go straight on up to the next T-junction. Turn left to reach a mini-roundabout and go down Cadogan Gardens to reach King's Road/Duke of York Square.

Turn right onto King's Road and take the second left into Walpole Road.

Useful refreshment stops
Café Fratelli, Duke of York Square, SW3 4LY. 020 7823 6800 www.fratellidelicafé.com

Gallery Mess Restaurant and Café, Saatchi Gallery, Duke of York's HQ, King's Road, SW3 4RY. 020 7730 8135 www.saatchi-gallery.co.uk

The Serpentine Bar and Kitchen, Serpentine Road, Hyde Park, W2 2UH. 020 7706 8114 www.serpentinebarandkitchen.com

Bike shops
Action Bikes Victoria (hire available) 19 Dacre Street, SW1H 0DJ. 020 7799 2233 www.actionbikes.co.uk

Cycle Surgery Victoria 26 Palace Street, SW1E 5JD. 020 7630 4959

Barclays Cycle Hire scheme – lots of stations around the route: www.tfl.gov.uk/cycling

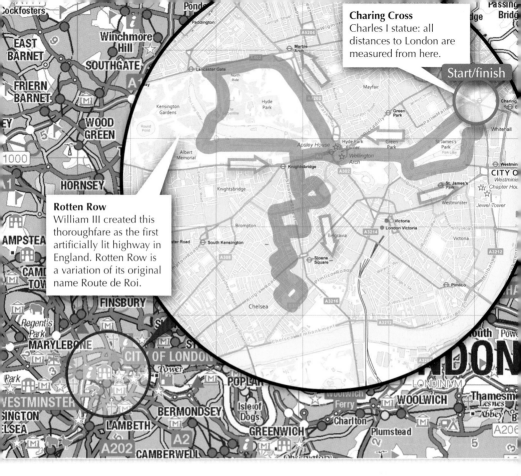

Charing Cross
Charles I statue: all distances to London are measured from here.

Start/finish

Rotten Row
William III created this thoroughfare as the first artificially lit highway in England. Rotten Row is a variation of its original name Route de Roi.

At the T-junction, turn right onto St Leonard's Terrace, then take the first left into Durham Place and do a circuit of the Royal Hospital / Burton's Court.

At the end of Franklin's Row, go down Cheltenham Terrace to reach King's Road. Turn right (or use the zebra crossing) and take the second left into Blacklands Terrace. At the T-junction, turn right into Draycott Place. At the mini roundabout turn left into Cadogan Gardens and go straight over the next mini-roundabout to reach Cadogan Square.

At the T-junction, turn right (or use the zebra crossing) onto Pont Street. Continue right up to Belgrave Square.

Turn left and take the second left into Wilton Terrace, then first left into Motcomb Street. At the T-junction, turn right onto Lowndes Street and go round Lowndes Square to return to Hyde Park via Albert Gate.

Turn right onto Rotten Row and at the end leave the park and retrace your route back to Buckingham Palace via Constitution Hill. At the start of The Mall cross the road and turn right to join the traffic. At the traffic lights, turn left down Spur Road to reach Birdcage Walk. Turn left and follow to Horse Guards Road, where you turn left to complete the ride just after Horse Guards Parade.

Regent's Park and Hampstead

Distance: 15 miles (24km)
Big hills: 1
Challenge: ★☆☆☆☆

A pleasant scenic route around some of the more tranquil areas of urban north London

From tourist attractions such as London Zoo to the peace and tranquillity of Hampstead Heath, a bike ride here makes for a pleasant urban trip. As this route consists of three loops you can do it in parts depending on time constraints.

Loop 1: From Marylebone station turn right onto Harewood Avenue. Go to Lisson Green Estate. Turn right onto Swain Street. Take the first left into Casey Close and join Regents Canal via the bridge and ramp. Follow the towpath east to London Zoo and explore Regent's Park.

Loop 2: Leave the canal at St Mark's Bridge and follow sign for Hampstead. Follow Regents Park Road. Pass the shops at Primrose Hill. Go over the graffiti bridge. Cross Adelaide Road and go up Eton College Road. Turn left and immediately right into Eton Villas. Turn left at the T-junction, bear right into Fellows Road. Turn right into Primrose Hill Road. At the fork bear left into Belsize Park Gardens. Take the first right into Belsize Grove. Cross Haverstock Hill and turn left into Lawn Road. Go over the crossroads to Cressy Road. Turn right then left into Mackeson Road. Turn right into Constantine Road and enter Hampstead Heath via the path (steps) on the left.

Bear right onto the cycle path. Turn left onto Highgate Road. On the hill turn left into Millfield Lane and re-enter Hampstead Heath via the cycle path.

Useful refreshment stops

Café Seventy-Nine, 79 Regent's Park Road, Primrose Hill, London NW1 8UY. 0207 586 8012

The Honest Sausage, The Broad Walk, Regent's Park. 0207 224 3872

The Garden Café, Queen Mary's Garden, Regent's Park. 020 7935 5729

The Flask, 77 Highgate West Hill, Highgate, London N6 6BU. 020 8348 7346

The Spaniards Inn, Spaniards Road, Hampstead, London NW3 7JJ. 020 8731 8406

Bike shops

Cycle Surgery, 42–48 Great Portland Street, London W1W 7LZ. 020 7436 9727

Cycle Surgery Camden, 44 Chalk Farm Road, London NW1 8AJ. 020 7485 1000

Evans Cycles, 86 Chalk Farm Road, London NW1 8AR. 020 7485 7293

Barclays Cycle Hire scheme – lots of stations around the route: www.tfl.gov.uk/cycling

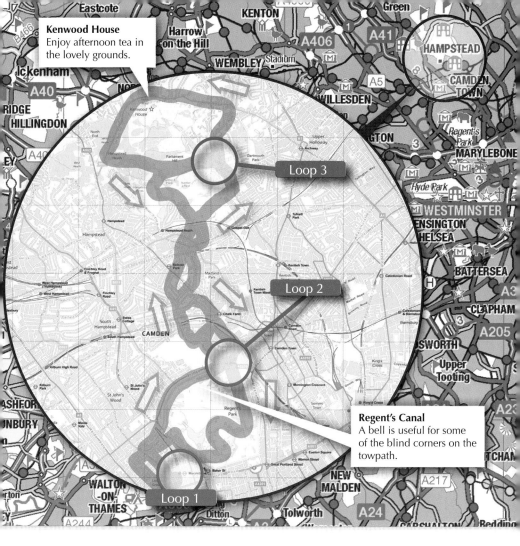

Kenwood House
Enjoy afternoon tea in the lovely grounds.

Loop 3

Loop 2

Regent's Canal
A bell is useful for some of the blind corners on the towpath.

Loop 1

Loop 3: Follow the cycle path to the summit and continue along Spaniards Road. Follow Hampstead Lane. Turn right into The Grove, then first right into Fitzroy Park (private road). Re-enter Hampstead Heath and follow the cycle path downhill. Turn left onto East Heath Road. Turn left into Parliament Hill, then right into Nassington Road. In Hampstead Heath leave via the steps and go down Roderick Road. Turn right at the T-junction, straight on at the lights and bear left into Parkhill Road. Cross Haverstock Hill and follow England's Lane. Turn left into Primrose Hill Road and retrace to St Mark's Bridge.

Cross and enter Regent's Park. Go down the Broadwalk. Right onto Chester Road, right onto the Inner Circle, right onto York Bridge. At the lights turn right onto the Outer Circle. At Hanover Gate turn left then right onto Park Road. Before the roundabout turn left onto Lodge Road, left onto Lisson Grove and left into Harewood Row to reach Marylebone station.

Royal Windsor

Distance: 20 miles (32km)
Big hills: 2
Challenge: ●●☆☆☆

A gently undulating ride around the landmarks of Windsor Great Park

Just 25 miles west of London there's a chance you'll be cycling in the presence of royalty. From Windsor Castle, to the Great Park and the various other grounds of the Royal Landscape, the London cyclist can make the most of these popular areas, care of the Crown Estate.

Useful refreshment stops
Chocolate Theatre Café, 57 Thames Street, Windsor SL4 1QW. 01753 736629 www.chocolatetheatrecafebar.com

Windsor Farm Shop Coffee Shop, Datchet Road, Old Windsor SL4 2RQ. 01753 623800

The Royal Stag, The Green, Datchet, Berkshire SL3 9JH. 01753 584231

Bike shops
Cyclelife Windsor, Trinity Yard, 59 St Leonards Road, Windsor SL4 3BX. 01753 751007 www.cyclelifewindsor.co.uk

Stows Cycles Windsor, Dedworth Road, Windsor, SL4 4JW. 01753 862734 www.stows.co.uk

Leave Virginia Water railway station and follow the B389 to the A30. Cross the road and enter Virginia Water Lake car park. Enter Windsor Great Park.

Turn left and follow the path through the woods and around the lake. Cross the bridge and go up the hill. Pass Smith's Lawn. Head towards Cumberland Lodge. Pass the Royal Lodge and go down the hill to The Village. Pass the estate and the Village Shop on the right. Follow the sign for Rangers Gate and then exit Windsor Great Park.

Cross the A332 and join a cycle path that runs parallel to the main road and through the woods. At the T-junction, turn left and through a car park. Follow the National Cycle Network Route 4 into Windsor. Head to Alexandra Gardens and the main road parallel to the river. Turn left at the traffic lights for Eton Bridge (optional).

Pass Eton Bridge and follow the main road to Datchet, continuing to Old Windsor. After the junction with the A308, take the first right for the local shops and follow the road through Old Windsor village. Turn right at the second church to join the unclassified road up Crimp Hill. At the junction, bear right into Wick Road and head for Savill Gardens. Turn right into Savill Gardens car park. Join the path into Windsor Great Park.

Turn left to go back to Virginia Water Lake. Cross the car park and the A30 to reach the B389/cycle path to Virginia Water station.

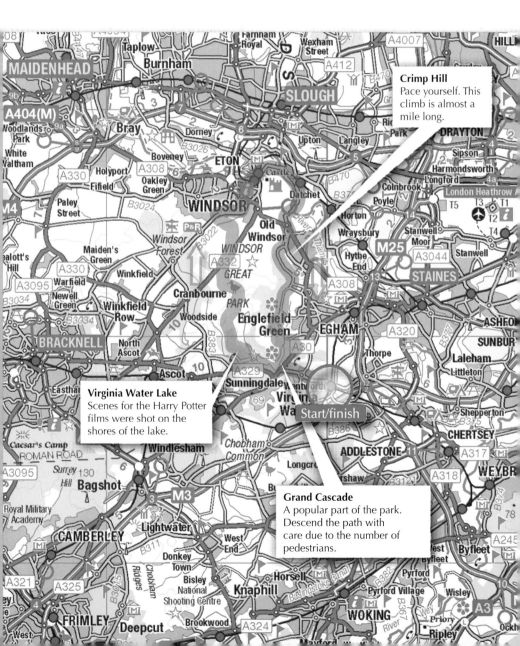

Crimp Hill
Pace yourself. This climb is almost a mile long.

Virginia Water Lake
Scenes for the Harry Potter films were shot on the shores of the lake.

Start/finish

Grand Cascade
A popular part of the park. Descend the path with care due to the number of pedestrians.

Hove to Shoreham

Distance: 17 miles (27.5km)
Big hills: none
Challenge: ●●☆☆☆

Cruise the back route from Hove to Shoreham along the coast and up the Adur valley, linking station, port and airfield

There's a great mix of surroundings on this ride which is coastal, urban and rural in various parts. From the beginning, the visual contrasts are startling, so it's just as well that the route is largely flat and often traffic-free.

Starting by an overgrown boating lake on the beach front in Hove called, the Lagoon, follow National Cycle Route 2 signs to Shoreham Beach. Beware speed humps and freight trucks along Basin Road, Hove. After Carats Café, cross the harbour locks, then cross the busy A259 (by the pelican crossing if necessary). Left at Southwick Green, then due west for one mile, taking cycle path left round allotments, then into Shoreham and over footbridge to the beach.

Useful refreshment stops
Restaurant in Shoreham Airport, Shoreham-by-Sea BN43 5FF. 01273 452300

The Royal Sovereign, Middle Street, Shoreham-by-Sea BN43 5DP. 01273 453518.

Bike shops
South Coast Bikes, 2 Quayside Buildings, Basin Road South, Hove BN41 1WF. 01273 202124
www.southcoastbikes.co.uk

Leave NCR2 at Kings Crescent, then take the third left into Fisherman's walk for a good crossing of the A259 and a path on to New Salts Farm Road. Skirt the airfield, cross the A27 at the lights into Coombes Road. After two miles, bear right onto a bridleway at St Botolphs, to cross the river footbridge. Stay on Downs Link cycle path (Regional Route 79) into Shoreham, then take the NCR2 back to Hove Lagoon.

South bank of River Adur
Floating homes of all shapes and sizes overlook a wetland conservation area. Even the mailboxes are home-made – out of disused electrical gadgets.

Start/finish

Western Esplanade
Millionaire's Row, Hove style. Fatboy Slim lives and records in the two westernmost houses.

Shoreham Road
Beeding Cement Works, a vast abandoned concrete structure that would befit a post-apocalypse landscape, yet it's on the edge of the verdant South Downs.

The Cuckoo Trail, East Sussex

Distance: 18 miles (29km)
Big hills: none
Challenge: ●●☆☆☆

An easygoing ride through some of the prettiest scenery the South East has to offer

The Cuckoo Trail is a surfaced path along a 14-mile stretch of disused railway, between Heathfield and Eastbourne, in East Sussex. Thanks to the efforts of the railway builders, back in the 1870s, the land is levelled off and the route is pan-flat from end to end. Better still, it's now owned and maintained by East Sussex County Council for the benefit of cyclists, runners and walkers.

This is 'Ride 2' from the council's 'Off the Cuckoo Trail: Circular Rides' leaflet. Starting in Horam, join the Cuckoo Trail opposite Wessons Café. Follow the trail south, towards Hailsham. Cross Upper Horsebridge Road; stay on the trail. Approaching Hailsham, take the right fork, signposted Michelham Priory. Turn right onto Hawks Road and at the roundabout, take the second exit on to Hempstead Lane.

Cross the A22 and continue straight ahead on Hempstead Lane – keep going when the tarmac ends and emerge from the woods onto Arlington Road, and turn right.

At a T-junction, in Upper Dicker, turn left. Take the first right on to Lower Wick Street, then right again on to Poundfield Road.

In Chalvington, bear right. At the Golden Cross, turn left, then right, crossing the A22, towards Chiddingly. At Muddles Green, turn left. After the Six Bells pub in Chiddingly, turn right, and right again at the end of the road. Turn left on to Smithlands Lane. At the junction with the A267, turn left and return to Horam.

Useful refreshment stops

Wessons Café, High Street, Horam, East Sussex TN21 0ER. 01435 813999

The Six Bells Chiddingly, East Sussex BN8 6HE. 01825 872 227

Plough Inn, Coldharbour Road, Upper Dicker, East Sussex BN27 3QJ. 01323 844859

Yew Tree Inn, Chalvington Road, Chalvington, East Sussex BN27 3TB. 01323 811326

Bike shops

Cycle Revival, Oxford House, Hailsham Road, Heathfield, East Sussex TN21 8AA. 01435 866118 www.cyclerevival.co.uk

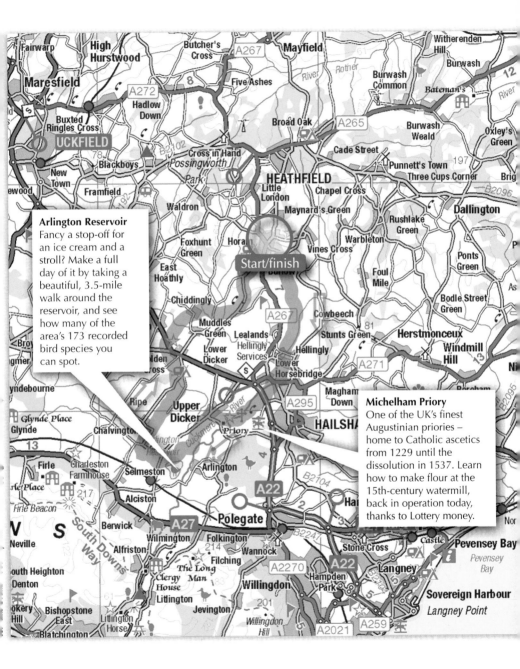

Arlington Reservoir
Fancy a stop-off for an ice cream and a stroll? Make a full day of it by taking a beautiful, 3.5-mile walk around the reservoir, and see how many of the area's 173 recorded bird species you can spot.

Michelham Priory
One of the UK's finest Augustinian priories – home to Catholic ascetics from 1229 until the dissolution in 1537. Learn how to make flour at the 15th-century watermill, back in operation today, thanks to Lottery money.

Start/finish

Guildford to the coast

Distance: 37 miles (60km)
Big hills: 1
Challenge: ❶❶❶☆☆

A predominantly flat and traffic-free route along the brilliant Downs Link, a path along a disused railway line

There's something special about riding a long distance and seeing a geographical change – it can really make a ride. The Downs Link stretches from the North Downs in Surrey to the South Downs of Sussex, mostly via dismantled railway lines. Add just a couple of miles on to each end and this ride route is formed – Guildford to the coast.

Useful refreshment stops

Westons Farm Shop, Fulfords Rd, Itchingfield, Horsham, West Sussex RH13 0NR. 01403 791228

The Cat and The Canary, Upper Station Road, Henfield, West Sussex BN5 9PJ. 01273 492509

Crown & Anchor, 33 High Street, Shoreham-by-Sea, West Sussex BN43 5DD. 01273 463500
www.crownandanchor-shoreham.co.uk

Bike shops

Southwater Cycles (hire available), 9 Lintot Square, Fairbank Road, Southwater, West Sussex RH13 9LA. 01403 732561

Don't let the 37-mile distance put you off, as there is just one notable hill on the entire route, and the rest is an endless supply of barely perceptible gradients perforated by villages and pubs.

From Guildford station, exit via the main entrance. Head right down towards the pedestrian crossing, but instead of going over it, look for the subway under the road. Go through it, then turn right up the ramp at the end. Follow the path to the left, and then head down to the river. Turn right, so that the river is now on your left-hand side.

Once you have passed under the bridge, take a left up the ramp and past the car park until you reach The White House pub. Take the road past the pub and follow it until you see a footbridge over the river on the left. Cross here, then head right onto the towpath next to the lock. Follow this towpath, keeping the river on your left for a couple of miles.

Pass St Catherine's lock, then ride under a large metal railway bridge. Keep an eye out on your right-hand side for a path and set of steps up on to a railway embankment. Head up on to the disused railway. Follow the path.

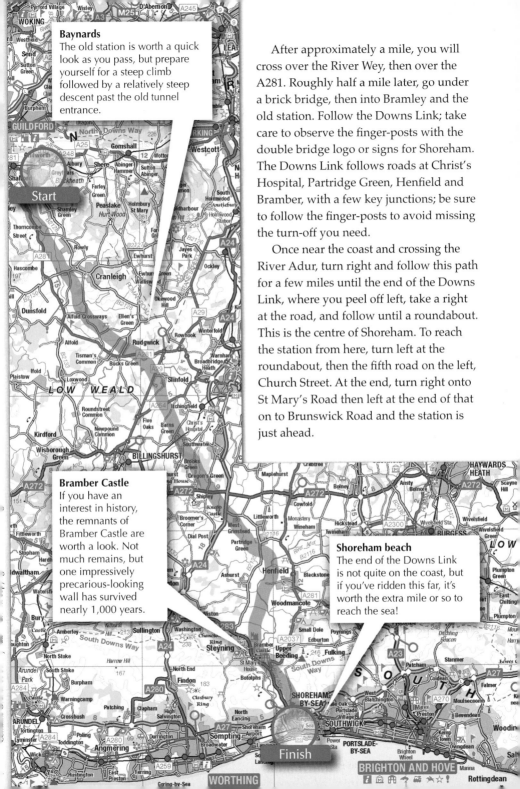

Baynards
The old station is worth a quick look as you pass, but prepare yourself for a steep climb followed by a relatively steep descent past the old tunnel entrance.

After approximately a mile, you will cross over the River Wey, then over the A281. Roughly half a mile later, go under a brick bridge, then into Bramley and the old station. Follow the Downs Link; take care to observe the finger-posts with the double bridge logo or signs for Shoreham. The Downs Link follows roads at Christ's Hospital, Partridge Green, Henfield and Bramber, with a few key junctions; be sure to follow the finger-posts to avoid missing the turn-off you need.

Once near the coast and crossing the River Adur, turn right and follow this path for a few miles until the end of the Downs Link, where you peel off left, take a right at the road, and follow until a roundabout. This is the centre of Shoreham. To reach the station from here, turn left at the roundabout, then the fifth road on the left, Church Street. At the end, turn right onto St Mary's Road then left at the end of that on to Brunswick Road and the station is just ahead.

Bramber Castle
If you have an interest in history, the remnants of Bramber Castle are worth a look. Not much remains, but one impressively precarious-looking wall has survived nearly 1,000 years.

Shoreham beach
The end of the Downs Link is not quite on the coast, but if you've ridden this far, it's worth the extra mile or so to reach the sea!

Start

Finish

Romney and Rye, Kent

Distance: 26 miles (42km)
Big hills: 1 (in Rye, optional)
Challenge: ●●☆☆☆

The flatlands of Romney and Rye make for an easygoing day out on the bike, on some incredibly flat but beautiful terrain

Rye, the ancient fortified town that commanded this area, is the starting point and the railway station puts you at the gateway to the Romney, Denge and Walland Marshes. An area of some 40 square miles crisscrossed by a network of lanes ranging from well surfaced B-roads to single tracks that have been abandoned and left to their fate because of a lack of traffic.

From Rye station, follow the road and bear left past the police station. Turn left at the T-junction, over a railway bridge, then first right. Take Military Road to the end at a T-junction, turn right over the canal then first right. Past the church, second left and at the next junction bear right to the main road.

Turn right then first left, pass an old 'looker's' cottage on the right then take the next two lefts onto a rough surfaced road. Left again and follow until a T-junction at

> **Useful refreshment stops**
> Plenty of choice in Rye –
> www.visitrye.co.uk
>
> **Bike shops**
> Romney Cycles (hire available),
> New Romney, 77 High Street, New
> Romney, Kent TN28 8AZ.
> 01797 362155
> www.romneycycles.co.uk
> Rye Hire (hire available), 1 Cyprus Place,
> Rye, East Sussex TN31 7DR.
> 01797 223033

Brookland. Turn right then first left and left again at another T-junction.

At a roundabout take the third exit then right at a T-junction, first left, first right by a cottage then keep going until the T-junction with Appledore Road.

Turn left then first right past Snargate church. At a crossroads turn left then straight across at a staggered crossroads. Over the railway and canal past a vineyard, left at a T-junction then left into Appledore.

Then it's right after the tea shop then left at every turn until finally right back onto Military Road and back to Rye.

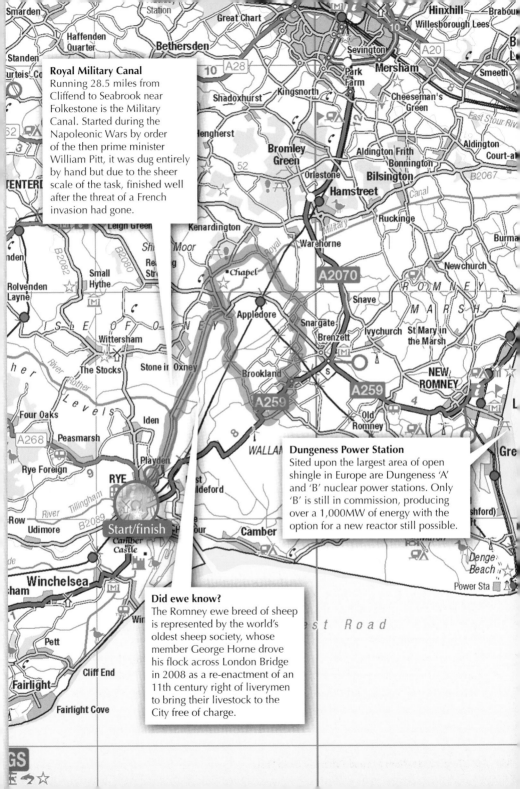

Royal Military Canal
Running 28.5 miles from Cliffend to Seabrook near Folkestone is the Military Canal. Started during the Napoleonic Wars by order of the then prime minister William Pitt, it was dug entirely by hand but due to the sheer scale of the task, finished well after the threat of a French invasion had gone.

Dungeness Power Station
Sited upon the largest area of open shingle in Europe are Dungeness 'A' and 'B' nuclear power stations. Only 'B' is still in commission, producing over a 1,000MW of energy with the option for a new reactor still possible.

Did ewe know?
The Romney ewe breed of sheep is represented by the world's oldest sheep society, whose member George Horne drove his flock across London Bridge in 2008 as a re-enactment of an 11th century right of liverymen to bring their livestock to the City free of charge.

North Downs and Surrey hills

Distance: 23.5 miles (38km)
Big hills: 2
Challenge: ✪✪✪☆☆

An off/on road ride on the North Downs Way for cyclo-cross fans and mountain bikers, taking in the rolling Surrey hills

The twisting lanes of Surrey offer much for the road cyclist, but in the hills of the North Downs exists a network of bridleways and tracks, appealing to mountain bikers and cyclo-cross riders alike. This ride is versatile, and can be ridden fast, for training, or slowly, to enjoy the varied surroundings.

Leave Redhill Station and go across the roundabout to the town centre. Through the town to join the road (A25, Station Road) towards Reigate. Go right into Oxford Road to the zebra crossing towards Donyings. Pick up the cycle lane at the far end of the car park.

Go right at the end and straight on across a small road junction until a gate onto Wray Common. Go diagonally across the common to Croydon Road and head right along the road (over a roundabout) and straight on. After the junction with Carlton Road on the right, look for a gated gravel track on the left, marked 'bridleway'.

Follow past stables and down to Gatton School, where it's left on the tarmac and left again onto a bridleway, uphill. Bear right and climb to Reigate Hill car park. Follow North Downs Way, over the bridge and on to Colley Hill, where you go straight on (through some gates). Stay on track until you turn right on a tarmac road. Turn left after crossing the M25, to follow bridleways to Walton Heath (golf course).

Stay on track to cross Dorking Road and continue (to the right of the driveway) to Walton on the Hill. Left on the B2220, keeping the pond on the right, and turn

Useful refreshment stops

The Spaghetti Tree, 1 Walton Street, Walton-on-the-Hill, Surrey KT20 7RW. 01737 819919

Box Hill Café, The Old Fort, Box Hill Road, Box Hill, Tadworth, Surrey KT20 7LB. 01306 885502

The Sportsman, Mogador Road, Lower Kingswood, Surrey KT20 7ES. 01737 246655

Fox and Hounds, Walton on the Hill, Tadworth, Surrey KT20 7RU. 01737 817744

Bike shops

C&N Cycles, 32 Station Road, Redhill, Surrey RH1 1PD. 01737 760857

next right (Sandlands Road). Turn left at the end, down an unmade road to a junction where you can turn right and straight on at junction onto a bridleway all the way to Langley Vale (with Epsom Racecourse to the right).

Just before the main road, take the bridleway left, uphill (crossing the road junction at the top). Staying in the direction of the track, downhill (speed bumps) into trees and a bridleway. Up, down, but always straight, on Stane Street (Roman road), taking care crossing road junctions, until the track splits after a pebbly downhill – take the right fork into trees (easy to miss).

Stay on this course, until a chalky downhill brings you to a road opposite Juniper Hill. Turn right, and then left and next left to cross road to a cycles only track to climb Box Hill.

Right at the road, past the café and turn left in the village at Headley Heath Approach, down to the gate on the right to Headley Heath. The track bears right, then left and up a short rise, where you bear right. Stay on track, and bear left when it splits, then left again at the junction with a large track, to lead to the second of two car parks.

Cross the road to the right of the cricket ground. A bridleway bears right from this track. Follow the route of the bridleway, bearing right, until the path splits after a short climb – stay right then cross the main road. Bear left, then right at a track junction, along the rutted track and down a steep hill – turning off it at the first left (before a steep bit). Follow the track, snaking down to exit the woods. Take the next left, up a short hill and right at the top to follow the bridleway back to Colley Hill and retrace back to Reigate Hill car park.

Crossing the road beyond the car park, a bridleway forks right, parallel with the road down to join it (keep bearing right). Follow the road to Wray Common, retracing your route back to the start.

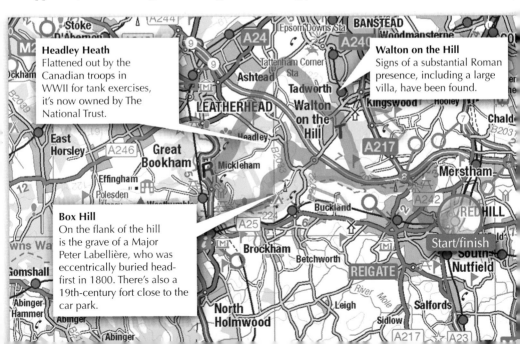

Headley Heath
Flattened out by the Canadian troops in WWII for tank exercises, it's now owned by The National Trust.

Walton on the Hill
Signs of a substantial Roman presence, including a large villa, have been found.

Box Hill
On the flank of the hill is the grave of a Major Peter Labellière, who was eccentrically buried head-first in 1800. There's also a 19th-century fort close to the car park.

Start/finish

Kent and Surrey

Distance: 24 miles (38km)
Big hills: 1 (to Markbeech)
Challenge: ●●●●☆

The garden of England is packed full of quiet lanes with beautiful views – this little loop on the Kent/ Surrey border is a perfect introduction

You don't have to venture deep into the hills or forests to experience a good ride, and this route, just outside the M25, shows what London's city dwellers have on their doorstep. Ten miles due south of Croydon, the ride begins in Crockham Hill, just outside the town of Oxted. Crockham Hill sits just on the Kent side of the Surrey/ Kent border, but there is a fair amount of historical interest in both counties, and there are plenty of great country lanes to explore.

From Crockham Hill take the B269 south-east to Four Elms. At the junction in Four Elms continue straight over on the B2027 then take the second right onto How Green Lane. Turn right at the end of How Green Lane onto Hever Road.

From Hever the route heads south, so turn left onto Uckfield Lane and continue to Markbeech. At the end of Uckfield Lane take a right turn to head west. Take care crossing the B2026, and follow Spode Lane

as it meanders to the village of Cowden. At the end of North Street in Cowden turn right onto High Street, down through a small S-bend and on under the trees. Take the next right, up an incline and head west.

Keep left until reaching a T-junction with Shepherds Grove Lane. Turn right

Useful refreshment stops

The Royal Oak, Main Road, Crockham Hill TN8 6RD. 01732 866335

The Wheatsheaf, Hever Road, Bough Beech TN8 7NU. 01732 700254

The Kentish Horse, Cow Lane, Markbeech TN8 5NT. 01342 850493 www.kentishhorse.co.uk

The Fountain, High St, Cowden, Edenbridge TN8 7JG. 01342 850528 www.fountain-cowden.com

The Plough, 44 Plough Road, Dormansland RH7 6PS. 01342 832933 www.ploughdormandsland.com

Haxted Mill Riverside Brasserie and Bar, Haxted Road, Haxted TN8 6PU. 01732 862914 www.haxtedmill.co.uk

Bike shops

London Cycles Ltd, Unit 3, Imberhorne Business Centre, Imberhorne Way, East Grinstead RH19 1RL. 01342 323494

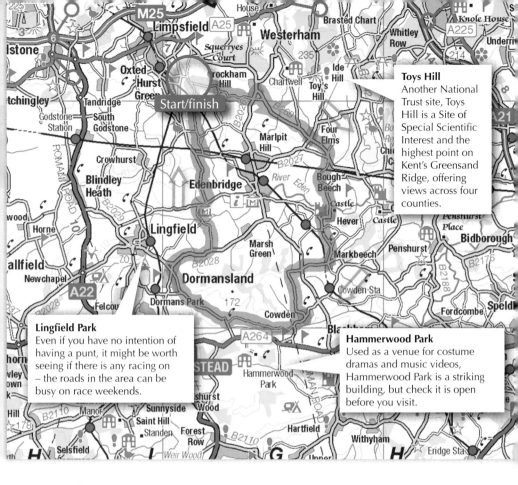

Toys Hill
Another National Trust site, Toys Hill is a Site of Special Scientific Interest and the highest point on Kent's Greensand Ridge, offering views across four counties.

Lingfield Park
Even if you have no intention of having a punt, it might be worth seeing if there is any racing on – the roads in the area can be busy on race weekends.

Hammerwood Park
Used as a venue for costume dramas and music videos, Hammerwood Park is a striking building, but check it is open before you visit.

here and the road will become Hollow Lane. Continue on Hollow Lane to Dormansland, heading around the fringes of East Grinstead.

At the crossroads at the end of Hollow Lane, turn right onto Plough Road, then go straight over onto the reasonably busy B2028 (Moor Lane) towards Marsh Green. Take the first left onto the extremely straight Starborough Road, ignore the first junction then keep right as the road forks to become Water Lane. At the next junction turn right onto Haxted Road towards Edenbridge, and ride past Haxted Mill.

Immediately after Haxted Mill take the next left turn onto Dwelly Lane, then the first right onto Honeypot Lane, then take the very next left turn onto Grants Lane, on the eastern edge of Hurst Green.

After crossing over the second railway bridge you come to Grants Lane, take a right turn onto Itchingwood Common Road. Head past the large roadside pond on the right-hand bend, then at the big triangular crossroads turn left onto Swaynesland Road and follow this all the way to the main road. Turn left onto the B2026 and you're back at your starting point at Crockham Hill.

Box Hill
and Surrey

Distance: 27 miles (43km)
Big hills: 3
Challenge: ●●●☆☆

A fine ride amongst the quiet lanes and lovely views of the Surrey Hills

The Surrey Hills are very popular with cyclists, thanks to their varied landscape, which appeals to riders of all ages and abilities. Wide open common land is contrasted with thick woodland, all set on gently rolling chalk downs.

A short train ride from Victoria or Waterloo will take you right to the heart of this area of outstanding natural beauty. From the capital, you can reach the stations at Dorking, Box Hill and Westhumble, Gomshall and Leatherhead. There are also train services from Redhill and Guildford. Although this is a region known for its hills, everything is rideable if you have a reasonable level of fitness.

Start at Dorking Station and leave the station via the subway under the A24. Turn right and follow the cycle path beside the main road. Turn left towards Westhumble, climb over the railway bridge and after two miles, turn left at Chapel Farm Fields to climb Ranmore Hill.

Useful refreshment stops

Ryka's (snack van), Burford Bridge car park

Box Tree Café, Box Hill, Tadworth KT20 7LB. 01306 885502 www.nationaltrust.org.uk/box-hill

The Stepping Stones Pub and Restaurant, Westhumble Street, Dorking RH5 6BS. 01306 889932

The Abinger Hatch, Abinger Common, RH5 6HZ. 01306 730737 wwwtheabingerhatch.com

Conservatory and Gallery Restaurants, Denbies Wine Estate, London Road, Dorking, RH5 6AA. 01306 876616 www.denbies.co.uk

Bike shops

Nirvana Cycles (hire available) 5 The Green, Guildford Road, Westcott RH4 3NR. 01306 740300

Cycles Dauphin, 2 Green Tiles, Box Hill Road, Tadworth KT20 7JE. 01737 844576 www.cyclesdauphin.com

Head for the Hills, 43 West Street, Dorking RH4 1BU. 01306 885007 www.head-for-the-hills.co.uk

Bike Hut, 111–113 High Street, Dorking RH4 1AL. 01306 878560

After 1.2 miles turn right at the T-junction. At the crossroads turn left into Whitedown Lane. Straight ahead at the next crossroads and next left up Abinger Hill Road and climb up to Leith Hill Road. Keep left for Coldharbour.

After Coldharbour village, drop down to Dorking. Turn left at the bottom, then left onto the one-way system. Turn right at the traffic lights onto the A25 towards Reigate and continue along the high street. Turn left opposite the petrol station and then join the cycle path on the A24.

Continue on to Westhumble again, but this time carry on and under the subway towards Burford Bridge. Go past the hotel and take the next right up Zig Zag Road. Follow the road through Box Hill village and then turn left at the T-junction onto Headley Common Road (B2033).

Take the next left through Headley village, then next left onto Lodge Bottom Road. At the T-junction, turn left back to Burford Bridge, onto the A24 cycle path and back to Dorking station.

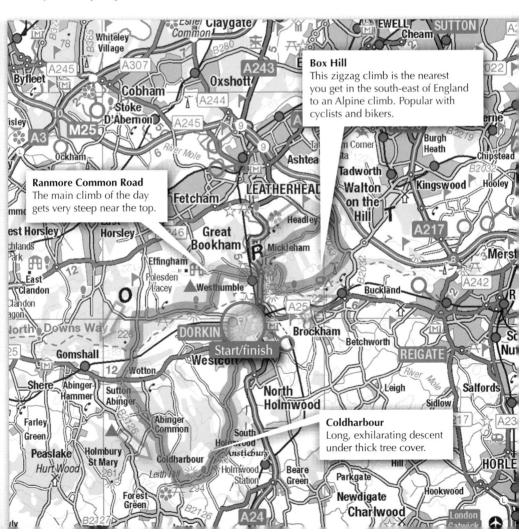

Box Hill
This zigzag climb is the nearest you get in the south-east of England to an Alpine climb. Popular with cyclists and bikers.

Ranmore Common Road
The main climb of the day gets very steep near the top.

Coldharbour
Long, exhilarating descent under thick tree cover.

Start/finish

South-east London parks

Distance: 16 miles (26km)
Big hills: 2
Challenge: ✪✪✪☆☆

A tour of the green spaces of south-east London

London is known for its abundance of parks, and the south-east of the city is no exception. Start at Crystal Palace railway station, enter the park and follow the road downhill. At the Jubilee Stand go through a gate on the right and enter the play area to do an anti-clockwise circuit of the park.

Leave the park at the top of Crystal Palace Park Road and at the double roundabout take Fountain Drive. Go down the hill and at the traffic lights turn left onto the cycle path. Take the first left into Alleyn Park. Go straight on at the traffic lights and then turn right

> **Useful refreshment stops**
> There are cafés in Crystal Palace Park, Brockwell Park, Dulwich Park and Peckham Rye.
>
> **Bike shops**
> Blue Door Bicycles (hire available), 5&7 Central Hill, London SE19 1BG. 020 8670 9767
>
> BC Bikes, 36 East Dulwich Road, London SE22 9AX. 020 7732 4170 www.bcbikes.co.uk
>
> Herne Hill Bicycles, 83 Norwood Road, London SE24 9AA. Tel: 020 8671 6900 www.hhbikes.co.uk

at the mini-roundabout onto Rosendale Road. Follow the road to the end and at the T-junction cross the road to enter Brockwell Park.

Do a clockwise circuit of the park and leave the park via the same Rosendale Road exit. Go down Rosendale Road and turn left onto Turney Road. Continue straight on through the traffic lights. Turn right into Boxall Road and right again into Dulwich Village. At the mini-roundabout take the first exit, then enter Dulwich Park via the College Road gate.

Follow the path through the park anti-clockwise and leave the park at the Court Lane gate. Go straight up Eynella Road. At the traffic lights go straight on into Barry Road then take the second right into Goodrich Road followed by the first left into Friern Road. Follow the road to the end and cross to enter Peckham Rye Park. Follow the cycle path (Strakers Road) and leave the park to enter Somerton Road.

At the T-junction turn left into Waveney Avenue and right into Forrester Road, then right again into Linden Grove. Follow the road to the double roundabout and turn right into Ivydale Road. Follow the road, which becomes Athenlay Road. At the end turn left and then immediately

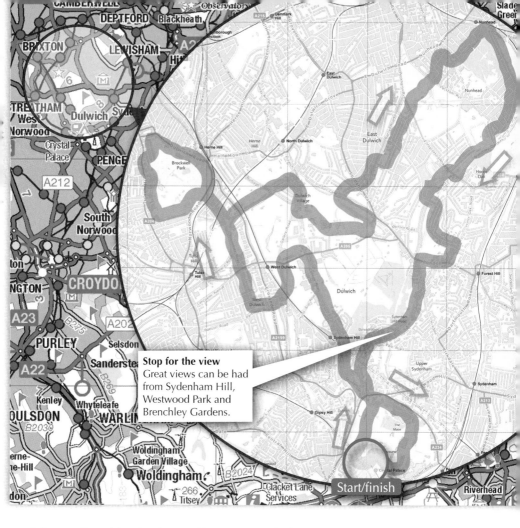

Stop for the view

Great views can be had from Sydenham Hill, Westwood Park and Brenchley Gardens.

right onto Brenchley Gardens. Follow the road to the end and turn right and then first left into Wood Vale. At the mini- roundabout turn left into Langton Rise and right into Westwood Park. (An alternative, from Brenchley Gardens, is to go straight on up Canonbie Road and take the first right into Westwood Park).

Follow Westwood Park to the top of the hill, then at the T-junction turn right onto Honor Oak Road. At the lights turn right onto London Road and then first left onto Eliot Bank. (Alternatively: at the foot of the hill on Westwood Park turn right onto the cycle path. At the end turn left onto London Road then right onto Eliot Bank).

At the top of the road go straight on into Sydenham Hill at the mini-roundabout. Follow the road to the end and turn left at the roundabout. At the crossing double back by crossing the road and going back up the hill. Enter Crystal Palace Park via the Crystal Palace Park Road gate. Ride across the top section of the park to return to the station.

St Michael's Mount to Lamorna

Distance: 20 miles (32km)
Big hills: 1
Challenge: ●●☆☆☆

A splendid ride through picture-postcard ports and flower-filled lanes

Starting in Marazion, this route takes in the picturesque village of Mousehole and some terrific views of St Michael's Mount, the island topped by a church used for worship during the Norman invasion of the area and the counterpart of Mont St Michel in France. The only access to the island is via boat or the road that only reveals itself at low tide.

Leaving Kings Road, Marazion, head along the coast on West End Road, turn into Long Road. The coast is on the left

of you and St Michael's Mount is behind. At the first traffic island take the second exit and continue on Long Road. At the next big traffic island, take the first exit on to the A30 in the direction of Land's End, Penzance. Take the first exit on the next traffic island, heading to Easter Green and Gulval, the B3311. Continue on to Chyandour Cliff and then to Eastern Green. The station will be on your left, take this left and then a slight right, bringing you onto Wharf Road.

At the end of the wharf head left onto the Western Promenade Road. Turn left at the Strand, continue until a slight right on the Parade and head up Parade Hill. Continue on Fore Street, which turns into Cliff Road. You will drop down into Mousehole.

Turn left at The Wharf, which becomes Portland Place, then left at Gurnick Street, continue straight on to St Clements Terrace then turn left at Raginnis Hill. At the top turn left and then the first right heading to Castallack. At Lamorna it's a sharp left onto Well Lane and follow it down to the sea.

Return up Well Lane and go sharp left at Lamorna. Take the first right on Well Lane, heading to the B3315. Turn

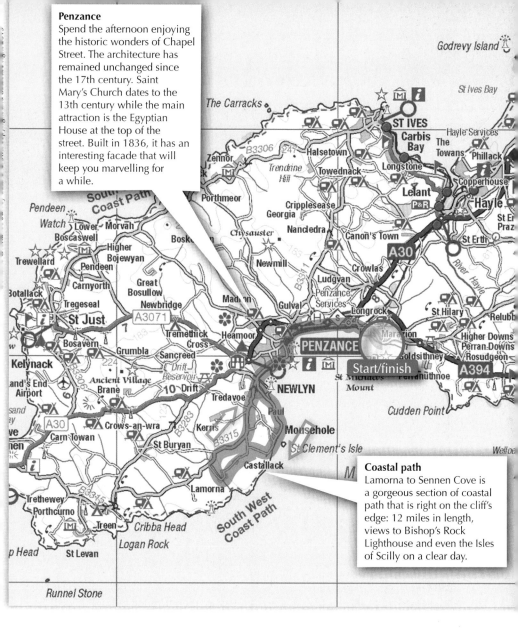

Penzance
Spend the afternoon enjoying the historic wonders of Chapel Street. The architecture has remained unchanged since the 17th century. Saint Mary's Church dates to the 13th century while the main attraction is the Egyptian House at the top of the street. Built in 1836, it has an interesting facade that will keep you marvelling for a while.

Coastal path
Lamorna to Sennen Cove is a gorgeous section of coastal path that is right on the cliff's edge: 12 miles in length, views to Bishop's Rock Lighthouse and even the Isles of Scilly on a clear day.

Start/finish

left towards the B3315. Turn right on to the B3315 to Penzance. Continue on the B3315 until Newlyn. This is New Road and the Western Promenade, where you retrace your route through Penzance harbour, past the train station on to the A30. Exit on to Long Road and back along West End Road. The coast will be on your right and St Michael's Mount in full view.

The New Forest

Distance: 18 miles (29km)
Big hills: 1 or 2 small hills on the Burley road
Challenge: ⬤⬤☆☆☆

Useful refreshment stops

The Old Farmhouse and Tea Rooms, The Cross, Ringwood Road, Burley, Hampshire BH24 4AB. 01425 402218 www.oldfarmhouseinburley.co.uk

The Foresters Arms, 10 Brookley Road, Brockenhurst, Hampshire SO42 7RR. 01590 623397

The Snakecatcher, Lyndhurst Rd, Brockenhurst, Hampshire SO42 7RL. 01590 622348

The Queens Head, The Cross, Burley, Ringwood, Hampshire BH24 4AB. 01425 403423 www.queens-head-pub-ringwood.co.uk

Bike shops

AA Bike Hire (hire available), Lyndurst. 023 8028 3349 www.aabikehirenewforest.co.uk

Country Lanes Cycle Hire (hire available), Brockenhurst. 01590 622627 www.countrylanes.co.uk

Cycleexperience Ltd (hire available), Brockenhurst. 01590 624204 www.newforestcyclehire.co.uk

Forest Leisure Cycling (hire available), Burley. 01425 403584 www.forestleisurecycling.co.uk

A gentle ride through the wilds of the New Forest

The New Forest is a wonderful place to cycle. In addition to the miles of sheltered country roads, there are over 100 miles of approved cycle routes throughout the forest, providing you with plenty of places to explore by bike. Starting in Brockenhurst, this ride makes its way to Burley by country road and then picks up the woodland gravel track trail loop for approximately five miles. Thereafter, it's a mixture of road and trail all the way back to Brockenhurst.

Leave the A337 at the Snakecatcher Pub and go straight down Brookley Road. At Lloyds Bank turn left into the B3055. Turn right into the Rise and left at the end of the road into Burley Road.

Follow the road until it becomes Station Road under the A35 and all the way into Burley. At the Queens Head pub in Burley turn right into Chapel lane. Follow the road and merge right onto Lyndhurst Road. At the sign for Burley Products turn left onto a gravel track. Go through the gate into the Woodland.

Cross Blackensford Brook and continue until you reach the Anderwood enclosure. Fork left here until you reach

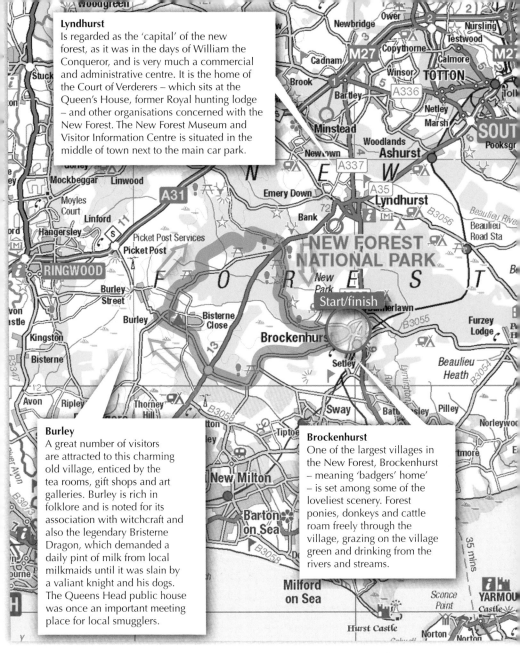

Lyndhurst
Is regarded as the 'capital' of the new forest, as it was in the days of William the Conqueror, and is very much a commercial and administrative centre. It is the home of the Court of Verderers – which sits at the Queen's House, former Royal hunting lodge – and other organisations concerned with the New Forest. The New Forest Museum and Visitor Information Centre is situated in the middle of town next to the main car park.

Burley
A great number of visitors are attracted to this charming old village, enticed by the tea rooms, gift shops and art galleries. Burley is rich in folklore and is noted for its association with witchcraft and also the legendary Bristerne Dragon, which demanded a daily pint of milk from local milkmaids until it was slain by a valiant knight and his dogs. The Queens Head public house was once an important meeting place for local smugglers.

Brockenhurst
One of the largest villages in the New Forest, Brockenhurst – meaning 'badgers' home' – is set among some of the loveliest scenery. Forest ponies, donkeys and cattle roam freely through the village, grazing on the village green and drinking from the rivers and streams.

the Boldenwood Ornamental Drive. Turn right and follow the road until you reach the A35.

Go over the A35 into Rhinefield Ornamental Drive. Follow until North Weirs. Turn right at North Weirs, signposted Brockenhurst and follow the track until reaching Burley Road. Turn left and follow the road back into Brockenhurst.

Bristol to Clevedon and back

Distance: 37 miles (59km)
Big hills: 1
Challenge: ●●●☆☆

A half-day ride on back roads and Sustrans routes

It's hard to imagine a route with a greater range of interest and contrast than one that starts in Bristol and goes around two loops of the National Cycle Network to the picture-postcard town of Clevedon on the Severn estuary. There are plenty of diversions in Bristol and then the blessed relief of escape from the city into country lanes, mostly chosen and signed by Sustrans (founded in Bristol), to the sea.

Take the A369 from the Clifton Suspension Bridge, signposted Portishead, and after 1.5 miles at Abbots Leigh village take the left turn, signposted National Cycle Network Route 334. Follow the arrows through the hamlet of Lower Failand to Portbury where you head left, following cycle route arrows towards Easton in Gordano. After about six miles, at B3124 Walton Road on the outskirts of Clevedon, take a right and then an immediate left onto Holly Lane, uphill into town, and then drop down to the seafront for beach cafés and sights.

Leave Clevedon by following signs to Bristol and pick up National Cycle Route 10 via West End, Chelvey, Brockley, Lulsgate Bottom and Felton, then turn back

onto the B3130 towards Barrow Gurney (take care crossing the A38!) and on to Long Ashton, still following National Cycle Route signs for Bristol.

After Long Ashton, enter the Ashton Court Estate via the gatehouse and follow signs through the park and past the campus of the University of the West of England. Follow bike signs down to the quayside and home.

Useful refreshment stops
Mud Dock Cycleworks and Café, 40 The Grove, Bristol BS1 4RB. 0117 934 9734

Scarlett's, 20 The Beach, Clevedon BS21 7QU. 01275 349032

Five the Beach, 5 The Beach, Clevedon BS21 7QU. 01275 341633 www.fivethebeachcafe.co.uk

The Black Horse, Clevedon Lane, Clapton in Gordano BS20 7RH. 01275 842105

The Royal Oak, 35 Copse Rd, Clevedon BS21 7QN. 01275 790420 www.royaloakclevedon.co.uk

The Blue Flame Inn, West End, Nailsea BS48 4DE. 01275 856910

Bike shops
Mud Dock Cycleworks and Café, (as above)

Bike Style, 25b Alexandra Road, Clevedon BS21 7QH. 01275 876572 www.bike-style.co.uk

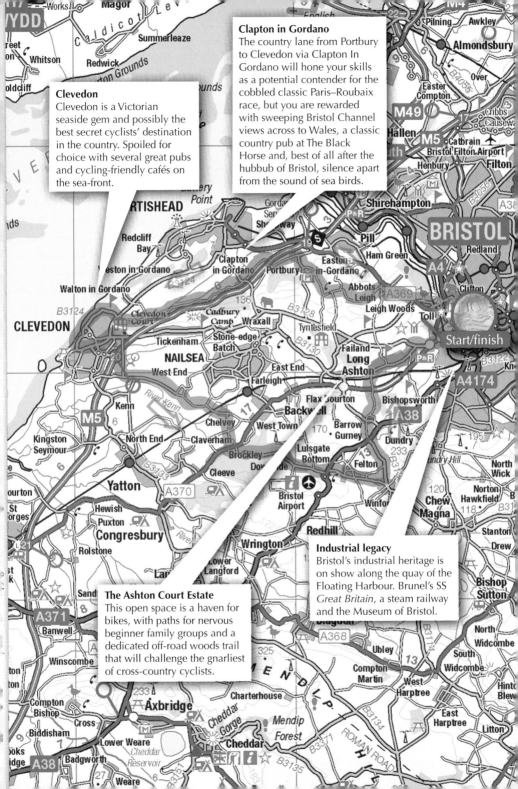

Clapton in Gordano
The country lane from Portbury to Clevedon via Clapton In Gordano will hone your skills as a potential contender for the cobbled classic Paris–Roubaix race, but you are rewarded with sweeping Bristol Channel views across to Wales, a classic country pub at The Black Horse and, best of all after the hubbub of Bristol, silence apart from the sound of sea birds.

Clevedon
Clevedon is a Victorian seaside gem and possibly the best secret cyclists' destination in the country. Spoiled for choice with several great pubs and cycling-friendly cafés on the sea-front.

The Ashton Court Estate
This open space is a haven for bikes, with paths for nervous beginner family groups and a dedicated off-road woods trail that will challenge the gnarliest of cross-country cyclists.

Industrial legacy
Bristol's industrial heritage is on show along the quay of the Floating Harbour. Brunel's SS *Great Britain*, a steam railway and the Museum of Bristol.

Minions and a Cornish tramway

Distance: 5.6 miles (9km)
Big hills: 1
Challenge: ●●☆☆☆

A leisurely amble through some lovely scenery on the southern fringes of Bodmin Moor

Cornwall's mining days are, of course, all over, but mine closures have left behind them beautiful expanses of countryside free for exploration as empty engine houses and mineshafts pepper the landscape, giving it a unique atmosphere and feel. This route takes you around one

such area: Caradon Hill on the southern fringes of Bodmin Moor. Caradon Hill is the most southerly of Bodmin Moor's hills, and all the way round the ride, the countryside drops away, leaving stunning views of Cornwall and the sea beyond.

Ride away from the eastern car park of the village of Minions keeping an eye out for a path heading off the road to the right. It's a steep track leading upwards on the right-hand side of the road on to the plateau of an old mining railway route or tramway.

From here, there's a clear path which heads towards the hill and bears to the left. When you reach Wheal Tor Café, continue on the lower branch of the track, parallel with the road. Eventually the path reaches a car park, from which the trail heads up the hill to the right. Once at the top, it flattens out. After passing two disused shafts, the path bears to the right and goes slightly downhill, leading to another engine house, with another one slightly below it.

Drop to the lower of the two, and turn left, following the path downwards, which then zigzags back on itself to the right along the valley floor. Cross a small stream and head down the valley once more. The path turns into a track and heads uphill

---

Useful refreshment stops

Hurlers Halt Tea Rooms, Minions, Liskeard, Cornwall PL14 5LE. 01579 363056 www.hurlers-halt.co.uk

The Cheesewring, Minions, Liskeard, Cornwall PL14 5LE. 01579 362321

Wheal Tor Hotel, Caradon Hill, Pensilva PL14 5PJ. 01579 363401

Bike shops

Bodmin Bike Hire (hire available), 3 Hamley Court, Dennison Road, Bodmin PL31 2LL. 01208 73192 www.bodminbikes.co.uk

Cornish Cycle Hire (hire available), Pensilva PL14 5PJ. 07526 317737

Liskeard Cycles, Pigmeadow Lane, Liskeard, Cornwall PL14 6AF. 01579 347696 www.liskeardcycles.co.uk

to your right. Follow it, heading uphill, turn back on yourself at the first junction you meet, follow the path around another hairpin and then turn right onto a road that eventually leads to a farmhouse named Downhill Farm.

When you reach the farmhouse, ride through it and head up a road that turns to the left before meeting a field. Next, head straight on into the field and follow a rutted track past another chimney and a disused mine on your right. Follow this rutted track until you hit the road. Then turn right and continue riding back to the village to arrive back in the car park.

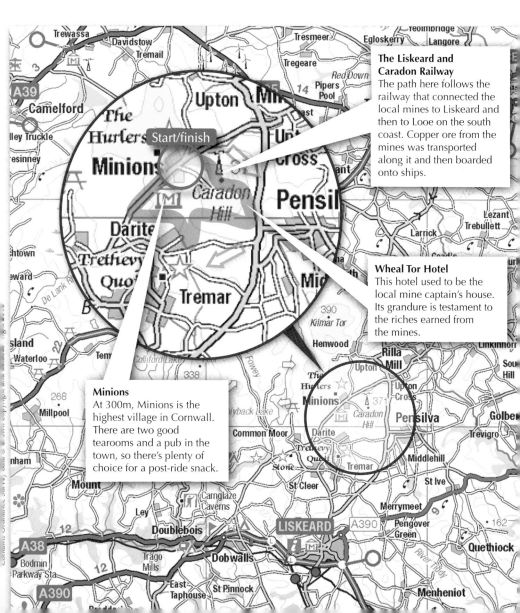

The Liskeard and Caradon Railway
The path here follows the railway that connected the local mines to Liskeard and then to Looe on the south coast. Copper ore from the mines was transported along it and then boarded onto ships.

Wheal Tor Hotel
This hotel used to be the local mine captain's house. Its grandure is testament to the riches earned from the mines.

Minions
At 300m, Minions is the highest village in Cornwall. There are two good tearooms and a pub in the town, so there's plenty of choice for a post-ride snack.

Purbeck and Corfe Castle

Distance: 25 miles (40km)
Big hills: several short sharp ascents
Challenge: ✪✪✪✪☆

A ride of two distinct halves with plenty of interesting spots to stop and two off-road stretches

Beginning in Studland, this route visits the majestic Corfe Castle, a picturesque lake and and an RSPB reserve.

Leave Studland to the west on the B3351. Take the first turn left (a fork) signed to Ulwell. Turn right into the village (signed to the Village Inn), follow the road as it bears left and then fork right. At a junction turn right (unsigned) then follow this road along the side of the ridge all the way to Corfe Castle.

At the junction with the A351 turn right and around the castle. Continue ahead at the roundabout then turn left off the main road to and through Norden Farm. Pass through the campsite to enter the wood in the far right corner. Continue in the same direction as before through the wood initially on its southern edge.

Emerging at a road, turn right and then take the first track on the right to the Blue Pool. Leave the Pool following the exit signs for cars, which brings you to the A351. Turn right and then, at the Halfway Inn, left onto a minor road across the heathland. At a T-junction turn

right (unsigned) to continue to Arne. (The bridleway to Shipstall Point starts opposite St Nicholas Church.)

Retrace your route to the first junction, where you bear left. After about 1.5 miles look out on your left for a fingerpost with the first in a series of blue waymarkers for the cycle route. They take you off-road along a bridleway to Studland (also Route 2 of the National Cycle Network) initially over an old stone bridge and then in and out of forests. Eventually, you emerge at the ferry road. Turn right to return to Studland.

Useful refreshment stops

The Bankes Arms, Studland BH19 3AU.
  01929 450225 www.bankesarmes.com

The Village Inn, Ulwell BH19 3DG.
  01929 427644
  www.villageinn-swanage.co.uk

Good choice of pubs and cafes in
  Corfe Castle: www.corfecastle.co.uk

The Blue Pool Tea Room, Norden BH20
  5AR. 01929 551408

The Halfway Inn, Norden, BH20 5DU.
  01929 480402
  www.thehalfwayinnwareham.co.uk

Bike shops

The Bikemonger, 137B High Street,
  Swanage BH19 2NB. 01929 475 833
  www.charliethebikemonger.com

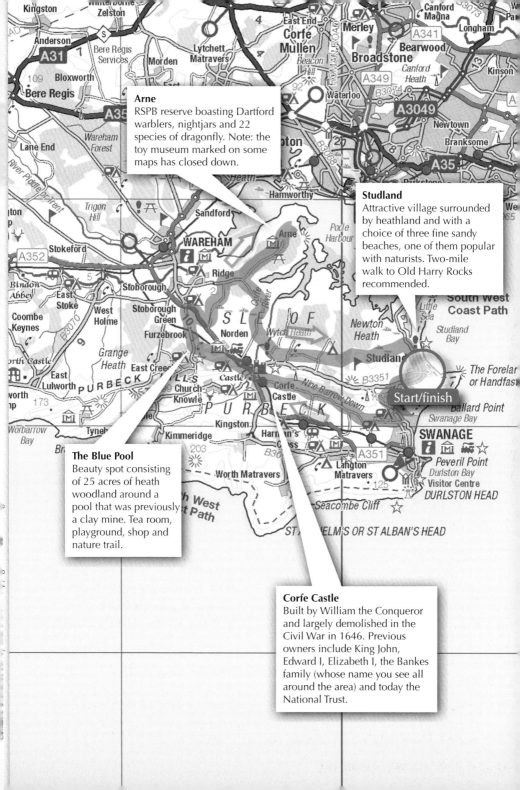

Arne
RSPB reserve boasting Dartford warblers, nightjars and 22 species of dragonfly. Note: the toy museum marked on some maps has closed down.

Studland
Attractive village surrounded by heathland and with a choice of three fine sandy beaches, one of them popular with naturists. Two-mile walk to Old Harry Rocks recommended.

The Blue Pool
Beauty spot consisting of 25 acres of heath woodland around a pool that was previously a clay mine. Tea room, playground, shop and nature trail.

Corfe Castle
Built by William the Conqueror and largely demolished in the Civil War in 1646. Previous owners include King John, Edward I, Elizabeth I, the Bankes family (whose name you see all around the area) and today the National Trust.

Wiltshire countryside

Distance: 20 miles (32km)
Big hills: none
Challenge: ★☆☆☆☆

A appealing tour on mixed terrain, using Sustrans paths

This quiet part of Wiltshire, just off the M4 motorway is a great place to ride, and if you are interested in Second World War history, you have definitely come to the right place. During the war, the whole area was a hive of activity, as it housed the US 101st Airborne Division, members of which were made famous nearly 60 years later by the TV series *Band of Brothers*. There aren't many obvious signs of the US occupation left, but if you look under the skin of the area you will find that the Yanks' time here is still very much remembered by the locals. The historic market town of Marlborough is the base for this ride and makes a perfect place for post-ride refreshments, which you can find in the many hostelries and cafés.

Starting in Marlborough High Street, head north then east towards Mildenhall/Ramsbury. This is a decent two-lane road all the way to Ramsbury. At the Bell Pub in Ramsbury take a left for Aldbourne. At the B4192 go left for Aldbourne – this is the busiest road on the ride, but nothing serious. At Aldbourne village centre, take a left, then immediate right onto Castle Street towards Woodsend.

This is the hardest, most exposed part of the route, but is a long drag rather than steep. Traffic, although little, can be quite fast, as it's a good stretch of road. At the top take care as the descent is steep, but wide. Go left at the flyover, just before Ogbourne St George and pick up the Marlborough to Chiceldon railway path, which is part of Sustrans National Route 45. This gravel path will take you back into Marlborough, but watch out for changes in the surface and sharp stones!

Useful refreshment stops

The Blue Boar, Aldbourne, Wilts
  SN8 2EN; 01672 540237
  www.thepubonthegreen.co.uk

The Bell, Ramsbury, Wilts SN8 2PE. 01672
  520 230 www.thebellramsbury.com

Silks on the Downs, Main Road,
  Ogbourne St Andrew, Marlborough
  SN8 1RZ. 01672 841229
  www.silksonthedowns.co.uk

Bike shops

Bertie Maffoon (hire available), Unit 1
  Glympton Court, Marlborough Business
  Park SN8 4AL. 01672 519119

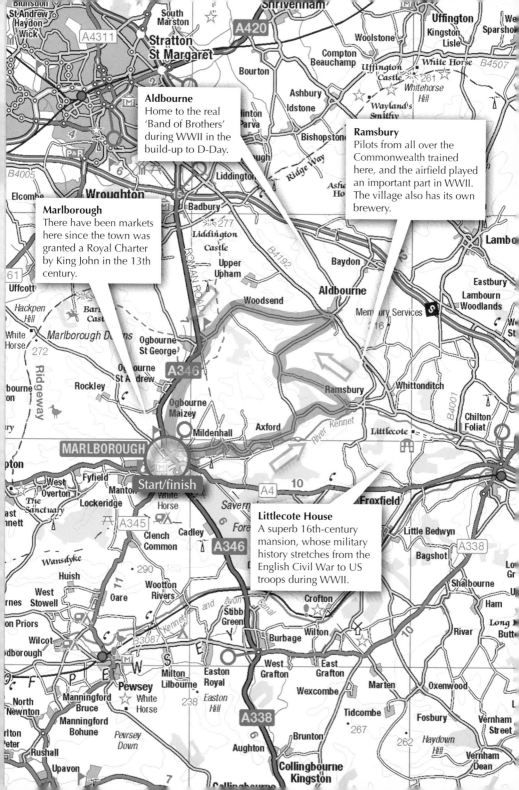

Aldbourne
Home to the real 'Band of Brothers' during WWII in the build-up to D-Day.

Ramsbury
Pilots from all over the Commonwealth trained here, and the airfield played an important part in WWII. The village also has its own brewery.

Marlborough
There have been markets here since the town was granted a Royal Charter by King John in the 13th century.

Littlecote House
A superb 16th-century mansion, whose military history stretches from the English Civil War to US troops during WWII.

MARLBOROUGH
Start/finish

The Tarka Trail, Devon

Distance: 33 miles (53km)
Big hills: 3 – and lots of little ones
Challenge: ✪✪✪✪☆

A day ride through North Devon's river country taking in the Tarka Trail cycle path

This ride starts in Great Torrington and explores the Taw valley before joining the Tarka Trail at Barnstaple. It's a circular ride, so like many similar ones in this area there are some tough hills in it. However, the purpose of the ride is to showcase the Tarka Trail, a family-friendly stretch of flat cycle path that goes south for over 50 miles from the north coast at Braunton inland to Meeth. The trail takes its name

from a classic of English literature, *Tarka the Otter*, written by Henry Williamson and first published in 1927.

Head east out of Great Torrington on the B3227, following signs to South Molton. This eight-mile leg is the hilliest of the ride, but the road surface is very good. Turn right onto the A377 and in Umberleigh turn left, with care, to cross the river Taw. Take the first left on the unclassified road that runs north alongside the Taw. The surface on this leg is more like the usual North Devon roads, with slippery mud and gunk that requires care in the wet.

Join the A377 and head into Barnstaple, taking the second left after the roundabout junction with the A39. This brings you out at a roundabout. After taking the first exit, cross a long bridge and at the second roundabout take the third exit, then turn right where you see the Tarka Trail signs. Follow the Trail, which is flat, apart from a drag before the tunnel, and is well surfaced. At the Puffing Billy turn right into the car park and then left onto the A386 for the tough but rewarding climb back into Great Torrington.

Useful refreshment stops

The Quay Café, Fremington, Bickington, near Barnstaple EX31 2NH. 01271 378783 www.fremingtonquay.co.uk

The Cyder Presse, Weare Giffard, Bideford EX39 4QR. 01237 425517 www.cyderpresse.co.uk

The Boathouse, Marine Parade, Instow EX39 4JJ. 01271 861292 www.instow.net/boathouse

Bike shops

The Bike Shed, The Square, Barnstaple, EX32 8LS. 01271 328628

Tarka Trail Cycle Hire, by Barnstaple Station. 01271 324202 www.tarkabikes.co.uk

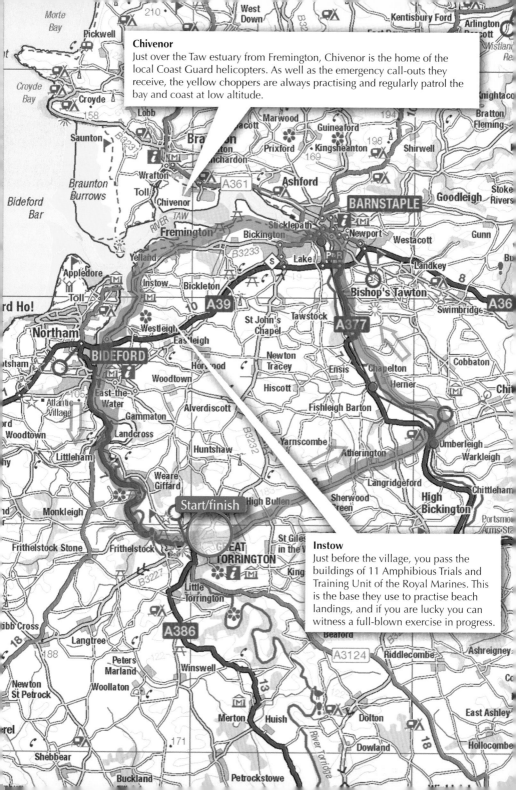

Chivenor
Just over the Taw estuary from Fremington, Chivenor is the home of the local Coast Guard helicopters. As well as the emergency call-outs they receive, the yellow choppers are always practising and regularly patrol the bay and coast at low altitude.

Instow
Just before the village, you pass the buildings of 11 Amphibious Trials and Training Unit of the Royal Marines. This is the base they use to practise beach landings, and if you are lucky you can witness a full-blown exercise in progress.

Start/finish

Cornwall coast to coast

Distance: 14 miles (22.5km)
Big hills: none
Challenge: ★☆☆☆☆

A comfortable ride on a section of the 'Coast to Coast' cycle path

Cornwall's mines were once connected by a network of rail lines, which also linked them with the sea, so coal could be hauled in for the engines and metal ore out to be exported. The lines were called tramways and, now removed, they make excellent routes for cycling. There are over 35 miles of usable trails, mostly with a hard surface, and because they are former rail lines there are hardly any hills, just gradual rises. You can link them all together for a big ride, but this route is on the 'Coast to Coast' – 12 miles each way from Devoran in the south to Portreath in the north – only going halfway across the county though and then doing a loop to take in a couple of interesting mines.

All tourist offices plus many hotels and other tourist locations stock a free map and information sheet on the trails – www.cornishmining.org.uk contains maps and a huge amount of information too. Basically though for this ride, if you start in Devoran, where there is ample space for parking, find the quay and follow the trail signposts north-west. You'll ride on country roads at first, but the off-road trail begins soon. Take care crossing the road just after the arsenic works, and head for the Bike Chain / Bissoe Bike Hire car park. Continue through this to Twelveheads, ignoring the sign to Wheal Busy, and head for Scorrier. Once in Scorrier follow the sign to Wheal Busy, and the route will loop back to the coast to coast route, from where you can retrace south-east back to Devoran.

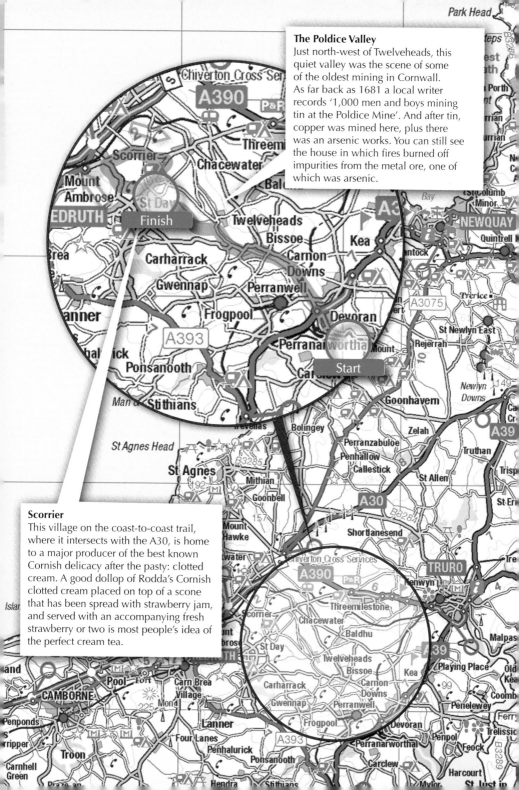

The Poldice Valley
Just north-west of Twelveheads, this quiet valley was the scene of some of the oldest mining in Cornwall. As far back as 1681 a local writer records '1,000 men and boys mining tin at the Poldice Mine'. And after tin, copper was mined here, plus there was an arsenic works. You can still see the house in which fires burned off impurities from the metal ore, one of which was arsenic.

Scorrier
This village on the coast-to-coast trail, where it intersects with the A30, is home to a major producer of the best known Cornish delicacy after the pasty: clotted cream. A good dollop of Rodda's Cornish clotted cream placed on top of a scone that has been spread with strawberry jam, and served with an accompanying fresh strawberry or two is most people's idea of the perfect cream tea.

Swindon and Marlborough

Distance: 38 miles (56km)
Big hills: 4
Challenge: ✪✪✪☆☆

A day ride from Swindon to Marlborough via a white horse and classic lanes

On Wood Street in the Old Town of Swindon, head west, turn left onto Devizes Road and then, after 500m, right onto Springfield Road. Follow Westlecot Road and Mill Lane, cross the M4 and after three miles, turn right at a T-junction onto Wharf Road.

Follow the road for approximately two miles and turn left at a T-junction signposted Broad Hinton. After three miles cross the A4361 and pass the Wroughton Airfield on your left. After about another 500m, turn right, signed Broad Hinton, and re-cross the A4361 into Broad Hinton.

In the village centre, take a left, signed Marlborough, and crossing the A4361 for the last time, follow Hackpen Hill up past the white horse and along seven miles until Marlborough centre.

To return, retrace 200m and take the right signed Mildenhall and then to Axford. After one mile take the left fork signed Aldbourne. At Aldbourne, take the left signed Ogbourne St George. After three miles, take care descending Snap Hill past the golf course to Ogbourne St George and take the right signposted Chiseldon. Follow signs to Swindon but a half-mile out of Chiseldon take a right signed Hodson. Follow the lane to Broome Manor. Keep going to the roundabout on Marlborough Road, then left and follow signs back to Old Town.

Useful refreshment stops

Old Town Cafe, 64 Devizes Road, Swindon SN1 4BD. 01793 542552

The Polly Tearooms, The Polly Tearooms, 27 High Street, Marlborough SN8 1LW. 01672 512146 www.thepolly.com

Applebys Café, 5 Old Hughenden Yard, High Street, Marlborough SN8 1LT. 01672 515200 www.applebycafe.com

The Crown Inn, Broad Hinton, Swindon SN4 9PA. 01793 731302 www.thecrownatbroadhinton.co.uk

Sun Inn, 90 High Street, Marlborough SN8 1HF. 01672 515011 www.thesunmarlborough.co.uk

The Crown, The Square, Aldbourne SN8 2DU. 01672 540214 www.thecrownaldbourne.co.uk

Bike shops

Bertie Maffoon (hire available), Unit 1 Glympton Court, Marlborough Business Park SN8 4AL. 01672 519119

Hargroves Cycles, Unit 9, Penzance Drive, Churchward Park, Swindon SN5 7RX. 01793 528208 www.hargrovescycles.co.uk

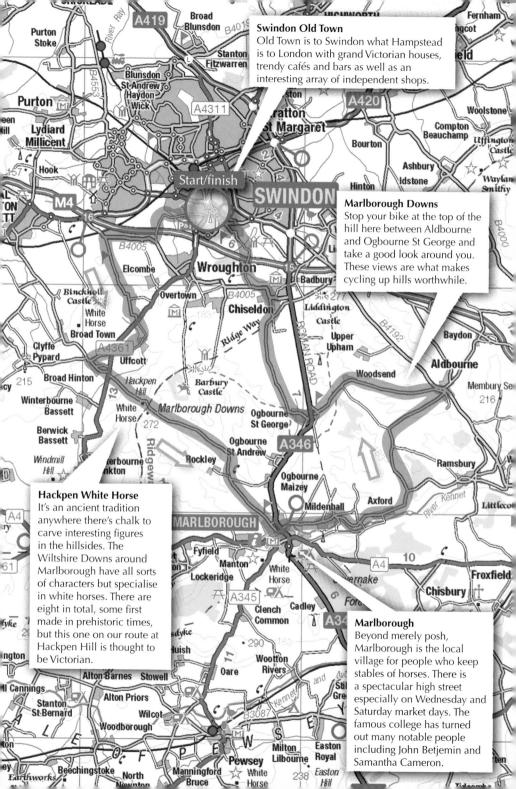

Swindon Old Town
Old Town is to Swindon what Hampstead is to London with grand Victorian houses, trendy cafés and bars as well as an interesting array of independent shops.

Marlborough Downs
Stop your bike at the top of the hill here between Aldbourne and Ogbourne St George and take a good look around you. These views are what makes cycling up hills worthwhile.

Hackpen White Horse
It's an ancient tradition anywhere there's chalk to carve interesting figures in the hillsides. The Wiltshire Downs around Marlborough have all sorts of characters but specialise in white horses. There are eight in total, some first made in prehistoric times, but this one on our route at Hackpen Hill is thought to be Victorian.

Marlborough
Beyond merely posh, Marlborough is the local village for people who keep stables of horses. There is a spectacular high street especially on Wednesday and Saturday market days. The famous college has turned out many notable people including John Betjemin and Samantha Cameron.

Start/finish

Dartmoor

Distance: 12.5 miles (20km)
Big hills: 1
Challenge: ✪✪☆☆☆

A short, very hilly mountain bike ride on Dartmoor, taking in the vista at Hound Tor

East Dartmoor – and Dartmoor on the whole, for that matter – has an abundance of routes on offer for mountain bikers of all abilities (crazy freeriders to freeflowing cruisers…with plenty of terrain in-between the two extremes). If you like the idea of sticking to dedicated trails, Haldon Forest Park is a short drive away from Dartmoor and a good option for families. Equally, there is an abundance of Sustrans routes in Devon. Check out www.sustrans.org.uk.

Useful refreshment stops
The Kestor Inn, Manaton TQ13 9UF.
01647 221626
www.thebullersarms.co.uk
Hound of the Basket snack wagon at Hound Tor car park
Plus lots of choice in Bovey Tracey

Bike shops
Nearest bike shops in Newton Abbot or Exeter

This is a route in Dartmoor National Park an, area of almost 370 square miles where any number of alternative rides are possible. Beginning at the renowned 'gateway to the moor', Bovey Tracey, head out towards Reddaford Water on the road, following signs to Manaton and Becky Falls. Just before arriving at Reddaford Water, there are signs on the left indicating the car park at Yarner Wood. At the Yarner Wood car park, beyond the small welcome hut, is a gate that marks the start of numerous footpaths. Take the main and larger one, heading out north-west, leading around the perimeter of the woodland.

It essentially leads you towards North Lodge, the furthest corner of the wood in tough steep and sometimes rocky trails. At North Lodge, make your way through another gate and head right for another uphill stretch, this time on a small road towards Blackhill and Hound Tor. Another hard climb and when the road levels off, you can see Black Hill on the left.

Continue towards Hound Tor, a granite hilltop poking out on the horizon, one of the many tors that characterise Dartmoor. Shortly after, cut left on to a sign-posted bridleway leading towards Hound Tor and the medieval settlement.

Following from the bridleway on to a small road through Leighton, you turn uphill again on a small road heading towards Hound Tor, with glimpses of the deserted medieval village nestled beneath. From the Hound Tor car park follow signs to Chagford and Manaton, past fields and open moorland through Hayne Down.

Once at Manaton, head towards Becky Falls, a tributary of the River Bovey. From Becky Falls, cut through the east Dartmoor woods and heaths National Nature Reserve of Trendlebere Down. The majority of this downhill section sends you gliding through the vast moorland, all the way back towards Bovey Tracey.

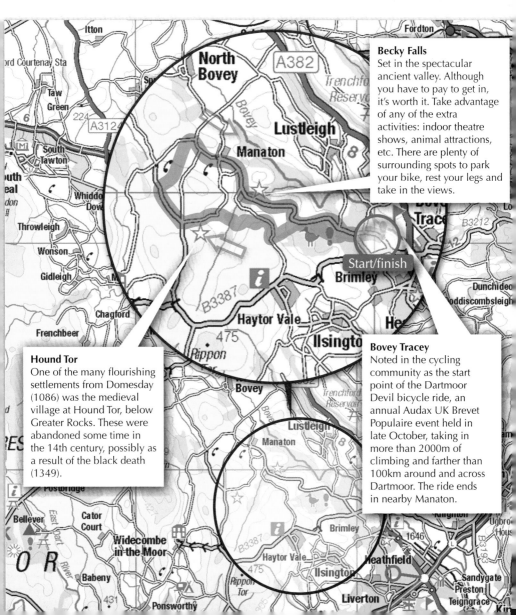

Becky Falls
Set in the spectacular ancient valley. Although you have to pay to get in, it's worth it. Take advantage of any of the extra activities: indoor theatre shows, animal attractions, etc. There are plenty of surrounding spots to park your bike, rest your legs and take in the views.

Hound Tor
One of the many flourishing settlements from Domesday (1086) was the medieval village at Hound Tor, below Greater Rocks. These were abandoned some time in the 14th century, possibly as a result of the black death (1349).

Bovey Tracey
Noted in the cycling community as the start point of the Dartmoor Devil bicycle ride, an annual Audax UK Brevet Populaire event held in late October, taking in more than 2000m of climbing and farther than 100km around and across Dartmoor. The ride ends in nearby Manaton.

Cornwall's Flat Lode Trail

Distance: 7.7 miles (12km)
Big hills: 1
Challenge: ●●☆☆☆

A short trail on the Great Flat Lode Trail taking in farmland and Cornwall's industrial heritage

From the Brea Inn (now closed) in Higher Brea, head up the hill to the point at which there are signs to the Great Flat Lode in either direction. On the right-hand side, there is a map of the area with all the local cycle paths clearly marked. Take the path on the same side of the road as the map, and head straight along a flat road which cuts along a hill.

At Chy, you meet the road and must turn right for a few metres and there is a T-junction with a steep path opposite you. It flattens out after a few hundred metres.

After this, there are a number of farms on either side of the path. This continues until the King Edward Mine Museum, where you must cross a quiet road, and the hedgerows open out to open, grassy areas and engine houses and mineshafts are frequent.

Continue past Lower Grillis Farm, and enter an open area where a huge number of mining buildings dominate the landscape. Cross the road at Piece, making sure that you do not drop lower than the path on the other side, as it emerges at two points. If you find yourself emerging on the road lower than South Wheal Frances, head up the road for a short time and the next part of the path becomes obvious and well signposted.

The path rises up to Carnkie, with Carn Brea Hill on your left, and a tumulus on your right. From here, the path continues through a number of farm areas until you reach a T-junction. Go left at the T-junction, and at the bottom of the hill, cross the crossroads back onto the cycle path which is signposted as Redruth and Chasewater Trail – this is a shared path for around 500m. The signposts resume, and the path passes between Carn Brea Hill and Carn Brea village, before an easy, straight path back to Brea. The path emerges opposite the starting point.

Useful refreshment stops
The Countryman, Piece, Carnkie, Redruth TR16 6SG. 01209 215960

Bike shops
Bike Chain Bissoe (hire available), Old Conns Works, Bissoe, Truro TR4 8QZ. 01872 870341
www.cornwallcyclehire.com

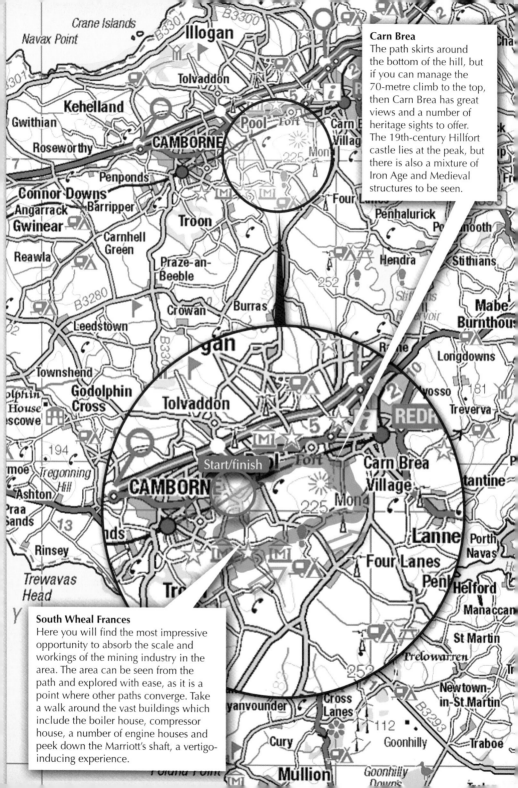

Carn Brea
The path skirts around the bottom of the hill, but if you can manage the 70-metre climb to the top, then Carn Brea has great views and a number of heritage sights to offer. The 19th-century Hillfort castle lies at the peak, but there is also a mixture of Iron Age and Medieval structures to be seen.

Start/finish

South Wheal Frances
Here you will find the most impressive opportunity to absorb the scale and workings of the mining industry in the area. The area can be seen from the path and explored with ease, as it is a point where other paths converge. Take a walk around the vast buildings which include the boiler house, compressor house, a number of engine houses and peek down the Marriott's shaft, a vertigo-inducing experience.

Cheltenham and the Gloucestershire countryside

Distance: 29 miles (46km)
Big hills: 2
Challenge: ❶❷☆☆☆

An easy 29-mile ride from Cheltenham into the Cotswolds and Laurie Lee country

For cyclists, the Cotswold hills, bounded by Stratford, Oxford and Gloucester, are some of the most beautiful in Britain, but they can be tough going with a good few ups and downs, usually rewarded at the tops with a breathtaking view. As long as you're avoiding the M5 and the busy cross-country A417, all roads towards the destination of this ride, Stroud, are good for cycling and clearly marked, the motorway having taken away the worst of the traffic from the A46 on which the route begins.

From Cheltenham, follow the A46, signed towards Stroud, then Painswick, for 11 miles. At the end of the village, take the left turn marked Stamage's Lane and follow this, signed Stroud, along Stepping Stone Lane, Wick St and finally Painswick Old Road until Stroud, at nearly 14 miles.

At both roundabouts, take the first exit signed B4070 Slad. Ride 7 miles until Birdlip. In the village centre, at the T-junction, go right and then immediately left, signed Cheltenham. After 200m, take the left signed with a brown 'view' sign and after a further 300m enter Barrow Wake viewing area, going through the car park until the gravel path merges into the main A417 dual carriageway (take care!)

There's a foot crossing around the Air Balloon roundabout, otherwise take the second exit signed Oxford and then left to Leckhampton, back to Cheltenham.

Useful refreshment stops

The Star Anise Arts Café, Five Valleys Foyer, Gloucester Street, Stroud GL5 1QG. 01453 840021 www.staraniseartcafe.com

Pepper Crescent, 12 Royal Crescent, Cheltenham GL50 3DA. 01242 572958 www.peppercrescent.co.uk

The Woolpack Inn, Slad, Gloucestershire GL6 7QA. 01452 813429

Fostons Ash Inn, Slad Road, Birdlip GL6 7ES. 01452 863262

Bike shops

Cheltenham Cycles, 61 Winchcombe Street, Cheltenham GL52 2NE. 01242 255414 wwww.cheltenhamcycles.co.uk

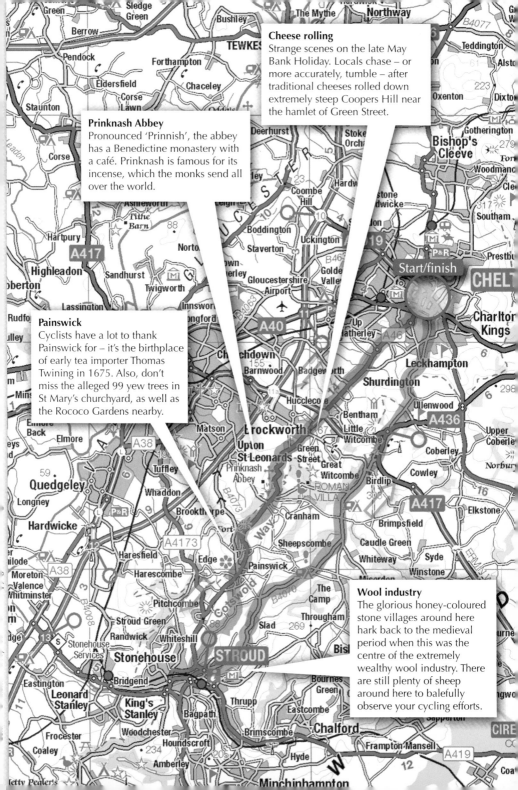

Cheese rolling
Strange scenes on the late May Bank Holiday. Locals chase – or more accurately, tumble – after traditional cheeses rolled down extremely steep Coopers Hill near the hamlet of Green Street.

Prinknash Abbey
Pronounced 'Prinnish', the abbey has a Benedictine monastery with a café. Prinknash is famous for its incense, which the monks send all over the world.

Painswick
Cyclists have a lot to thank Painswick for – it's the birthplace of early tea importer Thomas Twining in 1675. Also, don't miss the alleged 99 yew trees in St Mary's churchyard, as well as the Rococo Gardens nearby.

Wool industry
The glorious honey-coloured stone villages around here hark back to the medieval period when this was the centre of the extremely wealthy wool industry. There are still plenty of sheep around here to balefully observe your cycling efforts.

Start/finish

Suffolk coast

Distance: 13 miles (21km)
Big hills: none
Challenge: ●●☆☆☆

Explore beautiful beaches, commons, heathland and old railway lines along the North Sea coast

Rides like these, which are well off the beaten track, are the perfect way to discover those hidden gems – be they pubs, restaurants, places of interest or just traffic-free routes.

Starting in Sizewell, leave the car park at Sizewell Beach. Pass the Vulcan Arms then turn left signed to Sizewell Hall. Continue ahead at the Hall signed 'Waldens'. Where the Tarmac ends bear right onto an unsurfaced track signed as a byway. Take the second left signed 'byway' on a fingerpost. At the end, at a T-junction, turn right onto a broad, sandy track. After 200m bear left onto a grassy track signed as a byway and Suffolk Coast path. As you near Thorpeness's houses, bear left then immediately hard right onto a gravel road.

At Thorpeness, turn right at a small green and onto the road, then left in front of Ogilvie Hall and right down Uplands Road (unsurfaced) to view the windmill and House in the Clouds. Return along Uplands Road then turn right down The

Haven. Pass Thorpeness Meare and the Beach House Café, then turn left into a car park. Push your bike for a short distance along a boardwalk to reach the beach. Turn right and proceed towards Aldeburgh. Stay at the back of the beach where the surface is firmer until reaching a Tarmac path, which takes you into Aldeburgh via a car park.

Useful refreshment stops

Sizewell Beach Refreshment Café, Sizewell Gap, Leiston IP16 4UH. 01728 831108

The Meare Shop and Tea Room, Thorpeness, Meare, Leiston IP16 4NW. 01728 452156

Ives Ice Cream Parlour, High St, Aldeburgh IP15 5AQ. 01728 452264

Munchies Café, High St, Aldeburgh IP15 5AN. 01728 454566

The Vulcan Arms, Sizewell Gap, Sizewell IP16 4UD. 01728 830748 vulcanarms.freehostia.com

The Dolphin Inn, Peace Place, Thorpeness IP16 4NA. 01728 454994 www.thorpenessdolphin.com

Bike shops

Byways Bicycles (hire available), Priory Farm, Darsham IP17 3QD. 01728 668459

Go as far as you like into Aldeburgh then return along the Tarmac path to the car park. Just after you enter it turn left, across the road following signs for Church Farm and Ipswich (A1094).

After a few hundred yards look out for a sign indicating a public footpath through the caravan park. Pass through the width restriction and turn left, pushing your bike across the campsite. At the sign for Alde Meadow bear right, pass a phone box and the caravan park reception then left onto Deben Way. Leave the caravan park through a gap in the fence beneath a tree then turn right to join a path following the course of a disused railway line. Eventually, at a waterworks, the track becomes a concrete then Tarmac road.

At a T-junction in front of a white bungalow turn left onto the B1353. About 100m after a 'B&B next right' sign turn right to leave the road and enter a small car park within heathland. Take the right of the three tracks in front of you. At the end of the track turn right and follow the next track as it bears left (not into the trees).

Pass in front of three houses. Bear right then left, passing the golf course and pig farm. Cross over a farm track and keep straight ahead. Turn right at a crossroads of tracks onto Grimsey Lane. Pass Crownland's Cottage then left onto a very sandy track for about 300m.

At the end, cross over the road then follow signs (keeping in same direction) for Yoxford and Saxmundham. Take the first right turn and then right again down a broad track before Common Hall Cottages. Fork right at a fingerpost for a bridleway. At the end of it turn right, going slightly uphill. At the road turn left to return to Sizewell.

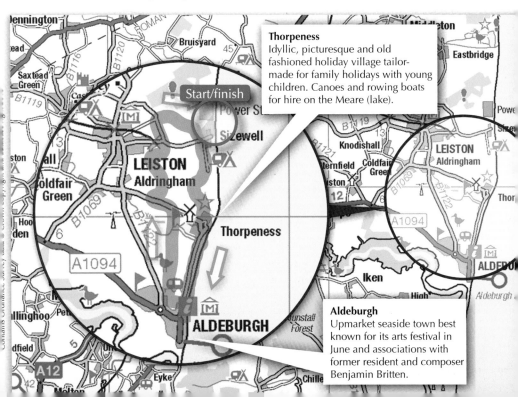

Thorpeness
Idyllic, picturesque and old fashioned holiday village tailor-made for family holidays with young children. Canoes and rowing boats for hire on the Meare (lake).

Aldeburgh
Upmarket seaside town best known for its arts festival in June and associations with former resident and composer Benjamin Britten.

Rutland Water

Distance: 25 miles (40km)
Big hills: gentle gradients but no major climbs
Challenge: ★☆☆☆☆

A picturesque and largely flat reservoir loop circumnavigating Rutland Water, mainly off-road, with a pub stop three-quarters of the way round

Rutland Water is perfect for cyclists. There's a largely traffic-free 25-mile course following the reservoir's shores on off-road trails. The route itself is entertainingly varied in terms of both cycling terrain and surroundings, so things never get boring. There are two great bike shops, one on the north shore, one on the south and a great pub, the Horse and Jockey pub, which judging by the ample bike racks is well used to welcoming cyclists.

The route itself could not be more straightforward: head out of the car park at Whitwell, keeping the reservoir to your left, and simply follow the signs all the way round.

Useful refreshment stops

Fox café kiosks around Rutland Water at Whitwell, Normanton and Empingham. 01780 460047

Horse and Jockey, St Mary's Rd, Manton LE15 8SU. 01572 737 335 www.horseandjockeyrutland.co.uk

Bike shops

Rutland Cycling Centre (hire available), Normanton Car Park, Rutland Water, Edith Weston, Nr Oakham LE15 8HD. 01780 720 888 www.rutlandcycling.com

Rutland Cycling Centre (hire available), Whitwell Leisure Park, Bull Brigg Lane, Whitwell, Nr Oakham LE15 8BL. 01780 460 705 www.rutlandcycling.com

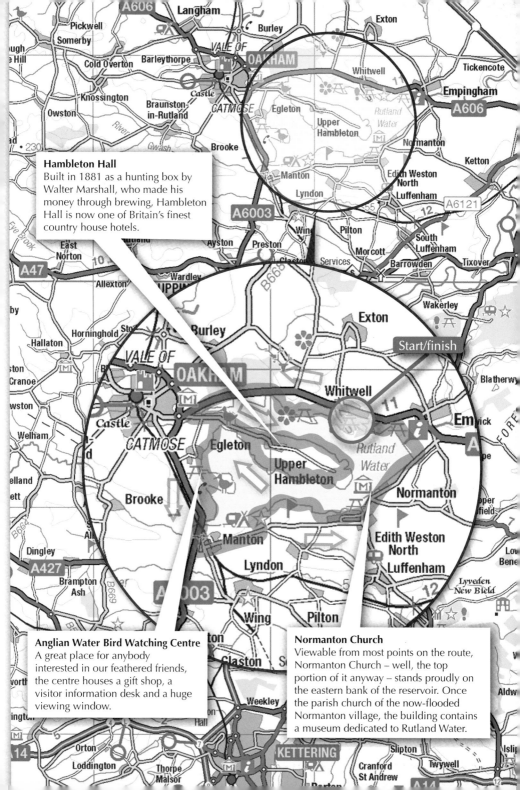

Hambleton Hall
Built in 1881 as a hunting box by Walter Marshall, who made his money through brewing, Hambleton Hall is now one of Britain's finest country house hotels.

Anglian Water Bird Watching Centre
A great place for anybody interested in our feathered friends, the centre houses a gift shop, a visitor information desk and a huge viewing window.

Normanton Church
Viewable from most points on the route, Normanton Church – well, the top portion of it anyway – stands proudly on the eastern bank of the reservoir. Once the parish church of the now-flooded Normanton village, the building contains a museum dedicated to Rutland Water.

Fertile, flat fenland

Distance: 20 miles (32km)
Big hills: none
Challenge: ★☆☆☆☆

Useful refreshment stops

Studio Café (tucked away at the back of home shop Etcetera), 7 York Row, Wisbech PE13 1EB. 01945 463440

The Globe Inn 1 School Road, Upwell, Norfolk PE14 9EW. 01945 773786

Chequers Inn, Friday Bridge, Cambs PE14 0HF. 01945 860059

Crown Lodge Hotel, Outwell PE14 8SE. 01945 773391 www.thecrownlodgehotel.co.uk

Bike shops

Discount Cycles, 114–115 Norfolk Street, Wisbech PE13 2LD. 01945 474635

A relaxing ride crossing fertile fields, beside deep ditches, to a real gem of a Georgian town

The land to the north of Cambridge is fertile and flat – perfect for growing fruit and veg and also ideal for pleasant and easy cycling.

Beginning at the village of Outwell, halfway between Downham Market and Wisbech, set out following the Nene–Ouse navigation canal south-west. Keep the canal on your right until the bridge at the Globe, then cross it to keep the water on your left. This dog-leg road crossing is hazardous.

Continue to Laddus Drove and head north. At the T-junction with Well End, go west (left) and at Friday Bridge clock, join the B1101 towards March. After half a mile, the road bends sharp left, so go straight ahead into Jew House Drove. Beware fast vehicles on the bend. Turn right along Belt Drove, part of National Cycle Route 63. Follow NCR 63 signs for four miles into Wisbech, crossing the main roads with care.

Leave Wisbech via the main traffic light junction on Downham Road into

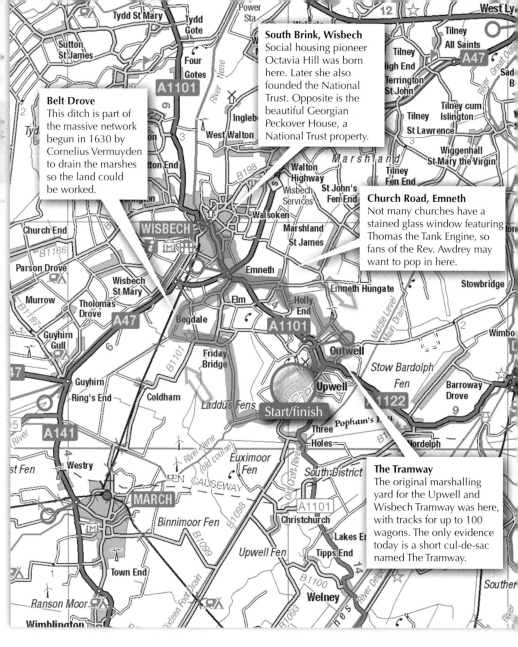

Belt Drove
This ditch is part of the massive network begun in 1630 by Cornelius Vermuyden to drain the marshes so the land could be worked.

South Brink, Wisbech
Social housing pioneer Octavia Hill was born here. Later she also founded the National Trust. Opposite is the beautiful Georgian Peckover House, a National Trust property.

Church Road, Emneth
Not many churches have a stained glass window featuring Thomas the Tank Engine, so fans of the Rev. Awdrey may want to pop in here.

The Tramway
The original marshalling yard for the Upwell and Wisbech Tramway was here, with tracks for up to 100 wagons. The only evidence today is a short cul-de-sac named The Tramway.

Norwich Road then along Elizabeth Terrace. Carefully cross Ramnoth Road, to Money Bank, then head due south down Quaker Lane. Care is needed crossing the A47 and again for 10 yards of the A1101 into Emneth. Ride through it, then follow Fendyke Road. Turn left when it ends, then first right to Marsh Road. Langhorns Lane leads back to Outwell and the A1122 to Downham Road.

Lincolnshire

Distance: 17.4 miles (28.5km)
Big hills: none
Challenge: ★☆☆☆☆

A leisurely ride discovering the history of the flatlands in this quiet area of Eastern England

Lincolnshire boasts a number of attractive market towns worth exploring. This ride begins in the market place at Horncastle. From here, turn left and go along the High Street. Turn right at the T-junction onto Bull Ring. Go straight on at the traffic lights and continue down the A153 for a short stretch. Take the first turning on the right after the built-up area. On reaching the white house, turn left into the public bridleway which is the Spa Trail, part of the Viking Way.

Follow the trail until it reaches a T-junction with a tarmac road. Turn right and follow the road to the end. Turn left at the staggered junction at Reeds Beck, and left again at the crossroads on to Stixwold Road. Turn left at the crossroads on to the Broadway just outside Woodhall Spa.

After passing the main shops, turn right into Kirkby Lane to head into Kirkby on Bain. At the T-junction in Kirkby, turn left and then right to cross Red Mill Bridge (Rimes Lane).

Turn left onto the A153 at the T-junction, then at Haltham turn right into Wood Enderby Lane. In Wood Enderby village, turn left and then, on reaching the crossroads, turn left onto the B1183 to join the A153 back to Horncastle.

Useful refreshment stops

The Ebrington Arms, Main Street, Kirkby on Bain LN10 6YT. 01526 354560

Hennys, St Lawrence Street, Horncastle LN9 5BJ. 01507 527805

Bike shops

Barnes Cycles (hire available), 6 Market Place, Horncastle, LN9 5GA. 01507 525754 www.barnescycles.co.uk

Cleveland Cycles, 91 High Street, Coningsby, LN4 4RB. 01526 342291 www.clevelandcycles.co.uk

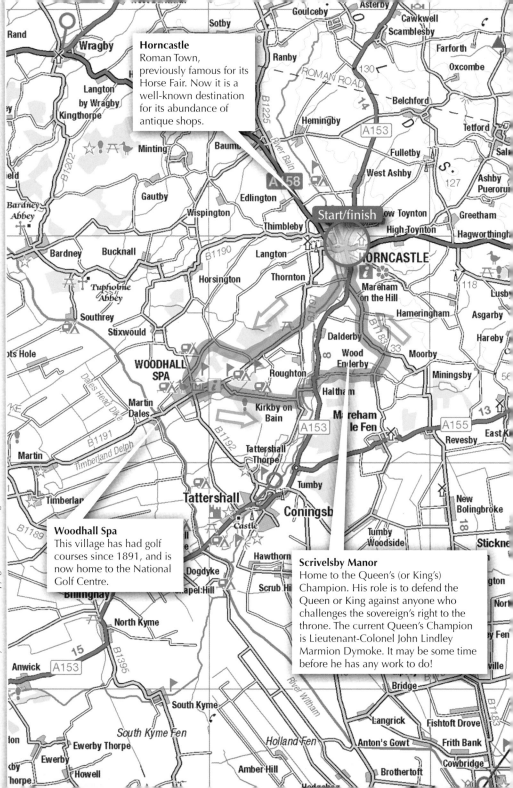

Horncastle
Roman Town, previously famous for its Horse Fair. Now it is a well-known destination for its abundance of antique shops.

Woodhall Spa
This village has had golf courses since 1891, and is now home to the National Golf Centre.

Scrivelsby Manor
Home to the Queen's (or King's) Champion. His role is to defend the Queen or King against anyone who challenges the sovereign's right to the throne. The current Queen's Champion is Lieutenant-Colonel John Lindley Marmion Dymoke. It may be some time before he has any work to do!

Start/finish

The National Byway in Rutland and Leicestershire

Distance: 50 miles (80km)
Big hills: 12
Challenge: ✪✪✪✪☆

Flat riding on the National Byway along lovely lanes visiting places of interest in Rutland and Leicestershire

One of the qualities of The National Byway is that the route is discreetly signposted all along the way which eliminates stops to consult a map and means that no detailed route description is necessary here. Start this ride in the centre of Oakham and head east from the town on the surfaced off-road Rutland Water cycle route

Along the route, the Byway signage is discreet brown-and-white boards. Signs are attached, wherever possible, to existing signposts which carry destination and mileage information. They are placed only at locations where the rider has to make a decision – if it is straight on at a junction, then there's no sign. So while you don't need a map, you do have to pay attention at junctions.

As a result of the permanent signs, it is easy to follow this ride route, starting at Catmose, the offices of the local council and site of the Rutland Museum in Oakham town centre.

Follow the Rutland Water Cycle Route signs round the lake to the Lyndon bird sanctuary, then follow the Byway signs from here. From Cranoe where the route joins Sustrans Route 64 (which the Byway does occasionally) there is joint signage, some of which has become faded and is due for replacement. From Owston the route is shared with Sustrans Route 63.

Useful refreshment stops
Fox café kiosks around Rutland Water at Whitwell, Normanton and Empingham. 01780 460047

Baines Bakery and Tea Shop, 3 High St, Uppingham LE15 9QB. 01572 823317

Bewicke, Hallaton LE16 8UB. 01858 555217 www.bewickearms.co.uk

Beans Coffee Shop, High St, Uppingham LE15 9PY. 01572 823953

Plus many village pubs on the route

Bike shops
Rutland Cycling Centre (hire available), Normanton Car Park, Rutland Water, Edith Weston, Nr Oakham LE15 8HD. 01780 720 888 www.rutlandcycling.com

Rutland Cycling Centre (hire available), Whitwell Leisure Park, Bull Brigg Lane, Whitwell, Nr Oakham LE15 8BL. 01780 460 705 www.rutlandcycling.com

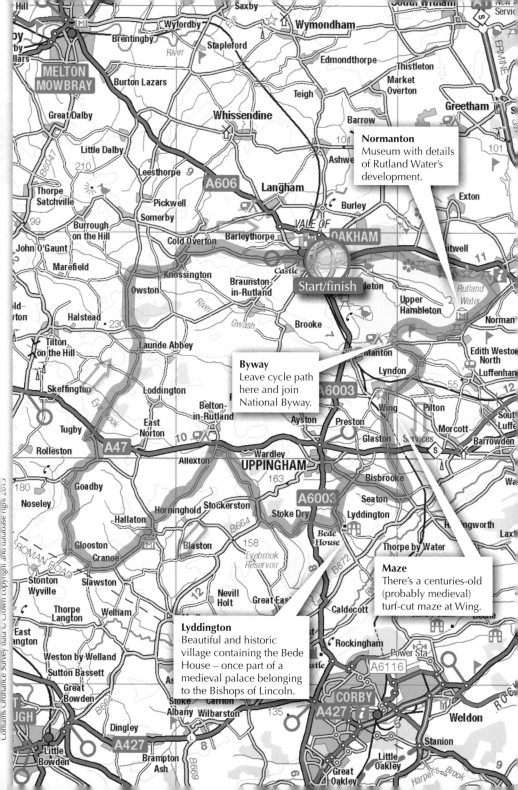

Cromwell's Cambridgeshire

Distance: 29 miles (48km)
Big hills: none
Challenge: ●●☆☆☆

Starting from the home town of Oliver Cromwell, this is a nice flat route in and around St Ives

Leave St Ives town centre via St Ives Bridge and head for Hemingford Grey then the thatched roofs of Hemingford Abbots. Go straight on to Common Lane and through the gates into the meadow. Exit at the other end and go left, taking caution with the narrow rough road, until reaching Godmanchester.

Take the long, fast road to Offord Cluny then turn right and take care on the level crossing. The road narrows for a mile or so until Buckden and then instead of crossing the busy roundabout on the A1 for Grafham Water, use the underpass on your right immediately before it.

Should you need a quick refreshment stop, the café at the visitor centre is in the car park on your right at the top.

From here retrace your route back to Offord Cluny and once you go over the level crossing go right for Offord D'Arcy.

> **Useful refreshment stops**
> Local Café, 10 The Broadway, St Ives, PE27 5BN. 01480 469 281
>
> Grafham Water Visitor Centre and Café, Marlow Park, Grafham, Huntingdon PE28 0BH. 01480 812154
>
> King William IV, High Street, Fenstanton, PE28 9JF. 01480 462467
> www.kingwilliamfenstanton.co.uk
>
> Axe and Compass, High Street, Hemingford Abbots, Huntingdon PE28 9AH. 01480 463605
> www.axeandcompass.co.uk
>
> Plus lots in St Ives town centre
>
> **Bike shops**
> Grafham Cycling (hire available), Marlow car park, Grafham Water, Huntingdon, PE28 0BX. 01480 812500
>
> Richardson's Cycles, 7 The Broadway, St Ives, PE27 5BX. 01480 463127

It's a straight run to Gravely then Hilton on wide, windswept roads and in from Hilton head towards Fenstanton. There is an underpass under the A14 which brings you out in the centre of Fenstanton, then it's signposted all the way back to St Ives.

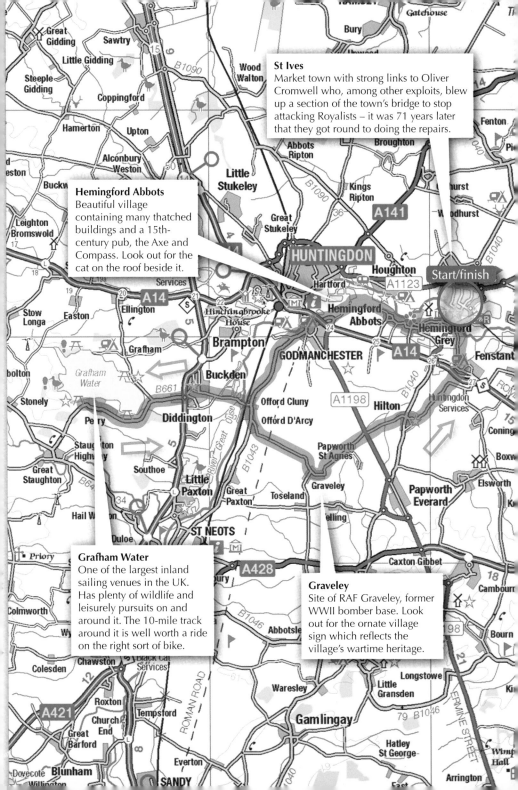

St Ives
Market town with strong links to Oliver Cromwell who, among other exploits, blew up a section of the town's bridge to stop attacking Royalists – it was 71 years later that they got round to doing the repairs.

Hemingford Abbots
Beautiful village containing many thatched buildings and a 15th-century pub, the Axe and Compass. Look out for the cat on the roof beside it.

Grafham Water
One of the largest inland sailing venues in the UK. Has plenty of wildlife and leisurely pursuits on and around it. The 10-mile track around it is well worth a ride on the right sort of bike.

Graveley
Site of RAF Graveley, former WWII bomber base. Look out for the ornate village sign which reflects the village's wartime heritage.

Start/finish

Constable's Essex

Distance: 16 miles (26km)
Big hills: 2
Challenge: ★☆☆☆☆

A quick, flat rural ride around the Essex border landscapes made famous by one of the best-known English painters

This route is a leisurely amble on the country lanes surrounding the River Stour. It is the type of ride that rolls along idly, where treats can be encountered along the way with very little effort.

Useful refreshment stops

The Red Lion, The Street, East Bergholt
  CO7 6TB. 01206 298332
  www.redlioneastbergholt.co.uk

Café Rio, 23 High Street, Manningtree
  CO11 1AG. 01206 393100

Fountain House Tea room, The Street, East
  Bergholt CO7 6TB. 01206 299955

Mistley Place Park Tea Rooms,
  New Road, Mistley, Manningtree
  CO11 1ER. 01206 393433

Flatford Bridge Cottage Tea Room,
  Flatford Mill, Flatford, East Bergholt,
  Suffolk, CO7 6UL; 01206 298260
  www.nationaltrust.org.uk/
  flatford-bridge-cottage

Bike shops

Globe G Sports, 26 St Botolphs Street,
  Colchester CO2 7EA. 01206 502502

From Manningtree railway station turn right onto the main road. At the roundabout take the first exit to go to Manningtree. Follow the road (B1352) through Mistley towards Bradfield. In Bradfield turn right towards Bradfield Heath and follow the road (Steam Mill Road).

At the T-junction turn right onto Clacton Road, following the B1035 back to Manningtree. At the roundabout take the first exit (B1352) to Lawford. At the T-junction turn right onto Cox's Hill (A137) and follow the road. Go straight on at the roundabout and under the railway bridge. At the roundabout turn left (B1070) to East Bergholt. Go up the hill and turn left to Flatford. Follow the one-way system to Flatford, following the signs for the Visitor Centre. To return to Manningtree station, follow the one-way system out of Flatford and turn right at the T-junction to retrace the route back to the station.

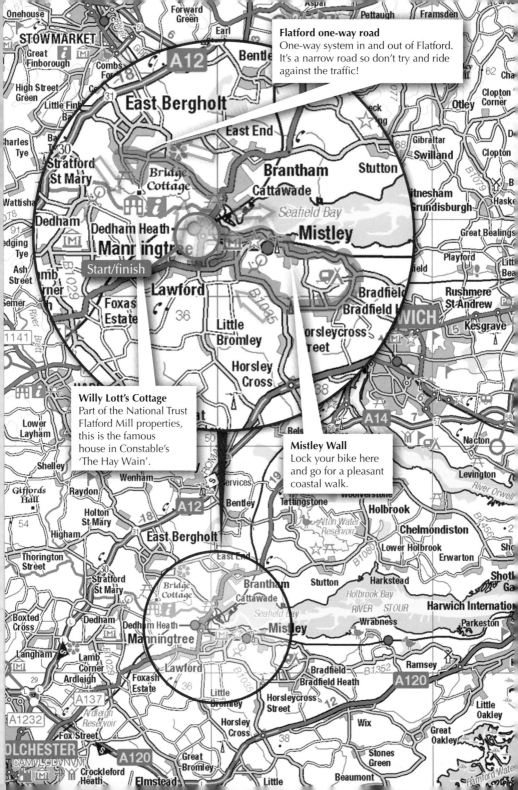

Flatford one-way road
One-way system in and out of Flatford. It's a narrow road so don't try and ride against the traffic!

Start/finish

Willy Lott's Cottage
Part of the National Trust Flatford Mill properties, this is the famous house in Constable's 'The Hay Wain'.

Mistley Wall
Lock your bike here and go for a pleasant coastal walk.

Yarmouth and the Norfolk Broads

Distance: 24 miles (39km)
Big hills: none
Challenge: ★☆☆☆☆

A family-friendly spin, mostly on lanes showcasing the traditional seaside along the Norfolk Coast

Great Yarmouth is famous as a traditional seaside resort and for its pleasure beach but only four or five miles outside the town you're into the Norfolk Broads national parkland – ideal for cycling, with quiet lanes and gently undulating landscape and scenic villages to explore.

Start out on Great Yarmouth seafront. Turn into Jellicoe Road and follow the road around past Great Yarmouth race course and out onto the cycle lane parallel with the A149. Follow the lane until you reach Caister-on-Sea and it then becomes Yarmouth Road. Go right through the village and out onto Ormesby Road. At the roundabout go straight over into Scratby Road and stay on it until you reach the crossroads at Hemsby village.

Go straight over into Waters Lane and follow the road out into the country, as it becomes Martham Road and then Hemsby Road. Stay on until you reach Martham village green. You will see the duck pond on your left and the Kings Arms pub on the right. Carry straight on into Repps Road then after 200m turn left

into Rollesby Road. Go past a piggery on your left and follow the road as it becomes Martham Road.

At the crossroads go straight over the A149 and past the Horse and Groom pub down into Fleggburgh Road, which takes you into the village of Rollesby. When you reach St George's church, bear left and stay on Rollesby Road until you go left again into Tower Road. You will see some ruins of an old church tower on your left. Directly after the ruins turn left onto the A1064 and go over Filby Broad, and into the village of Filby. Turn right into Thrigby Lane, past the Fox and Hounds pub and

Useful refreshment stops

The Old Manor Café, Manor Road, Caister-on-Sea NR30 5HG

The Kings Arms, The Green, Martham NR29 4PL. 01493 740204 www.thekingsarmsmartham.co.uk

Fox & Hounds, Thrigby Road, Filby NR29 3HJ. 01493 369804

Bike shops

Broadland Cycle Hire (hire available), 2 Littlewood Lane, Hoveton NR12 8DZ. 07887 480331 www.norfolkbroadcycling.co.uk

Clippesby Cycle Hire at Clippesby Hall (hire available), Clippesby, Great Yarmouth NR29 3BL. 01493 367800 www.clippesby.com/cyclehire

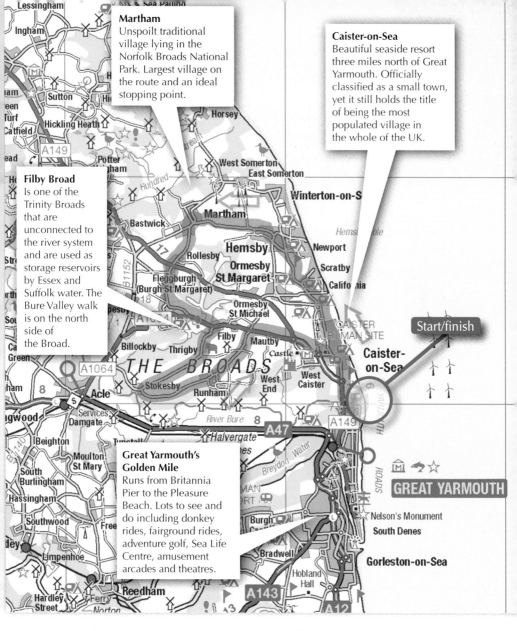

Martham
Unspoilt traditional village lying in the Norfolk Broads National Park. Largest village on the route and an ideal stopping point.

Caister-on-Sea
Beautiful seaside resort three miles north of Great Yarmouth. Officially classified as a small town, yet it still holds the title of being the most populated village in the whole of the UK.

Filby Broad
Is one of the Trinity Broads that are unconnected to the river system and are used as storage reservoirs by Essex and Suffolk water. The Bure Valley walk is on the north side of the Broad.

Start/finish

Caister-on-Sea

GREAT YARMOUTH

Nelson's Monument
South Denes

Gorleston-on-Sea

Great Yarmouth's Golden Mile
Runs from Britannia Pier to the Pleasure Beach. Lots to see and do including donkey rides, fairground rides, adventure golf, Sea Life Centre, amusement arcades and theatres.

back out into the country. After a mile, fork right into Stokesby Road and follow it onto Filby Road all the way into Stokesby.

Once there, veer left onto Runham Road and stay on it until Runham Village. Out of Runham, follow Mautby Lane, past Mautby village until you reach the A1064.

Turn right and stay on the road until you come to a large roundabout. Take the A149 for about a mile and come off at the next roundabout into Norwich Road. Carry on along this road until you're back into Caister-on-Sea. From there, it's back through the village into Yarmouth.

The Lincolnshire Wolds

Distance: 19.5 miles (31km)
Big hills: 3
Challenge: ❶❶❶☆☆

An undulating voyage of discovery in a hidden corner of the Lincolnshire Wolds

Beginning at the railway station in Market Rasen, go to the bottom of the road and turn right. At the T-junction turn left over Jameson bridge and head towards Tealby. In Tealby turn right into Cow Lane and follow Front Street through the village to get back to the main B1203.

At the crossroads turn right onto Papermill Lane and climb up Bully Hill. Turn left at the crossroads and then take the right fork to Stainton le Vale. Follow the road through the village. At the T-junction turn left (second left) and follow the road through woodland and past farm buildings. Follow the road to reach the main B1225 and turn right onto to it towards Caistor.

Just after the crossroads and near the disused windmill bear left down Whitegate Hill. Cross the Caistor bypass and go into the town centre. Pass a school and bear left into Butter Market, eventually to reach the market place.

Retrace the route back out of Caistor and go back to the B1225 via Whitegate Hill. At the crossroads turn right and go down Mansgate Hill. On the edge of Nettleton turn left into Normanby Road. Follow over Nettleton Top and continue into Normanby le Wold.

Turn left at the T-junction then left again. Turn right at the T-junction and pass the radar station, then right again onto the B1225. Take the right fork to Walesby then turn right again down Walesby Hill. In Walesby turn left to return to Market Rasen.

Useful refreshment stops
Sunnyside Up Tea Room and Farm Shop, Poplar Farm, Tealby Road, Market Rasen, Lincs LN8 3UL. 01673 843840 www.sunnyside-up.co.uk

Tealby Tea Rooms, 12 Front Street, Tealby, Market Rasen, Lincs LN8 3XU. 01673 838261 www.tealbytearooms.co.uk

King's Head, 11 Kingsway, Tealby, Market Rasen, Lincs LN8 3YA. 01673 838347 www.kingsheadtealby.com

Nettleton Lodge Inn, Off Moortown Road, Nettleton, Market Rasen, Lincs LN7 6HX. 01472 851829 www.nettletonlodgeinn.co.uk

Bike shops
Nearest cycle shops in Lincoln or Grimsby

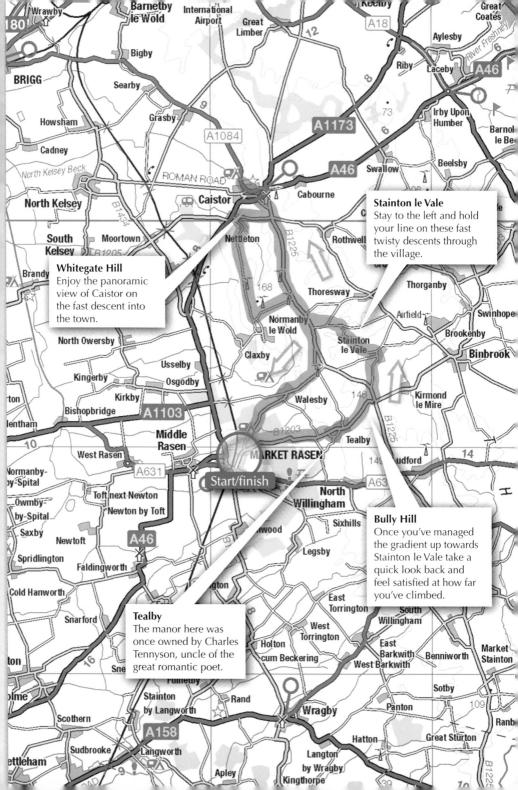

Whitegate Hill
Enjoy the panoramic view of Caistor on the fast descent into the town.

Stainton le Vale
Stay to the left and hold your line on these fast twisty descents through the village.

Bully Hill
Once you've managed the gradient up towards Stainton le Vale take a quick look back and feel satisfied at how far you've climbed.

Tealby
The manor here was once owned by Charles Tennyson, uncle of the great romantic poet.

Start/finish

Northamptonshire

Distance: 50 miles (80km)
Big hills: none – but several lumpy bits
Challenge: ❶❶❶☆☆

A day's ride with lots of small climbs to liven things up

Northamptonshire isn't known for its mountains, or indeed any kind of extreme terrain. Nevertheless, this route around the county shows that it can provide plenty of challenges for cyclists of all levels, thanks to countless lumps and bumps and some fairly exposed areas.

Beginning from Brackley, head to Halse, then take a right turn and head uphill to Greatworth. Cross the B4525 and head through the villages of Sulgrave, Moreton Pinkney and Canons Ashby. Follow this lumpy road all the way to the A5.

Cross the A5 and head to Bugbrooke, bear right and cross the railway line. Go straight over the crossroads and up a short hill into Gayton.

Enjoy the descent into Blisworth, taking care as you cross the narrow canal bridge. From Blisworth you'll ride parallel with the Blisworth canal tunnel, before taking a left downhill into Stoke Bruerne and the Canal Museum. After the stop, head back up the hill and continue straight on up another little rise to the A5.

Cross the A5 and head to Whittlebury, then Silverstone. Pass the race circuit on your left and continue to Dadford. Then take a right in Water Stratford – this tiny lane could easily be missed! Continue to Finmere and then Fulwell. A left in Fulwell takes you along an exposed lane until you reach a right turn for Mixbury. After Mixbury, head to Evenley.

After Evenley, you'll reach the A43. Take the cycle path on your right back to Brackley. Take care crossing the road to Brackley.

Useful refreshment stops
National Waterways Museum Café, Stoke Bruerne NN12 7SE. 01604 862229

The Navigation, Bridge Road, Stoke Bruerne NN12 7SY. 01604 864988 www.navigationpubtowcester.co.uk

The Boat Inn, Stoke Bruerne NN12 7SB. 01604 862428 www.boatinn.co.uk

The Red Lion, 39 The Green, Evenley NN13 5SH. 01280 703469 www.redlionevenley.com

Bike shops
Corley Cycles, Stacey Bushes, Milton Keynes MK12 6HS. 01908 311424 www.philcorleycycles.co.uk

Baines Racing, Unit 14, Silverstone Circuit NN12. 8TL 01327 858510 www.silverstonecycle.co.uk

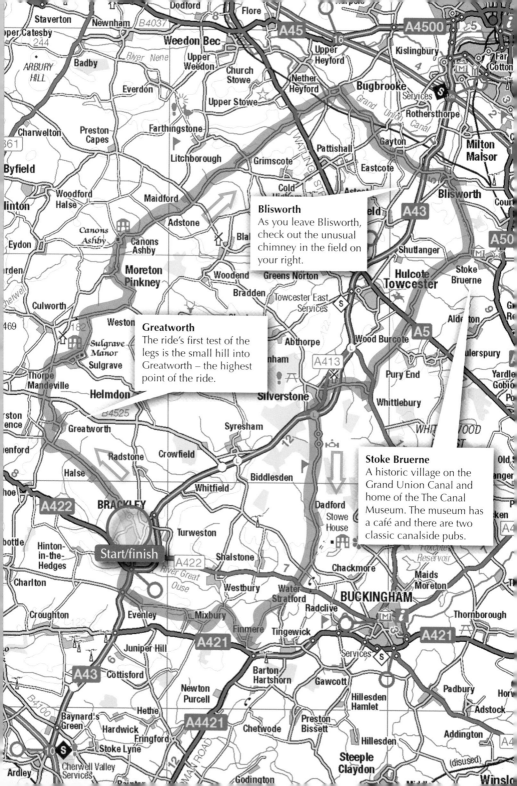

Blisworth
As you leave Blisworth, check out the unusual chimney in the field on your right.

Greatworth
The ride's first test of the legs is the small hill into Greatworth – the highest point of the ride.

Stoke Bruerne
A historic village on the Grand Union Canal and home of the The Canal Museum. The museum has a café and there are two classic canalside pubs.

Start/finish

Canalside Birmingham

Distance: 12 miles (19km)
Big hills: none
Challenge: ★☆☆☆☆

An amble along the Birmingham Mainline Canal to Sandwell and back again

The network of waterways in Birmingham is extensive and they add a fascinating dimension to Britain's second city. Within earshot of the bustling city streets there's a tranquil other-world, with its own lives, its own people and its own stories.

Start at Gas Street, which is right in the city centre, so there is plenty of multi-storey car parking surrounding it. It's right opposite The Mailbox, one of the city's most famous shopping centres, and one which is well signposted.

Head north-west from the basin, passing under a short tunnel, which brings you to the Old Turn Junction, and the island signpost. Bear left and go over the bridges at the next two left-hand canal junctions, keeping the Mainline Canal on your right.

After that the route is simple: just head north-west to follow the Mainline, which is signposted at all canal junctions anyway. For this route turn back in Sandwell, about 1000m further than the last of a set of locks just after Soho, but if you want you can follow the canal to Wolverhampton, more than 20 miles from Gas Street. If you then continue to Aldersley Junction, you can connect with the Staffordshire and Union Canal.

Useful refreshments stops
Canalside Café, Gas Street Basin
   35 Worcester Bar, Gas Street,
   Birmingham B1 2JT. 0121 643 3170

Plus lots of choice in Birmingham and
   suburbs along the route

Bike shops
On Your Bike (hire available), 33–40
   Bradford St, Birmingham B5 6HX.
   0121 666 6933 www.onyourbike.com

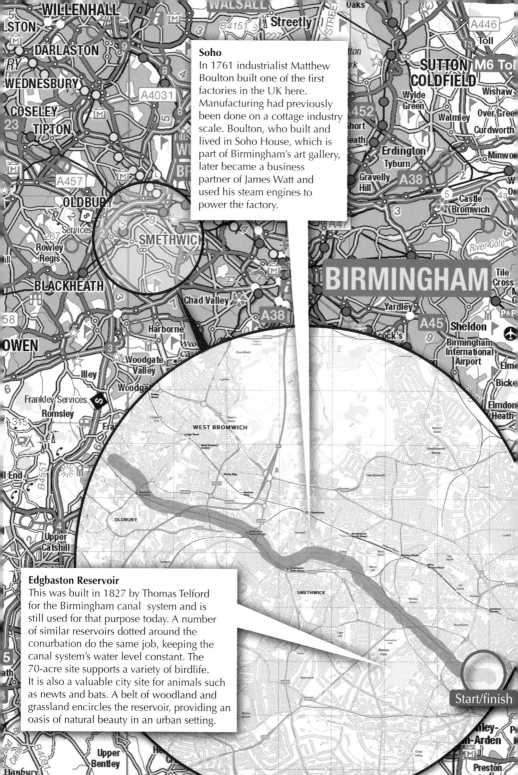

Soho

In 1761 industrialist Matthew Boulton built one of the first factories in the UK here. Manufacturing had previously been done on a cottage industry scale. Boulton, who built and lived in Soho House, which is part of Birmingham's art gallery, later became a business partner of James Watt and used his steam engines to power the factory.

Edgbaston Reservoir

This was built in 1827 by Thomas Telford for the Birmingham canal system and is still used for that purpose today. A number of similar reservoirs dotted around the conurbation do the same job, keeping the canal system's water level constant. The 70-acre site supports a variety of birdlife. It is also a valuable city site for animals such as newts and bats. A belt of woodland and grassland encircles the reservoir, providing an oasis of natural beauty in an urban setting.

Start/finish

Derwent Reservoir, Derbyshire

Distance: 10 miles (34km)
Big hills: none
Challenge: ✪✪☆☆☆

An easy ride round Derwent Reservoir taking in its famous dams and industrial history

This is a circular route around the Derwent Reservoir with a quiet road section and some off-road paths. The route is not completely flat, there are some short climbs but nothing unrideable.

Start the ride at Fairholmes car park. This makes a great starting point for visitors without their own bike, as there is a bike hire centre. There is also a café and toilets with drinking water.

From the A57 follow the signs to the Fairholmes car park and cycle hire centre. Once parked, head out of the car park and turn right. This road takes you along the side of the dam. From then on simply follow the marked cycle trail around the reservoir. As you come back down the opposite side of the reservoir the path will eventually meet the road. Turn right onto the road which will lead you back to the car park.

This ride around the reservoir is the simplest but there are longer and more challenging routes to suit any level of rider. It is the perfect destination for mixed-ability groups so whoever tags along is sure to enjoy something on this scenic ride.

Useful refreshments stops

Upper Derwent Visitor Centre Café, Fairholmes, Bamford, Hope Valley S33 0AQ. 01453 650953

The Ladybower Inn, Ladybower, Bamford, Hope Valley S33 0AX. 01433 651241

Yorkshire Bridge Inn, Ashopton Road, Bamford, Hope Valley, Derbyshire S33 0AZ. 01433 651361 www.yorkshire-bridge.co.uk

Bike shops

Derwent Cycle Hire (hire available) Fairholmes Car Park, Derwent, Bamford, Sheffield S33 0AQ. 01433 651261

Alive Bike Hire (hire available), The Old Stables, 8 Castleton Road, Hope, Hope Valley S33 6RD. 07538 892065 www.alivebikehire.co.uk

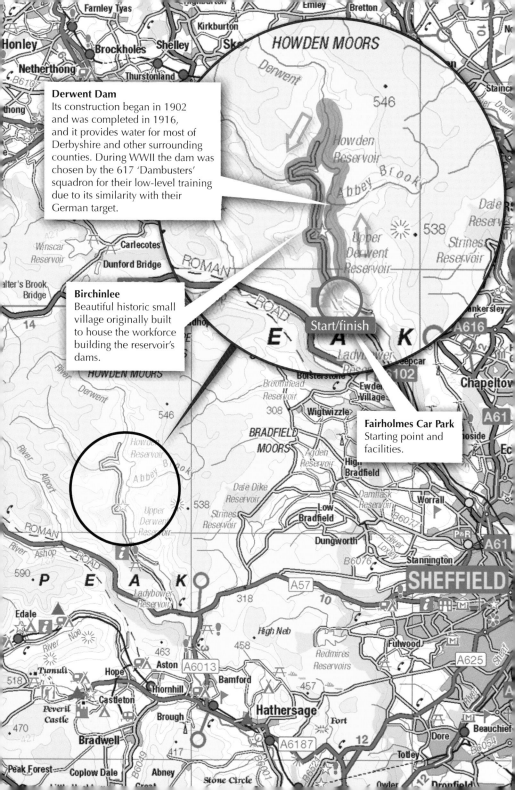

Derwent Dam
Its construction began in 1902 and was completed in 1916, and it provides water for most of Derbyshire and other surrounding counties. During WWII the dam was chosen by the 617 'Dambusters' squadron for their low-level training due to its similarity with their German target.

Birchinlee
Beautiful historic small village originally built to house the workforce building the reservoir's dams.

Start/finish

Fairholmes Car Park
Starting point and facilities.

The Peak District

Distance: 34 miles (55km)
Big hills: none
Challenge: ⊘⊘☆☆☆

Two disused railway lines provide plenty of traffic-free riding on this tour of the southern Peak District

The National Cycle Network's routes on the old Cromford and High Peak, and Ashbourne to Buxton railway lines are well used. Closed to trains since the sixties, the lines come alive again at weekends with all ages and types of cyclist – toddlers, tandems, grandparents and tourers.

Join the Tissington Trail in Tissington and head north towards Parsley Hay for 10 miles until a sign saying 'refreshments 800 yards'. Then either continue to Parsley Hay station (in view) or turn right onto the High Peak Trail. Leave the trail at Middleton Top before the visitor centre via a track on the right.

Turn left at the T-junction, then at the B5035, turn left to Wirksworth. Turn right at the crossroads by The Rising Sun down Middleton Road, right beside the Hope and Anchor and through the marketplace.

Just after the sign to Hopton turn left off the road, pass through a five-bar gate and bear left to join the Carsington Water Circular Route. It is well waymarked (in

blue) with one exception: at the Millfields car park and toilets pass a wooden sculpture, then at the barrier, turn right down a track then immediately left, signed 'viewing area, dam wall and

Useful refreshments stops

Parsley Hay Station, (kiosk only), just off the A515, SK17 0DG. 01298 84888

Middleton Top Visitor Centre, DE4 4LS. 01629 823204

Le Mistral Bistro, 23 Market Place, Wirksworth DE4 4ET. 01629 824840

Mainsail Restaurant, Carsington Water Visitor Centre, Ashbourne DE6 1ST. 01629 540363

The Old Coach House Tea Room, Tissington Hall, Ashbourne DE6 1RA. 01335 350501 www.tissintonhall.co.uk

The Knockerdown Inn, Knockerdown, Ashbourne DE6 1NQ. 01629 540209. www.knockerdown-inn.co.uk

The Bluebell Inn, Tissington DE6 1NH. 01335 350317 www.bluebellinn-tissington.co.uk

Bike shops

Parsley Hay Cycle Hire (hire available), Nr Buxton SK17 0DG. 01298 84493

Middleton Top Cycle Hire (hire available), Middleton Top Visitor Centre DE4 4LS. 01629 823204

Ashbourne Cycle Hire (hire available), Mapleton Lane, DE6 2AA. 01335 343156

visitor centre'. Cycle along the top of the embankment to the visitor centre and playground.

Leave Carsington Water via the main exit and turn right to Kniveton, Wirksworth and Matlock. At the Town Farm campsite fork left to join the signed National Cycle Route 54A. Follow signs through Bradbourne (left at T-junction).

On the descent from Bradbourne turn left onto a traffic-free section of Route 54A (easy to miss – at Valley View Barn). Follow the route over a bridge, across a road and then (back on road) over another bridge beside a ford and up a steep hill to Tissington.

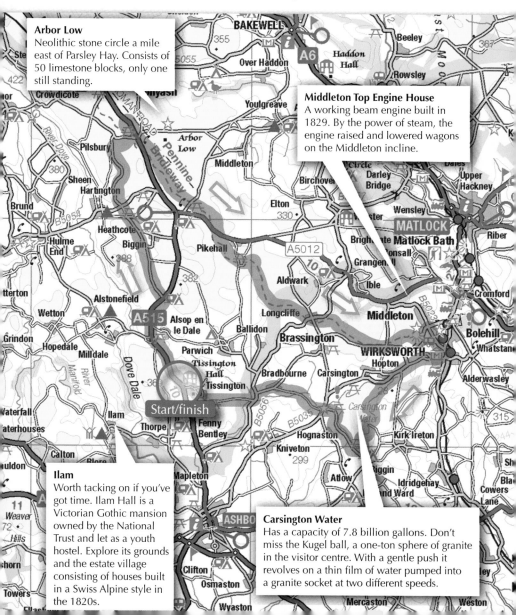

Arbor Low
Neolithic stone circle a mile east of Parsley Hay. Consists of 50 limestone blocks, only one still standing.

Middleton Top Engine House
A working beam engine built in 1829. By the power of steam, the engine raised and lowered wagons on the Middleton incline.

Ilam
Worth tacking on if you've got time. Ilam Hall is a Victorian Gothic mansion owned by the National Trust and let as a youth hostel. Explore its grounds and the estate village consisting of houses built in a Swiss Alpine style in the 1820s.

Carsington Water
Has a capacity of 7.8 billion gallons. Don't miss the Kugel ball, a one-ton sphere of granite in the visitor centre. With a gentle push it revolves on a thin film of water pumped into a granite socket at two different speeds.

Elgar's Worcestershire

Distance: 16 miles (24km)
Big hills: 1
Challenge: ★☆☆☆☆

A gentle rolling spin through classic countryside with a classical composer as a spiritual companion

Edward Elgar, the Worcestershire native who wrote the music for the rousing final song of the Last Night of the Proms, was a late adopter of the bicycle. At the age of 40, he learned how to ride a bike in the county's lanes and it's easy to see why he quickly became addicted to cycling.

Useful refreshments stops

The Mayfly Café: Cob House Fisheries, Worcester Road, Wichenford, Worcester WR6 6YE. 01886 888 517 www.cobhouse.org/mayfly

The Fox Inn, Monkwood Green, Hallow, Worcester WR2 6NX. 01886 889123

The Dewdrop Inn, Bell Lane, Lower Broadheath WR2 6RR. 01905 640012 www.thedewdrop-inn.co.uk

Saffrons Bistro, 15 New Street, Worcester WR1 2DP. 01905 610505 www.saffronsrestaurant.co.uk

Bike shops

The Green Bike Co, Bromyard Road, St Johns, Worcester WR2 5ER. 0844 888 2008. www.thegreenbikecompany.co.uk

Starting at the Green Bike Company shop in Bromyard Road on the western edge of the county town of Worcester on the A44, ride west with care on the busy road and take the cycle path on the right to the avoid giant roundabout after half a mile.

Leave the main road at Crown East Church, passing Broadheath Common, then straight over the crossroads and along Ankerdine Road. Bear right a mile later, signed to Wichenford. Left onto the B4204 and then first right at Mason's Arms, onto Venn Lane to Wichenford, then right down Moseley Road.

Right onto the busy A443 where great care is needed because of traffic and poor surface. Through Hallow, then right at Royal Oak. Ignore Shoulton Lane, but bear left at the bend 700m later, up a short, sharp climb.

In Lower Broadheath turn left onto B4204 and right at the Bell Inn into Bell Lane. At the further end of the common, turn left into Crown East Lane and retrace your route to Green Bike Company.

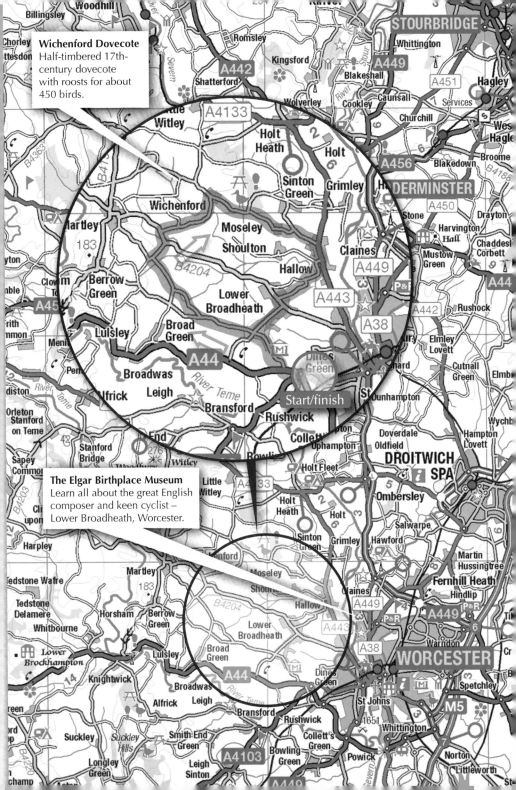

Wichenford Dovecote
Half-timbered 17th-century dovecote with roosts for about 450 birds.

The Elgar Birthplace Museum
Learn all about the great English composer and keen cyclist – Lower Broadheath, Worcester.

Start/finish

Chatsworth

Distance: 10 miles (16km)
Big hills: 2
Challenge: ●●☆☆☆

A quick blast round the stunning grounds of Chatsworth and surrounding Peak District lanes

This is a short but sweet ride ride, with a bit of climbing, that takes you to the heart of Derbyshire.

Start this ride in the village of Rowsley situated on the A6 between Matlock and Bakewell. Heading down the A6 towards Matlock turn left after the Grouse and Claret pub, by the art gallery. Continue out of the village along this road past the village of Beeley. Up over the humpbacked bridge and into Chatsworth Park.

Continue along this road over the hill and down the other side past the village of Edensor. Still on the same road climb up out of Chatsworth with the golf course on your right. At the peak of the climb turn left towards Pilsley. Follow this road past the farm shop and the village and then descend back down to the main road.

Take a left at the T-junction, signposted back to Bakewell. This road is a long run back into the town but take the second left before the bridge and then right by the car park, thus avoid riding through the traffic

in the centre of town. When the road runs out, turn left over the pedestrian bridge (you might have to hop off your bike here) and then right out the other side by the agricultural centre. Follow the drive that leads you back to the A6 – turn left and this road will lead you straight back to Rowlsey.

> **Useful refreshments stops**
> Caudwell's Mill Café. Bakewell Rd, Rowsley DE4 2EB. 01629 733185 www.caudwellsmill/craftcentre.co.uk
>
> Tiroler Stuberl Austrian Coffee Shop Water Street, Bakewell DE45 1EW. 01629 813899 www.tirolerstuberl.co.uk
>
> The Tea Cottage, Edensor Village, Chatsworth Park, Nr Bakewell, Derbyshire. 01246 582315 www.edensorteacottage.co.uk
>
> The Devonshire Arms, Devonshire Square, Beeley, Nr Matlock DE4 2NR. 01629 733259 www.devonshirebeeley.co.uk
>
> **Bike shops**
> Stanley Fearn Cycles, 19 Bakewell Rd, Matlock DE4 3AU. 01629 582089 www.stanleyfearns.co.uk

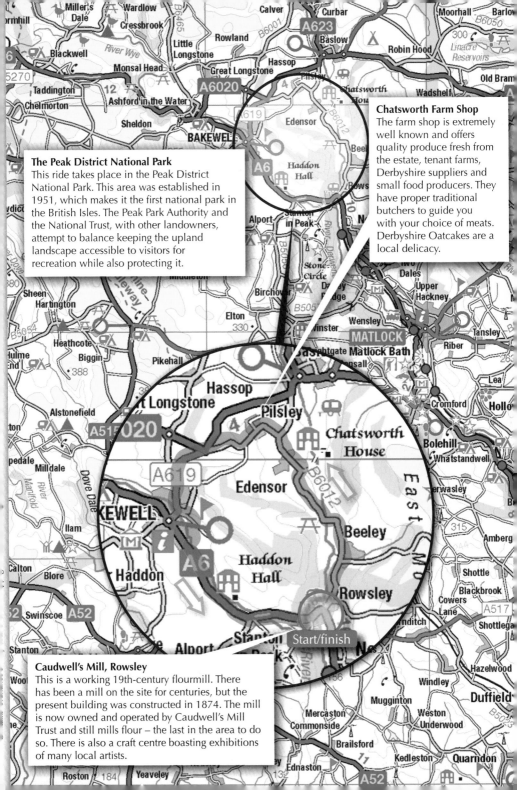

The Peak District National Park
This ride takes place in the Peak District National Park. This area was established in 1951, which makes it the first national park in the British Isles. The Peak Park Authority and the National Trust, with other landowners, attempt to balance keeping the upland landscape accessible to visitors for recreation while also protecting it.

Chatsworth Farm Shop
The farm shop is extremely well known and offers quality produce fresh from the estate, tenant farms, Derbyshire suppliers and small food producers. They have proper traditional butchers to guide you with your choice of meats. Derbyshire Oatcakes are a local delicacy.

Caudwell's Mill, Rowsley
This is a working 19th-century flourmill. There has been a mill on the site for centuries, but the present building was constructed in 1874. The mill is now owned and operated by Caudwell's Mill Trust and still mills flour – the last in the area to do so. There is also a craft centre boasting exhibitions of many local artists.

Start/finish

Wendover and Great Missenden

Distance: 18 miles (29km)
Big hills: 3
Challenge: ●●☆☆☆

An appealing ride taking in the scenes that inspired children's author Roald Dahl

Nestled among the Chilterns are the pretty villages of Wendover and Great Missenden. The latter was home to the children's author Roald Dahl and there are a number of sights and attractions in the area associated with his books.

Starting at Great Missenden railway station, turn right out of the station then right at a mini roundabout and go down the High Street. Turn right into Whitefield Lane (signposted 'route 57/Prestwood'). Ride up the lane and bear right onto a bridleway (signposted 'Chilterns Heritage trail route 57') through the woods.

At the road turn right, then left onto the A4138 (Prestwood High Street). When you reach the Chequers pub turn right into Honor End Lane. After 1000m take the first bridleway on the left. Cross farm fields and at the end turn left onto the road.

At the crossroads go straight on and as the road swings left, turn right onto a gravel track to enter Hampden House.

Go straight on through the woods which descend and ascend sharply through farm fields. The road swings left at Green Hailey Farm to the main road. Turn right and then left down Kop Hill. At the T-junction turn right onto Brimmers Road. After 200m turn right onto the Icknield Way Trail.

Follow the trail to the main Aylesbury Road. Turn right onto a bridleway through Pulpit Wood. After the small car park bear left up a steep, rooty bridleway. Follow the twisty trail (signposted 'bridleway'). At the crossroads of bridleways turn right (signposted 'Icknield Way Rider's Route').

Useful refreshments stops
Café Twit, The Roald Dahl Museum, High St, Great Missenden HP16 0AL. 01494 865113

Wendover Café in the Woods, Wendover Woods HP22 5NF. 01420 520212 www.cafeinthewoods.co.uk

Red Lion, Whiteleaf, Princes Risborough HP27 0LL. 01844 344476 www.theredlionwhiteleaf.co.uk

Bike shops
The Bicycle Workshop (hire available), Rookwood, Frith Hill, Great Missenden, Bucks HP16 0QS. 01494 868607 www.cyclefleet.com

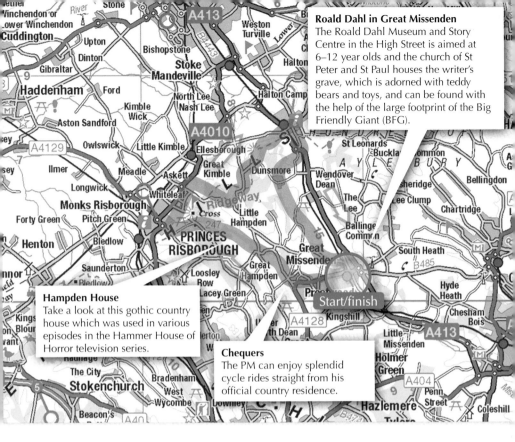

Roald Dahl in Great Missenden
The Roald Dahl Museum and Story Centre in the High Street is aimed at 6–12 year olds and the church of St Peter and St Paul houses the writer's grave, which is adorned with teddy bears and toys, and can be found with the help of the large footprint of the Big Friendly Giant (BFG).

Hampden House
Take a look at this gothic country house which was used in various episodes in the Hammer House of Horror television series.

Chequers
The PM can enjoy splendid cycle rides straight from his official country residence.

Start/finish

Continue through the woods to reach a road. Cross the road to a bridleway opposite and ride parallel to the road. Follow the trail round to the right. Cross a lane to another bridleway (signposted 'The Ridgeway, Wendover 4.4km'). Turn left at the crossroads of trails.

At the road turn right to ascend Lodge Hill. Go straight through a car park to reach a bridleway. At a fork bear right down Bacombe Hill. At the bottom of the hill turn right onto the road into Wendover.

Cross the railway line and the A413 then turn right (signposted 'Icknield Way'). After the petrol station turn right into Bacombe Lane. Cross the A413 and

the railway line, then immediately turn left onto a bridleway. At a roundabout bear right along the minor road. When the road swings sharply to the left continue straight on over a gravel track between houses. Go through the left-hand gate and follow the Icknield Way bridleway to Dunsmore.

After Dunsmore ignore the Icknield Way sign to turn right and continue straight on to Cobblershill Farm (signposted 'South Bucks Way'). Descend the trail, which becomes the tarmacked Mapridge Green Lane. Turn left onto Rignall Road. At the T-junction turn right, and right again at the mini roundabout to reach Great Missenden Station.

The Monsal Trail, Peak District

Distance: 17 miles (27km)
Big hills: none
Challenge: ✪✪☆☆☆

A pleasant rural ride along a well-surfaced traffic-free bike route

The Monsal Trail in the Derbyshire Peak District takes in eight-and-a-half miles of the old Midland Railway line route from Bakewell to Blackwell Mill near Buxton. A chance to ride on the footplate once more and experience the landscape and scenery from the old Midland line, there and back again.

It has been open for recreational use since the 1980s, allowing access along the former track bed, which closed to trains back in 1968. However, there were several sections of the trail that remained closed, at four of the longer tunnels along the route at Headstone, Cressbrook, Litton and Chee Tor, for safety reasons. Footpaths diverted around these points before rejoining the trail from Bakewell to Blackwell Mill near Buxton. After a period of refurbishment, those tunnels have now been reopened allowing walkers, cyclists, horse riders and wheelchair users to experience the full, uninterrupted length of this section of the former mainline London to Manchester route.

Start in Bakewell at the old station on Station Road off Coombs Road. Pick up the Monsal Trail from behind the station building there and head west calling at Hassop, Longstone, Monsal, Millers Dale and Blackwell Mill. Retrace your route to return to Bakewell.

Useful refreshments stops

Hassop Station, Bakewell, Derbyshire DE45 1NW. 01629 815668 www.hassopstation.co.uk

Lazy Days Tuck Shop, Blackwell Mill, (see bike shops below)

Bike shops

Hassop Station Bike Hire & Repairs (hire available), Hassop Station, Bakewell, Derbyshire DE45 1NW. 01629 810588 www.hassopstation.co.uk

Blackwell Mill Cycle Hire (hire available), Wye Dale, Buxton SK17 9TE. 01298 71986 www.peakblackwellcyclehire.com

---

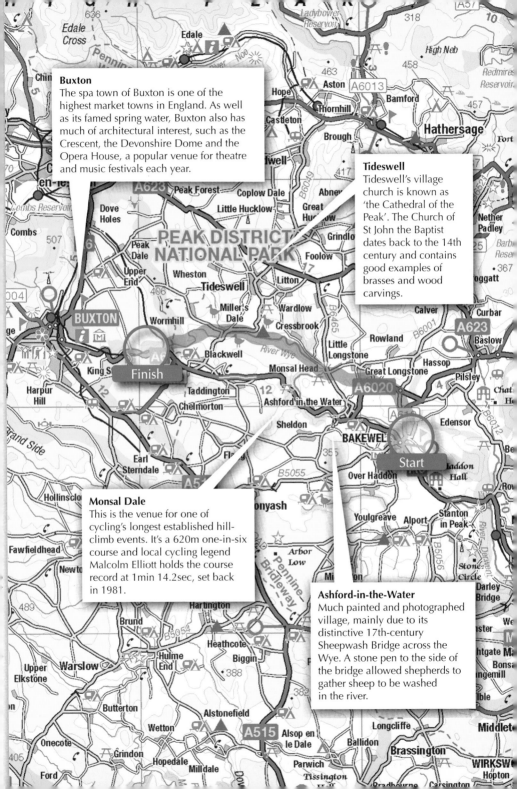

Buxton
The spa town of Buxton is one of the highest market towns in England. As well as its famed spring water, Buxton also has much of architectural interest, such as the Crescent, the Devonshire Dome and the Opera House, a popular venue for theatre and music festivals each year.

Tideswell
Tideswell's village church is known as 'the Cathedral of the Peak'. The Church of St John the Baptist dates back to the 14th century and contains good examples of brasses and wood carvings.

Monsal Dale
This is the venue for one of cycling's longest established hill-climb events. It's a 620m one-in-six course and local cycling legend Malcolm Elliott holds the course record at 1min 14.2sec, set back in 1981.

Ashford-in-the-Water
Much painted and photographed village, mainly due to its distinctive 17th-century Sheepwash Bridge across the Wye. A stone pen to the side of the bridge allowed shepherds to gather sheep to be washed in the river.

Shakespeare's Stratford

Distance: 10 miles (16km)
Big hills: none
Challenge: ❶☆☆☆☆

An easy, magical history tour of Shakespeare's life on good towpaths and some roads, suitable for all

Starting from the Greenway, a disused railway path running into historic Stratford-upon-Avon, set off from the bike hire shop at Seven Meadows Road and head along the right-hand path

that soon runs beside the River Avon. Dismount on the passageway marked 'no cycling' and join Mill Lane which takes you to Holy Trinity Church.

Past the church, turn left into Old Town and pass Halls Croft. Turn right onto Church Street, passing Nash's House and New Place, where Shakespeare's house used to stand. Continue down Chapel Street and High Street to the busy roundabout and junction with Bridge Street. Take the second exit and dismount up pedestrianised Henley Street; pass Shakespeare's Birthplace and turn right into Windsor Street, then left to follow the cycle path on Birmingham Road.

Join the canal towpath at the lights and follow all the way to Wilmcote, following signs at the road to Mary Arden's Farm. Turn left onto Church Road then Billesley Road, then left on the Ridgeway back towards Stratford. At the end, cross the busy A422 onto West Green Drive, right into Hathaway Green Lane then follow Cottage Lane to Anne Hathaway's Cottage. At the mini roundabout go straight ahead, follow the one-way system, then turn into Hathaway Lane. Left on Evesham Road then right on Aintree Road. A cycle path on the left will return you to Severn Meadows car park.

Useful refreshments stops

Carriages Café 34644, The Greenway, Stratford-upon-Avon CV37 8JW. 07771 916192 www.carriagescafé.co.uk

Mary Arden Inn, The Green, Wilmcote CV37 9XJ. 01789 267030 www.mary-arden.co.uk

The Garrick Inn, 25 High Street, Stratford-upon-Avon CV37 6AU. 01789 292186 www.garrick-inn-stratford-upon-avon. co.uk

Bike shops

Stratford Bike Hire (hire available), The Stratford Greenway, Seven Meadows Road, Old Town, Stratford upon Avon, CV37 6GR. 07711 776340 www.stratfordbikehire.com

Traditional Cycle Shop (hire available), The Chandlery, Stratford Marina, Stratford Upon Avon, Warwickshire, CV37 6YY. 01789 290703 www.traditionalcycleshop.co.uk

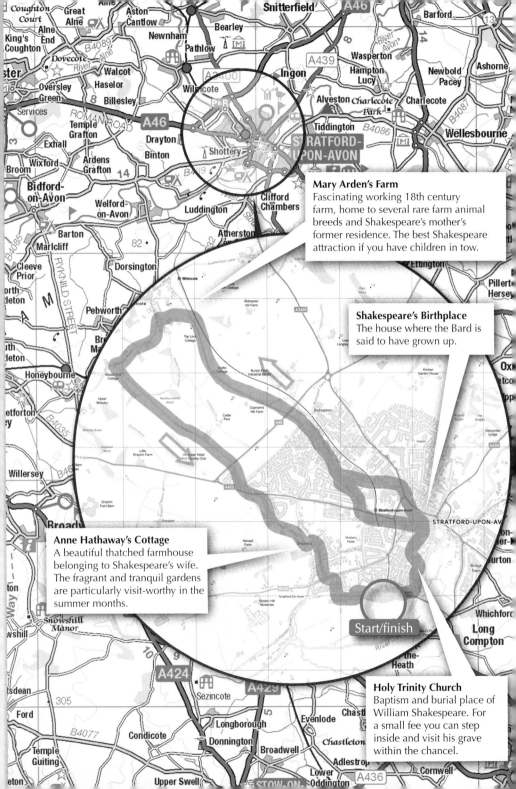

Mary Arden's Farm
Fascinating working 18th century farm, home to several rare farm animal breeds and Shakespeare's mother's former residence. The best Shakespeare attraction if you have children in tow.

Shakespeare's Birthplace
The house where the Bard is said to have grown up.

Anne Hathaway's Cottage
A beautiful thatched farmhouse belonging to Shakespeare's wife. The fragrant and tranquil gardens are particularly visit-worthy in the summer months.

Start/finish

Holy Trinity Church
Baptism and burial place of William Shakespeare. For a small fee you can step inside and visit his grave within the chancel.

Nottingham countryside

Distance: 30 miles (48km)
Big hills: none
Challenge: ❶❶☆☆☆

Escaping from the hubbub of urban life, this is a beautiful country route, just a stone's throw from Nottingham

Start the ride from Lenton in Nottingham picking up the cycle path signs towards West Bridgeford. This path takes you straight out of the city without having to tangle with any complicated junctions. Turn right down Lenton Lane (south-east direction). Turn left onto the cycle path and follow the blue signs to West Bridgeford.

At the end of the cycle path cross the A453 onto the Robin Hood Way. Turn right towards the Victoria Embankment and cross the footbridge over the River Trent. Continue straight through Wilford. Straight on at the next crossroads, along a road through the industrial estate.

Continue into Ruddington and turn left on Kirk Lane to the A60. Turn right at the lights and continue south to Bradmore. Take the second left on Pendock Lane. On Wysall Road take the right turn opposite the farm, signposted 'Bunny'.

Turn left on the A60 then take the right on Gotham Lane. Follow to the end then

Useful refreshments stops
Philo's Delicatessen, 2a High Street, Ruddington, Nottingham NG11 6EH. 01159 144440

The Bakery, 471 Tamworth Road, Long Eaton, Nottingham NG10 3GR. 0115 972 2218

The Lakeside Arts Centre Café Lakeside Arts Centre, University Park, Nottingham NG7 2RD. 0115 846 7179 www.lakesidearts.org.uk

The Boat Inn, 9 Priory Street, Nottingham NG7 2NX. 0115 978 0267 www.theboatinnlenton.co.uk

Bike shops
Freewheel, 34–36 Goose Gate, Nottingham NG1 1FF. 0115 952 0200 www.freewheelshop.co.uk

turn left to East Leake. In East Leake turn right at the T-junction onto main street. Proceed out of East Leake and take the right onto Brickyard Lane. Continue onto Melton Lane and go straight over the crossroads towards Kegworth. Turn right onto Long Lane and follow this narrow lane through to Sawley Marina.

At Sawley marina turn right towards Sawley (B6540). Turn right at the next roundabout by Long Eaton station, along

Fields Farm Road. Proceed straight over the next roundabout. Turn right onto station street at the lights.

At the A6005 Nottingham road turn right and follow this road for approx three miles until the roundabout with University Boulevard. Take the second exit then turn right at the next roundabout into the university campus. Turn first right then immediately left up a cut through lane and turn right after the university buildings down Kneighton Hill. Turn left at the bottom then left after the security hut to complete the route.

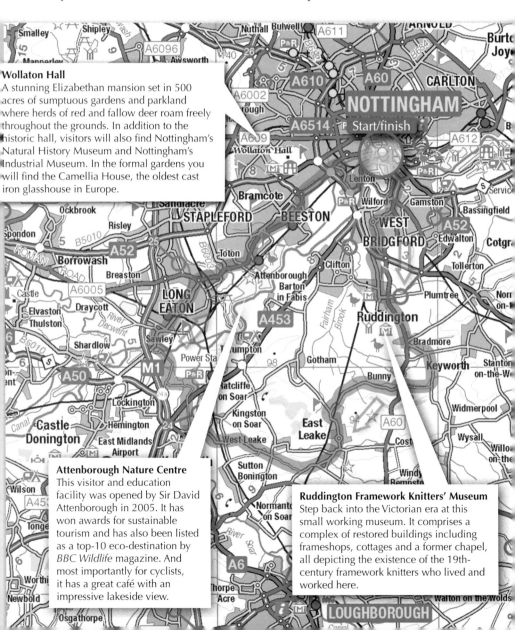

Wollaton Hall
A stunning Elizabethan mansion set in 500 acres of sumptuous gardens and parkland where herds of red and fallow deer roam freely throughout the grounds. In addition to the historic hall, visitors will also find Nottingham's Natural History Museum and Nottingham's Industrial Museum. In the formal gardens you will find the Camellia House, the oldest cast iron glasshouse in Europe.

Attenborough Nature Centre
This visitor and education facility was opened by Sir David Attenborough in 2005. It has won awards for sustainable tourism and has also been listed as a top-10 eco-destination by *BBC Wildlife* magazine. And most importantly for cyclists, it has a great café with an impressive lakeside view.

Ruddington Framework Knitters' Museum
Step back into the Victorian era at this small working museum. It comprises a complex of restored buildings including frameshops, cottages and a former chapel, all depicting the existence of the 19th-century framework knitters who lived and worked here.

Oxford and beyond

Distance: 28 miles (45km)
Big hills: a few undulations but no big hills
Challenge: ❂❂☆☆☆

A half-day loop, taking in the dreaming spires of central Oxford and the peaceful lanes of north Oxfordshire

Cyclists in Oxford have it pretty good, with an abundance of dedicated cycle paths and 2,500 public cycle parking spaces in the city, not to mention a juicy choice of riding destinations outside the city itself. Enticing countryside beckons from all directions, and this is a route that would appeal to keen roadies and adventurous beginners alike. Featuring no significant hills, this loop could be ridden at a good speed or equally at a more leisurely pace, taking time to enjoy the many appealing views.

Head north out of Oxford on the Woodstock Road (A4144). At the Wolvercote roundabout, take the fourth exit down Five Mile Drive. Turn left onto the A4165, then continue to the Gosford roundabout and take the third exit. Take the left fork at the mini-roundabout, followed by a left into a lane. Head through Hampton Poyle and then uphill to Bletchingdon.

In Bletchingdon take a left and then the second right-hand turn towards Kirtlington. At the T-junction turn right onto the A4095. Head out of the village and keep left on the lane towards the Heyfords, then turn left onto the B4030. At the bottom of the hill turn left into Lower Heyford. Head over the bridge, then turn left towards Rousham. Follow the road uphill to the A4260.

Useful refreshments stops

Kizzie's Waterside Bistro, Heyford Wharf OX25 5PD. 01869 340348 www.oxfordshire-narrowboats.co.uk/kizzies-bistro

Zappi's Bike Café, 28–32 St Michael's St, Oxford OX1 2EB. 01865 728877 www.zappisbikecafe.com

The Oxford Arms, Kirtlington, OX5 3HA. 01869 350208, www.oxford-arms.co.uk

Bike shops

Summertown Cycles (hire available), 202 Banbury Road, Summertown, Oxford OX2 7BY. 01865 316885 www.summertowncycles.co.uk

Beeline Bicycles, 59–65 Cowley Road, Oxford OX4 1HR. 01865 246615 www.beelinebicycles.co.uk

Bike Zone, 28–32 St Michael's St, Oxford OX1 2EB. 01865 728877 www.bike-zone.co.uk

---

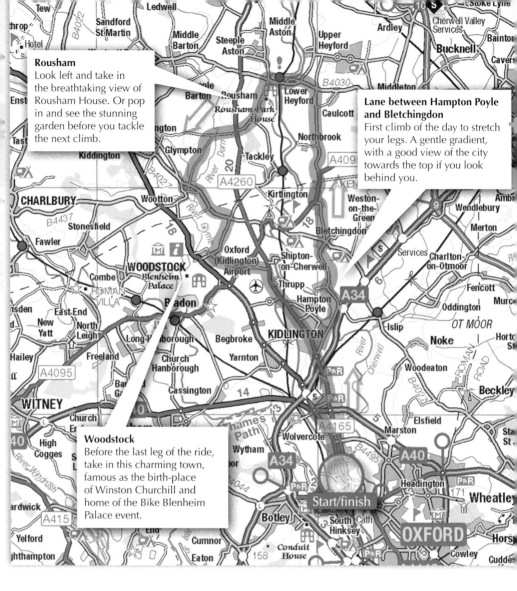

Rousham
Look left and take in the breathtaking view of Rousham House. Or pop in and see the stunning garden before you tackle the next climb.

Lane between Hampton Poyle and Bletchingdon
First climb of the day to stretch your legs. A gentle gradient, with a good view of the city towards the top if you look behind you.

Woodstock
Before the last leg of the ride, take in this charming town, famous as the birth-place of Winston Churchill and home of the Bike Blenheim Palace event.

Take a left and then immediate right towards Wootton, watching out for gravel on the first descent. After a couple of miles turn left at the crossroads onto the B4027. Follow it into a dip and up the other side, then after another mile take a right-hand turn towards Woodstock.

Turn left at the mini-roundabout onto the Shipton Road. Take a left onto the A4095 and then immediate right, passing the airfield. Turn right onto the A4260. Head back to Oxford through Kidlington, retracing your earlier steps back to the city centre.

Beautiful Birmingham

Distance: 30 miles (48.3km)
Big hills: 1
Challenge: ●●☆☆☆

From urban sprawl to rolling pastures, this 30-mile loop out of Birmingham city centre scythes through ever-changing scenery

Three hours riding at a good clip, four hours at a more leisurely pace, this route takes you from cityscape to rural landscape and back.

Start at the Custard Factory arts and media quarter and turn right onto Digbeth High Street. Follow the one-way system around the Selfridges building and past Moor Street Station onto the B4114. Over the island (Ashted Circus) and onto the A47 Nechells Parkway.

Keep on the A47 – its name changes from Nechells Parkway to Heartlands Parkway to Fort Parkway, but it's the same stretch of road. Follow signs to the Fort Retail Park.

At Spitfire Island, go straight over the roundabout onto Tangmere Drive and into the Castle Vale estate. At the first round-about, bear right onto Farnborough Road and follow it to its finish. Turn right onto Park Lane and go under the railway bridge.

At the T-junction swing right onto Water Orton Lane. Follow this road over the River Tame, past the station and left into Marsh Lane (B4118). Follow the road under the M42 and past the rugby club.

At the T-junction turn right. Be careful – this is the busy A446 Lichfield Road. After about 300m take the first left into Gorsey Lane, bisecting the Coleshill Industrial Estate. Turn right at the first island onto Station Road.

Follow Station Road until it merges into the High Street at Coleshill. Once over the little stone bridge it's uphill for a

Useful refreshments stops

Yumm Café, Custard Factory, Gibb Street, Digbeth, Birmingham B9 4AA. 0121 224 7365

Café Rouge, Bull Ring, Upper Mall West, Birmingham B5 4BG. 0121 616 1463

The Beehive, Beehive Lane, Curdworth, Sutton Coldfield, West Midlands B76 9HG. 01675 470223

The Cock Inn, Bulls Lane, Wishaw, Sutton Coldfield B76 9QL. 0121 313 3960 www.cockinnwishaw.co.uk

Bike shops

On Your Bike (hire available), 33–40 Bradford Street, Birmingham B5 6HX. 0121 666 6933

Specialized Concept Store, Unit 1A, Fort Dunlop, Fort Parkway, Birmingham B24 9FD. 0121 747 3444

The Tyburn House
Dating from 1730, this Georgian Inn was almost certainly a place of execution. Local legend has it that for many years the lintel over the front door was taken from the gallows itself.

The Bull Ring
The major commercial area of Birmingham since the Middle Ages. Covered in 15,000 shiny aluminium discs, the Selfridges building was inspired by a Paco Rabanne sequined dress.

quarter of a mile before a left into Blythe Road (B4114). Once over the River Blythe start looking for Station Road – the first 'proper' left turn. Station Road passes some water works and Holmsdale Farm before a left turn, signposted Whitacre Heath, takes you onto the Birmingham Road and through the village itself.

Over the River Tame again, second left into Church Lane, before a sharp jink right, into Hams Lane. Watch this manoeuvre either at speed or in the wet – it can be treacherous. Head along Hams Lane, past the electricity substation, before you are forced left by a one-way system, along Faraday Avenue. At the island, hook back on yourself along Faraday Avenue, over the island on the Lichfield Road (A446) and into the village of Curdworth.

Following the signs for Wishaw, carefully cross the Kingsbury Road (A4097) into Wishaw Lane. Ride past the Cock Inn and ready yourself for the climb up Bulls Lane.

Having caught your breath, turn left into Ox Leys Road, over the A38 Sutton Coldfield bypass. Once over the bridge, take the first left into Fox Hollies Road. At the end you have no choice but to follow the road to the right, before emerging onto the Thimble End Road.

Turn right at the roundabout into Walmley Village before picking up the B4148, which becomes the A38 all the way to Spaghetti Junction.

Once beneath this wonder of civil engineering (not as scary as it sounds on a bike!) turn left onto the A5127 Lichfield Road. At the first set of lights turn left, over Cuckoo Bridge, past the Star City leisure complex and then retrace your steps along the A47 to the start.

The beauty of this route is that all roads lead to Rome (or in this case Birmingham). You are never very far away from a major route back into town – and all are well signposted. Get tired or break down and you can easily cut it short.

Melton Mowbray

Distance: 17 miles (27km)
Big hills: 1
Challenge: ❷❷☆☆☆

A rolling ride on lanes south of Melton Mowbray with a mile on unmade tracks

Melton Mowbray, once home to the oldest and busiest cattle market in the country, lies between the M1 and A1 roads, pretty much in the very centre of England. The A roads are also busy with commercial and local traffic but between the bigger towns and north-south transport links lies a web of sleepy lanes and villages perfect for cycling.

Park next to the church just off the A606 in Burton Lazars and continue down Sawgate Road, bearing east in the direction of Stapleford. Turn right at the corner of the estate and along the lane up Cuckoo Hill to Jericho Lodge where you should turn left, then immediately right to reach the junction with the A606.

Drive straight over (taking great care of the busy traffic) and then continue on the lane to Pickwell village and into Somerby. Ride through Somerby bearing right as you leave in the direction of Burrough Hill. Descend through Burrough Hill turning right onto Melton Lane just outside the village. Turn left to Great Dalby on Burrough Road skirting south

of the village and continue on it to a right turn into Kirby Lane just before the junction with the A607.

Continue on this lane and at the junction with Dalby Road, cross over through a set of bollards onto a gravel track. Stay on this until the junction with the A606 Burton Road. Turn right and shortly after, head left onto an unmade road then continue to a junction where you can turn right and return to Burton Lazars.

> **Useful refreshments stops**
> The Stilton Cheese Inn, High Street, Somerby LE14 2PZ. 01664 454 394 www.stiltoncheeseinn.co.uk
>
> Ye Olde Pork Pie Shoppe (Dickinson and Morris), 10 Nottingham Street, Melton Mowbray LE13 1NW. 01664 482 068 www.porkpie.co.uk
>
> **Bike shops**
> Halfords, Norman Way, Snow Hill, Melton Mowbray LE13 1JE. 01664 566 923

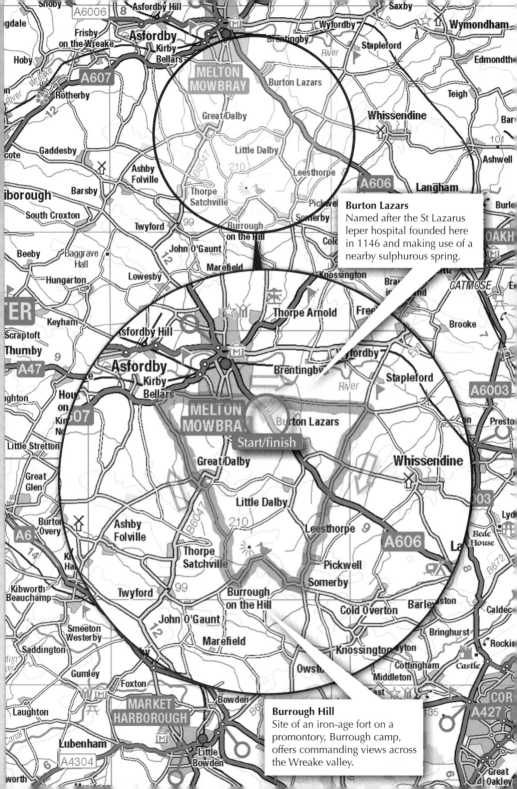

Burton Lazars
Named after the St Lazarus leper hospital founded here in 1146 and making use of a nearby sulphurous spring.

Burrough Hill
Site of an iron-age fort on a promontory, Burrough camp, offers commanding views across the Wreake valley.

Start/finish

Leicestershire lanes

Distance: 26 miles (45km)
Big hills: 2
Challenge: ●●●☆☆

An undulating roll through rural Leicestershire's charming countryside

A somewhat lumpy ride with some modest challenges along the way. This route passes through old gravel pits, now the delightful Watermead Country Park, uses a stretch of the National Route 6 of the Cycle Network and passes along some very good lanes, even passing the birthplace of Lady Jane Grey along the way.

Start at Mill Lane car park, Thurmaston which is tucked behind a shop – a red pillarbox marks the entrance. Meander north through Watermead Park but take enormous care when going west on the busy A46 then north on the A6.

Right at Rothley station then left towards Woodhouse Eaves, turning north onto Brand Lane. Sharp left by the church into Forest Road, then Beacon Road and right into Breakback Road and north on Woodhouse Lane to the Priory.

Turn left to climb up Nanpantan Road then left again at the top – a dangerous crossroads, so take care. Follow three straight miles to Bradgate Park's north entrance and swing downhill through Newton Linford and Anstey, bearing north in the village towards Thurcaston and signs to Birstall. At the water's edge follow the cycle path back to Watermead and cross to Mill Lane.

Useful refreshments stops

Old Bull's Head, Woodhouse Eaves, Loughborough LE12 8RZ. 01509 890 255 www.theoldbullshead.co.uk

Ellis Tea Rooms, Rothley Station LE7 7LD. 01509 632343

Bike shops

City Cycles, 1A Humberstone Lane, Thurmaston, Leicester LE4 8HJ. 0116 2640654

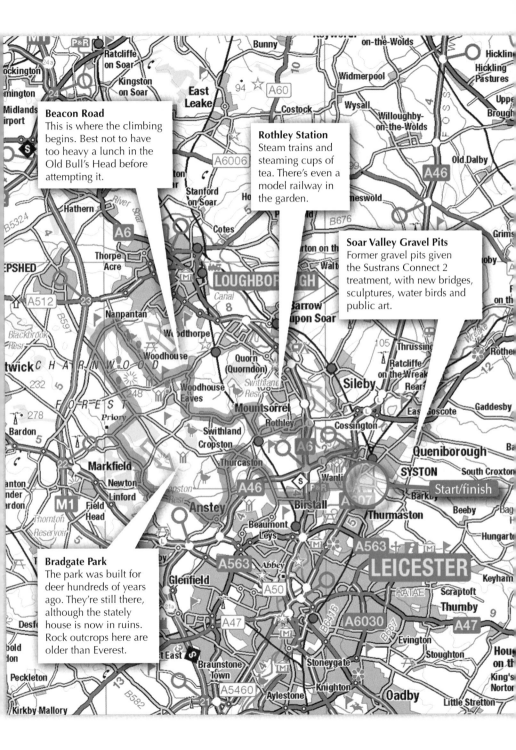

Beacon Road
This is where the climbing begins. Best not to have too heavy a lunch in the Old Bull's Head before attempting it.

Rothley Station
Steam trains and steaming cups of tea. There's even a model railway in the garden.

Soar Valley Gravel Pits
Former gravel pits given the Sustrans Connect 2 treatment, with new bridges, sculptures, water birds and public art.

Bradgate Park
The park was built for deer hundreds of years ago. They're still there, although the stately house is now in ruins. Rock outcrops here are older than Everest.

Start/finish

Derbyshire Dales

Distance: 30 miles (50km)
Big hills: 4
Challenge: ★★★☆☆

A ride off the beaten track in the Dales with plenty of ups and downs, as well as a few cracking views

The Derbyshire Dales have long been known for their stunning views and the exciting things there are to do there, plus their rolling profile makes it perfect for cyclists with an enthusiasm for a bit of climbing. This ride takes you away from the hustle and bustle of what is often a busy tourist destination, off the beaten track and onto the most picturesque, leafy countryside lanes. It explores a part of Derbyshire often overlooked by visiting crowds, but is extremely popular with local riders.

Head west out of Blackbrook on the A517 main road and in approximately 1000m turn left at Shottlegate, onto Over Lane. Climb onto the Ridgeway and then turn right at the church, downhill through Hazelwood. Turn right at the B5023 and then left in approximately 500m. Take the first left down Gunhills Lane.

In about a mile keep left onto Woodfall Lane and follow the road south to the crossroads. Turn right here. In another 1000m turn righ onto Kedleston Road, and next left to Kedleston village. The hall and park are on the left.

Follow the sharp right in the village and then follow the road (Mercaston Lane) north-west for approximately five miles through Mercaston and to the A517. Turn left here and in 500m turn right, heading north-east towards Carsington Water.

Follow this road, forking left after a mile-and-a-quarter, until you reach the reservoir, where you have the perfect opportunity to stop for a cuppa if required.

Continue, turn right at Knockerdown onto the B5035 and follow it round the northern edge of the reservoir. Shortly

Useful refreshments stops

Kedleston Hall, Quarndon DE22 5JH. 01332 842191 www.nationaltrust.org.uk

Carsington Water Visitor Centre, Ashbourne DE6 1ST. 01629 540696 www.moretoexperience.co.uk

The Bluebell Inn, Farnah Green, Belper DE56 2UP. 01773 826495

The Miners Arms, Carsington, Matlock DE4 4DE. 01629 540207

Bike shops

Stanley Fearn Cycles, 19 Bakewell Road, Matlock DE4 3AU. 01629 582089 www.stanleyfearns.co.uk

after losing sight of the water, turn right opposite Sycamore Farm, to climb steeply up Stainsbro Lane. Once over the hill, take the first left towards Wirksworth.

After a descent, turn left and then right onto the B5023. Follow this south for around four-and-a-half miles, enjoying the fast, smooth ride, and turn left shortly before the A517 onto White Lane and climb up past Shottle Hall. Right at the top to the A517, where you turn left for the last stretch back to the start.

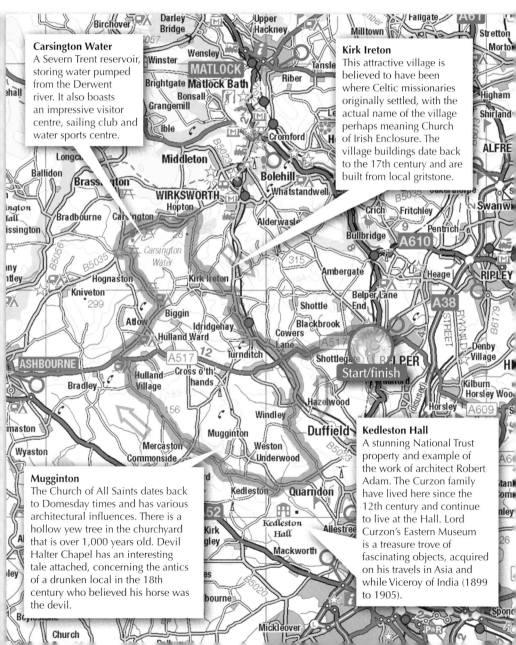

Carsington Water
A Severn Trent reservoir, storing water pumped from the Derwent river. It also boasts an impressive visitor centre, sailing club and water sports centre.

Kirk Ireton
This attractive village is believed to have been where Celtic missionaries originally settled, with the actual name of the village perhaps meaning Church of Irish Enclosure. The village buildings date back to the 17th century and are built from local gritstone.

Mugginton
The Church of All Saints dates back to Domesday times and has various architectural influences. There is a hollow yew tree in the churchyard that is over 1,000 years old. Devil Halter Chapel has an interesting tale attached, concerning the antics of a drunken local in the 18th century who believed his horse was the devil.

Kedleston Hall
A stunning National Trust property and example of the work of architect Robert Adam. The Curzon family have lived here since the 12th century and continue to live at the Hall. Lord Curzon's Eastern Museum is a treasure trove of fascinating objects, acquired on his travels in Asia and while Viceroy of India (1899 to 1905).

Bridlington and East Yorkshire

Distance: 22 miles (35.4km)
Big hills: 1
Challenge: ●●☆☆☆

A rural ride in and around Bridlington taking in coast and farmland, featuring seabirds and the country's tallest standing stone

Nestled between the Pennines, the North York Moors and the North Sea, the Yorkshire Wolds is a hidden retreat for those looking for sights off the beaten track. For birdwatchers, walkers and culture vultures, the Wolds has a lot to offer.

Starting from the Expanse Hotel in North Marine Drive, Bridlington turn left and ride along North Marine Drive to the junction with Sewerby Road. Turn right and follow the road to Sewerby. At Marton Hall turn left onto Jewison Lane and follow the road to Bempton. At Bempton church go straight on and follow Cliff Road to visit the nature reserve. Retrace the route back to Bempton village and turn right towards Buckton.

At Manor Farm turn left and gently climb the hill. Take the first right immediately after the level crossing and follow Grindale Road to the T-junction, where you turn right and pass through Grindale village. At the crossroads, next to

Argam Cottages, turn left and follow the signs to Rudston.

Go into Rudston village and take the first left to reach the church, then turn right and right again to exit the village. At the crossroads turn left towards Burton Agnes and climb the hill. At the summit turn left to Bridlington. Follow the road right to the end.

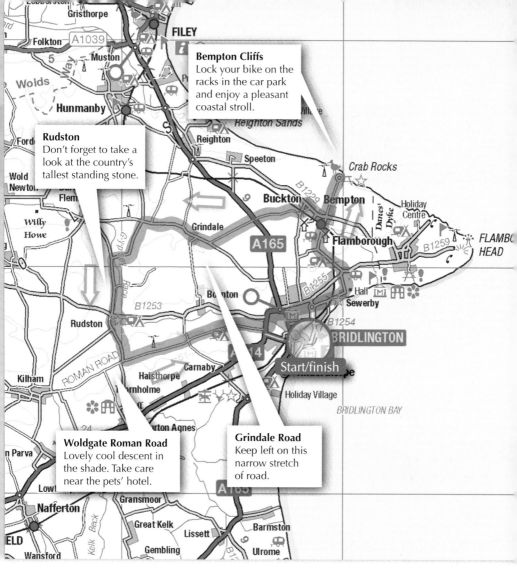

Bempton Cliffs
Lock your bike on the racks in the car park and enjoy a pleasant coastal stroll.

Rudston
Don't forget to take a look at the country's tallest standing stone.

Woldgate Roman Road
Lovely cool descent in the shade. Take care near the pets' hotel.

Grindale Road
Keep left on this narrow stretch of road.

Cross the main A165 to ride on the cycle path and follow National Cycle Network Route 1 through the residential estate to reach Bridlington Old Town.

Go down the High Street and continue straight on at the roundabout. At the next junction, just before the level crossing, turn right onto North Marine Drive to reach the beach.

Doncaster and beyond

Distance: 15 miles (24km)
Big hills: 1
Challenge: ❶❶❶☆☆

A leisurely multi-terrain ride along the Trans Pennine Trail and surrounding lanes of the Doncaster suburbs

There's beauty to be discovered all around in this former coal mining area.

From Doncaster railway station, cross the dual carriageway and go through the shopping precinct. Take the first left to pass the main shops and cross another dual carriageway. Cross the bridge using the cycle path. At the end turn right for Bentley and cross the busy A638/A19 using the footbridge.

Follow the sign for Scawsby, also signposted 'Sprotbrough via the subway' using the cycle path. On the other side of the subway turn right and ride along the cycle path parallel to the York Road (A19), passing various out-of-town superstores.

After about a kilometre as the path goes downhill away from the traffic take the left-hand blue bicycle sign for the Trans Pennine Trail, towards Barnsley. It is also signposted as 'Cusworth Cycle Trail'.

Follow the trail to the River Don and swing sharply to the right under an iron railway bridge. Continue parallel to the river, passing Sprotbrough Lock.

At Conisbrough Viaduct turn right sharply and go up the steep hill. At the top turn right towards Cadeby. At the junction, go straight on along the tarmac road that goes uphill. At Cadeby, go straight on at the crossroads into Cadeby Lane to reach High Melton. Turn left at the crossroads into High Melton.

At the university campus turn right into Hangman's Stony Lane (signposted as a cul-de-sac and bridleway). The residential road becomes a farmer's track; go straight on through the farm field. As the farm track goes left, swing sharply to the farm track on the road (not signposted). Follow the farm track round

Useful refreshment stops
Cushworth Hall Tea Room, Cusworth Hall and Park, Cusworth Lane, Doncaster DN5 7TU. 01302 782342

The Boat Inn, Nursery Lane, Sprotbrough, Doncaster DN5 7NB. 01302 858500

The Cadeby Inn, Main St, Cadeby, Doncaster DN5 7SW. 01709 864009 www.cadebyinn.co.uk

Bike shops
Don Valley Cycles, 10 Chequer Road, Doncaster, DN1 2AF. 01302 769531 www.donvalleycycles.com

to reach Melton Wood. At the wood go straight on to reach the central point, marked by a meeting of six bridleways and benches. Take the second turning on the right, a fast descent to the car park.

Turn left onto the country road to leave the woods. Go down Little Lane to join Back Lane and go uphill under the A1(M) to reach Cusworth Hall.

Go up to Cusworth Hall towards the tearoom and pass the driveway. Go down a road which says 'no unauthorised vehicles' and continue downhill through Cusworth village. Pass a church, and take the second turning on the right, signposted 'Cusworth Cycle Trail/ Orchard Lane'.

At the bottom of Orchard Lane turn left at the pond. Take the right-hand fork past some fields and a football pitch. Go through the trees to reach the Trans Pennine Trail and turn left to retrace the same route back to Doncaster as was taken on the outward journey.

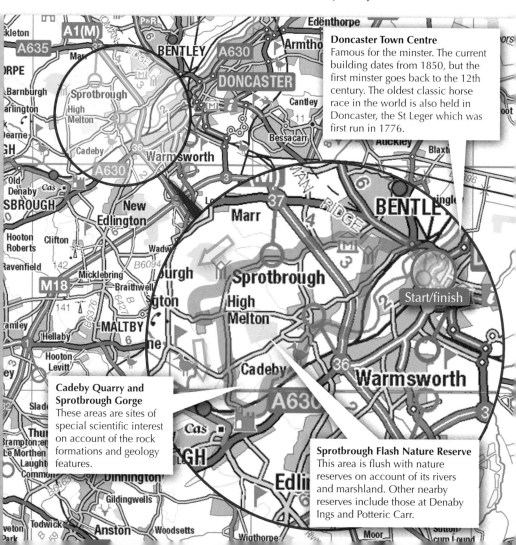

Doncaster Town Centre
Famous for the minster. The current building dates from 1850, but the first minster goes back to the 12th century. The oldest classic horse race in the world is also held in Doncaster, the St Leger which was first run in 1776.

Cadeby Quarry and Sprotbrough Gorge
These areas are sites of special scientific interest on account of the rock formations and geology features.

Sprotbrough Flash Nature Reserve
This area is flush with nature reserves on account of its rivers and marshland. Other nearby reserves include those at Denaby Ings and Potteric Carr.

Around Newcastle

Distance: 10 miles (16km)
Big hills: climbing up from the Tyne can be hard
Challenge: ❶☆☆☆☆

Useful refreshment stops
Pitcher and Piano, The Quayside
108 Quayside, Newcastle NE1 3DX.
0191 232 4110

The Quayside Bar, 35–37 The Close,
Newcastle upon Tyne. 0191 211 1050

Café 21, Trinity Gardens, Quayside,
Newcastle upon Tyne, NE1 2HH.
0191 222 0755
www.cafetwentyone.co.uk

Bike shops
The Cycle Hut (hire available), Quayside,
Newcastle upon Tyne NE6 1BU. 0191
276 7250 www.thecyclehub.org

Cyclelogical, 44 Forest Hall Road, Forest
Hall, Newcastle upon Tyne NE12 9AL.
0191 216 9222

A short ride in the historic and vibrant Geordie city

This ride is unusual because it's entirely within a city and neither is it a circuit, it's L-shaped, running from the northern suburb of Gosforth, south to the quay and its glorious waterfront and the iconic bridges over the River Tyne. It's also a journey through the history of the city and the renovation of Newcastle, delving deep into the heart of Geordie culture.

From Gosforth – there is plenty of street parking on Gosforth – find the South Gosforth Metro station and head east on Station Road, until you see signs for Jesmond Dene and head south on the Dene Cycleway.

Soon after the start there's a section that uses suburban streets, but direction signs are plentiful and clear. You return to the cycleway shortly after entering Jesmond. Continue south through Armstrong Park and Heaton Park, where again you will be directed onto a few quiet streets and traffic-free roads, until you pass under the railway viaduct and into Byker.

Proceed downhill using the Byker Link and onto the Quayside, where you head west under the bridges and for as long as you want before retracing your tracks.

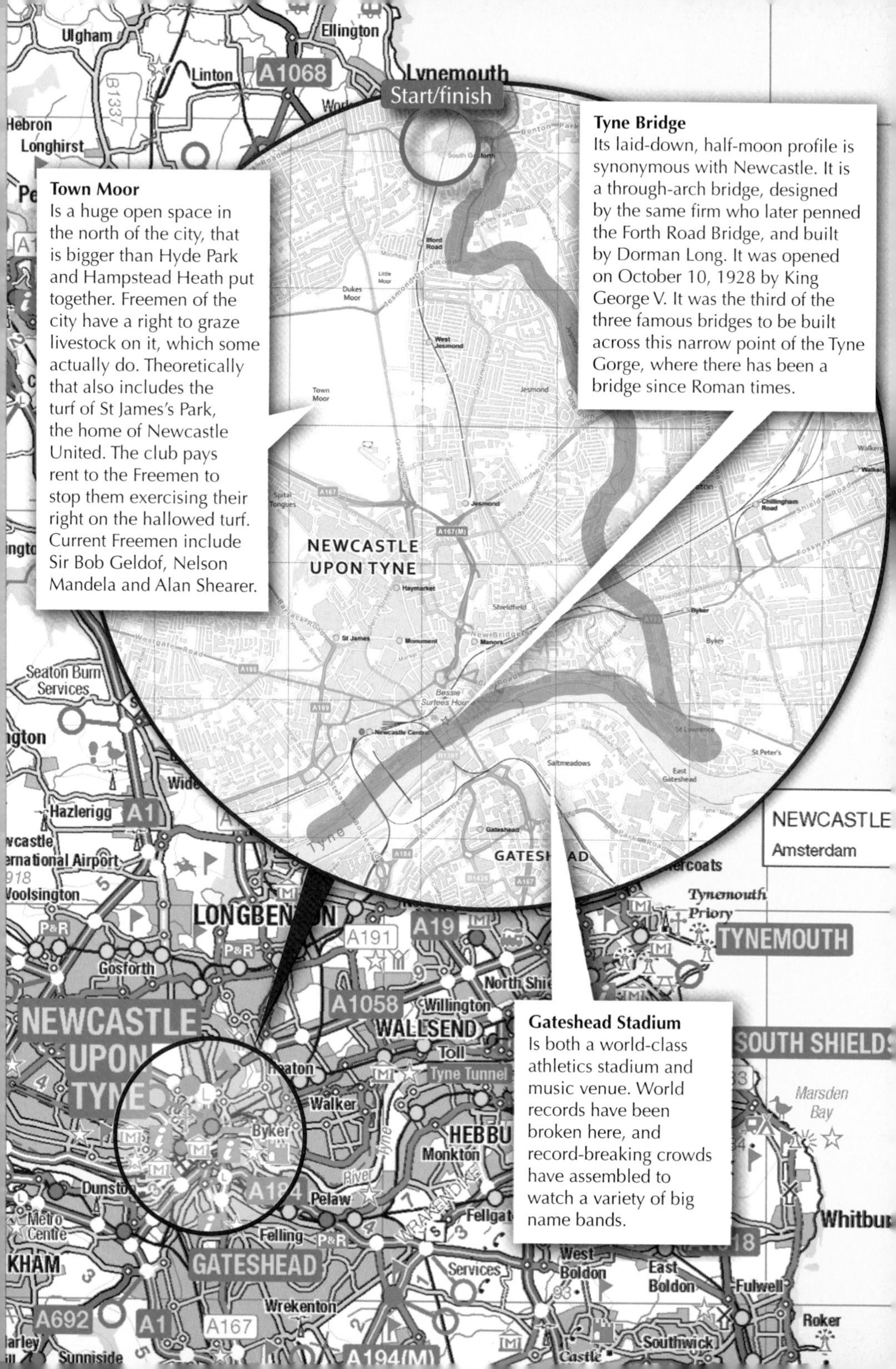

Town Moor

Is a huge open space in the north of the city, that is bigger than Hyde Park and Hampstead Heath put together. Freemen of the city have a right to graze livestock on it, which some actually do. Theoretically that also includes the turf of St James's Park, the home of Newcastle United. The club pays rent to the Freemen to stop them exercising their right on the hallowed turf. Current Freemen include Sir Bob Geldof, Nelson Mandela and Alan Shearer.

Tyne Bridge

Its laid-down, half-moon profile is synonymous with Newcastle. It is a through-arch bridge, designed by the same firm who later penned the Forth Road Bridge, and built by Dorman Long. It was opened on October 10, 1928 by King George V. It was the third of the three famous bridges to be built across this narrow point of the Tyne Gorge, where there has been a bridge since Roman times.

Gateshead Stadium

Is both a world-class athletics stadium and music venue. World records have been broken here, and record-breaking crowds have assembled to watch a variety of big name bands.

Start/finish

NEWCASTLE UPON TYNE

Kielder Water

Distance: 27 miles (43km)
Big hills: none
Challenge: ⊘⊘☆☆☆

A full day's expedition around the largest man-made lake in Britain

Kielder Water on the border between England and Scotland is perfect for exploration by bike. With the recent completion of the final stretch of Lakeside Way it is possible to cycle all the way around the shore of the lake and one can obviously start at any point. Knowe Visitor Centre is the southernmost tip, and a easy place for most people to get to but Kielder village at the northern end is the lake's capital, as such, and makes a better base if you're there for a night or two.

The multi-user path – this means it's used by walkers, runners, wheelchair users and horse riders too – is well signposted throughout. Since it's pretty obvious what you're cycling around (cycle clockwise and keep the water on your right), it's very hard to get lost, leaving you free to enjoy the views without constant map-checking.

Start at the roundabout beside Kielder Castle. Take the exit that leads steeply downhill, past the Anglers Arms. At the T-junction turn left, then almost immediately right down a track through

Useful refreshment stops
Duke's Pantry Tea Room, Kielder Castle NE48 1ER. 01434 250100 www.dukespantry.co.uk

Falstone Old School Tea Room, Falstone NE48 1AA. 01434 240459 www.falstonetearoom.co.uk

Café on the Water, Tower Knowe Visitor Centre, Falstone NE48 1BX. 01434 240436 www.visitkielder.com

The Anglers Arms, Kielder Village NE48 1ER. 01434 250072 www.anglers-arms.com

The Blackcock Country Inn, Falstone NE48 1AA. 01434 240200 www.blackcockinn.co.uk

The Pheasant Inn, Stannersburn, Falstone NE48 1DD. 01434 240382 www.thepheasantinn.com

The Boat Inn, Leaplish NE48 1BT. 01434 2510004

Bike shops
The Bike Place (hire available), Station Garage, Kielder Village NE48 1HX. 01434 250457 www.thebikeplace.co.uk

Ferry
Terminals are at Tower Knowe and Leaplish, where you can book in advance. Alternatively, call 01434 251000. You can also board or disembark at Belvedere. Check timetables at www.visitkielder.com

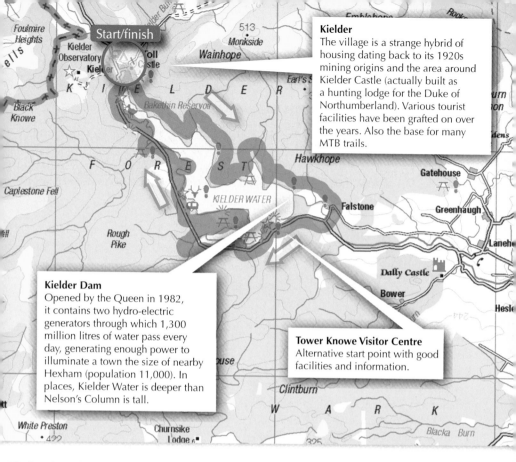

Kielder
The village is a strange hybrid of housing dating back to its 1920s mining origins and the area around Kielder Castle (actually built as a hunting lodge for the Duke of Northumberland). Various tourist facilities have been grafted on over the years. Also the base for many MTB trails.

Kielder Dam
Opened by the Queen in 1982, it contains two hydro-electric generators through which 1,300 million litres of water pass every day, generating enough power to illuminate a town the size of nearby Hexham (population 11,000). In places, Kielder Water is deeper than Nelson's Column is tall.

Tower Knowe Visitor Centre
Alternative start point with good facilities and information.

Viaduct Wood. Emerging at a road turn left over a bridge, then right to pick up the Lakeside Way. It winds its way up and around a sewage works, then hugs the northern shore of Bakethin Reservoir, then Kielder Water. At the car park to the north of the dam, pass by and continue in the same direction.

Take care at the farm at Hawkhope. Don't speed ahead but turn right just past the farm and down a track across fields that becomes a lane to Falstone. At the T-junction in the village turn right, then right again at the junction with the main road. Just after the dam cross over the road and pick up Lakeside Way again.

After the sailing centre either turn right to go around Bull Crag or keep ahead. The two routes join up at Freya's Cabin.

Pass through Leaplish and proceed north to the Matthew's Linn car park where the route swings away from the lake briefly to pass under the road and cross Lewisburn Bridge. Pass back under the road and shortly after the 'Mirage' turn left at a T-junction of tracks, then right just before the road to proceed to Kielder village. At the track's end turn right onto the road, then first left down the track through Viaduct Wood to the village centre.

Killer climbing in Yorkshire

Distance: 32 miles (51km) – 21m/34km return o

Big hills: 6 and lots of lumps

Challenge: ✪✪✪✪✪

A punishing but rewarding tour of the jarring cobbled climbs of West Yorkshire

Inspired by the great Tour of Flanders bike race this route sets some real challenges on the hilly terrain between Keighley and Halifax. To ride the whole loop leave the centre of Halifax and take the A629 from a giant roundabout heading north-west. To keep things simple, follow this same road all the way to Keighley.

Once you arrive in Keighley, take a right onto the A6035 Worth Way, pass the railway station, then take the very next left onto Dalton Lane. Follow Dalton Lane up to the point where the road bends round to the left. Leave it here and turn right across Thwaites Bridge then leave it left opposite the Shoulder of Mutton pub. Follow through the small industrial area to the bottom of Thwaites Brow Road (cobbled climb No. 1).

Follow the natural progression of the road to the T-junction at the top, take a right, then following a fast descent, your second left onto Hainworth Wood Road. At the end of this road turn left again onto Hainworth Lane (cobbled climb No. 2).

Useful refreshment stops

Rossi's Café, 102 Cavendish Street, Keighley, BD21 3DE. 01535 604813

Wilson's Fish Restaurant, Lawkholme Lane, Keighley, West Yorkshire BD21 3DX. 01535 608254

3 Acres Pub, Bingley Road, Lees Moor, Keighley, BD21 5QE. 01535 644895

Platform 4 Sandwich Station, Station Road, Haworth. 01535 644744

Bike shops

Pedal Sport, 193–195 King Cross Road

King Cross, Halifax, West Yorkshire HX1 3LN. 01422 361460

Aire Valley Cycles, Millennium House, 74 South Street Keighley, BD21 1DQ. 01535 610839
www.airevalleycycles.com

Follow Hainworth Lane, which turns into Goff Well Lane, turn right at the top onto Bingley Road and follow it down to the A629. Turn right onto the A629, then at the mini roundabout turn left and continue down into the centre of Haworth.

Ride past the station and carry straight on, then left as the main road banks right over a bridge and heads up the super-steep Brow Road to join the A6033.

Cross the A6033 onto the B6144 and take the first right onto Black Moor Road. Climb up and over the moor then drop onto the B6141, take a left and follow this back to the A629. Turn right then third left onto the A644, a one-way street. Exit the one-way section and at a junction where

three roads meet from the right at the same spot, take the last of the three, Roper Lane, to bypass Queensbury and join the A647 where you turn right.

Follow this round until the fifth left turn, Ploughcroft Lane (cobbled climb No. 3). Head straight up, turn right at the top, follow the hill down, take a left at the bottom and follow this road to the A58.

500m later, take the right onto Kell Lane then the next left onto Blake Hill, follow this down, past the Shibden Mill Inn to join Lee Lane and the base of Shibden Wall (cobbled climb No. 4). Once at the top, go straight across down Ploughcroft Lane, left at the bottom and follow the A647 back into the centre of Halifax.

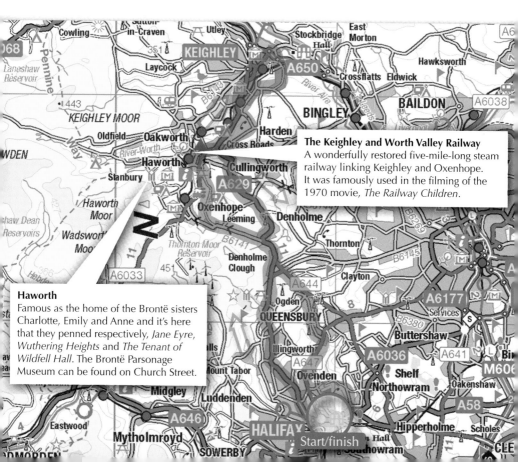

The Keighley and Worth Valley Railway
A wonderfully restored five-mile-long steam railway linking Keighley and Oxenhope. It was famously used in the filming of the 1970 movie, *The Railway Children*.

Haworth
Famous as the home of the Brontë sisters Charlotte, Emily and Anne and it's here that they penned respectively, *Jane Eyre*, *Wuthering Heights* and *The Tenant of Wildfell Hall*. The Brontë Parsonage Museum can be found on Church Street.

Barnsley easy paths

Distance: 17.5 miles (28km)
Big hills: none
Challenge: ❶☆☆☆☆

A leisurely ride along the Trans Pennine Trail

This ride is actually a choice of routes around a semi-urban area just south of Barnsley in Yorkshire. Using the Trans Pennine Trail, it's easy going and equally suited to children or older folk.

The RSPB's Old Moor wetlands centre is in the middle of the route and you can head either due west to the Worsbrough Mill and Country Park, or south-west to the Elsecar Heritage Centre.

To Worsborough: Head out of the Old Moor car park over the bridge and take a right, under a road bridge and up the other side. Join the Trans Pennine Trail and follow straight ahead, crossing the road and going through the A-frame gate. The road forks twice – at the first head left, and at the second head right. In both cases follow the signs for Worsbrough. You will pass under a couple of large bridges as you get nearer to the country park, and then you will see signs for the park to your left. Head down the steep, gravelly path directly in front of you then over a couple of small bridges to the mill.

To Elsecar: Head out of the Old Moor car park over the bridge and head right again, under a road bridge and up the

Useful refreshment stops
Gannets Café, Old Moor RSPB Wetlands Centre, S73 0YF. 01226 751593 www.rspb.org.uk

Brambles Tea-Room, Elsecar Heritage Centre, Wath Rd, Elsecar S74 8HJ. 01226 741915

Button Mill Inn, Worsbrough, Barnsley S70 5LJ. 01226 282639

Bike shops
Geared Up, 23 Barnsley Road, Barnsley S73 8HT. 01226 756281 www.gearedupcycles.co.uk

Racescene, 210–212 Upper Sheffield Rd, Barnsley S70 4PG. 01226 292111 www.racescene.co.uk

other side. Follow the same route to Worsbrough for a couple of hundred metres until you see a sign for Elsecar Greenway on your left. Follow that and head straight on. There are a couple of much more significant roads to cross on this route so take care. Eventually you will reach the disused Dearne and Dove Canal, then through a brief, muddy wooded section, then down and under a stone bridge. Once past the pretty little pond you will have to head up a slope to cross Tingle Bridge Lane. Then resume the trail and you'll soon be at Elsecar.

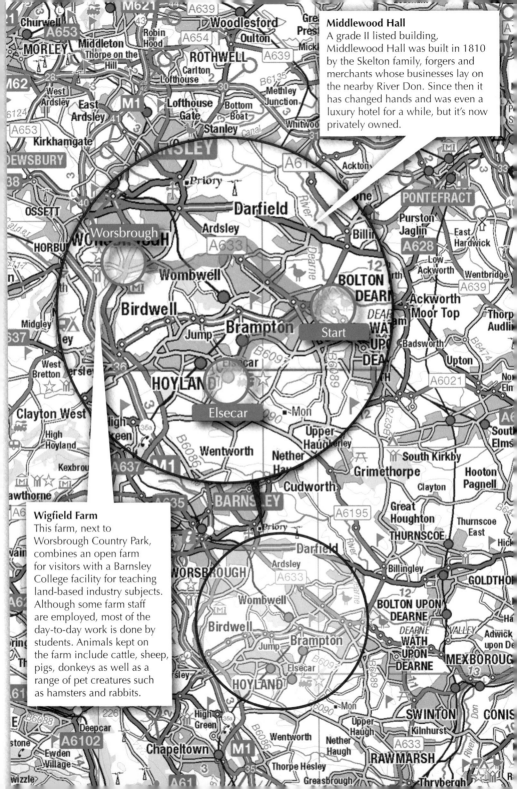

Middlewood Hall

A grade II listed building, Middlewood Hall was built in 1810 by the Skelton family, forgers and merchants whose businesses lay on the nearby River Don. Since then it has changed hands and was even a luxury hotel for a while, but it's now privately owned.

Wigfield Farm

This farm, next to Worsbrough Country Park, combines an open farm for visitors with a Barnsley College facility for teaching land-based industry subjects. Although some farm staff are employed, most of the day-to-day work is done by students. Animals kept on the farm include cattle, sheep, pigs, donkeys as well as a range of pet creatures such as hamsters and rabbits.

Start

Teesdale forest and moor

Distance: 17 miles (27km)
Big hills: 3
Challenge: ●●●●☆

A challenging off-road ride through coniferous forest and over the open, heather-covered moorland of Teesdale

Hamsterley Forest is the county's largest woodland area, a 5,000-acre expanse of coniferous and broad-leaved trees over the sides of a sheltered valley offers lots of opportunities for cyclists of all levels – from leisure mountain bike trails to freeride and 4X.

Our ride starts at The Grove in Hamsterley Forest and follows the Packhorse Trail through the forest and into Teesdale. The area is a convenient meeting point, as not only is there a car park but there is also ample space to park bicycles and tether horses, and further up the road is the café and a cycle hire / repair shop.

Starting at the Grove car park, leave the car park and turn right on the Forest Drive. Just before the barrier turn right on the uphill track. Turn left at the crossroads. Just as the climb gets steeper turn left on the level track. Turn left to follow the slightly downhill track (signposted 'Brown Horse Riding Trail'). At the junction with the bridleway continue straight ahead and round to the right of the track. Go straight ahead, then straight ahead again at the crossroads.

Continue uphill and straight ahead at the next two junctions. At the crossroads of five tracks take the first left (signposted 'bridleway'). Continue straight ahead at the next junction to the edge of the forest.

At the forest edge when the track turns to the right, bear left through a gate opposite a bench. Follow the bridleway across the moor. The route is rutted and rough in places. Turn right onto the stone track then turn left onto the road. (There is an alternative route which avoids

> **Useful refreshment stops**
> Hamsterley Forest Tea Rooms, Redford, Bishop Auckland DL13 3NL.
> 01388 488822
> Three Tuns Inn, Church Bank, Eggleston, Barnard Castle DL12 0AH.
> 01833 650289
>
> **Bike shops**
> Spitfire Cycles, 44 Galgate, Barnard Castle DL12 8PQ. 01833 690640
> www.spitfirecycles.co.uk

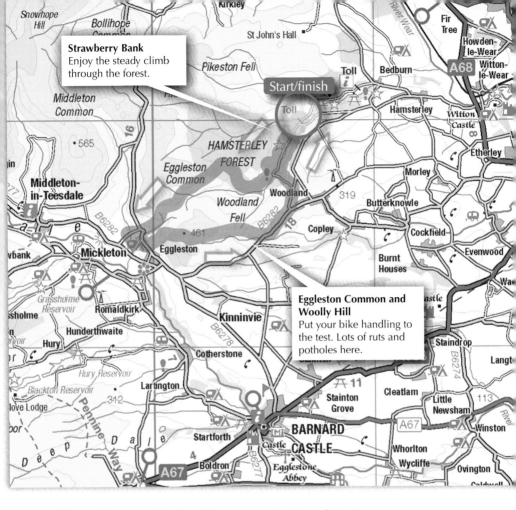

Strawberry Bank
Enjoy the steady climb through the forest.

Start/finish

Eggleston Common and Woolly Hill
Put your bike handling to the test. Lots of ruts and potholes here.

some of the road – go straight ahead for 500m, cross the bridge and turn left along the Teesdale Way. Cross two fords and continue straight ahead uphill. Turn left when you reach the road and right, at the top of the climb back onto the road.)

Take the first left after the Moorcock pub (signposted Neamour Road). At the top of the road follow the bridleway track straight ahead. At the top of the steep climb bear left (signposted 'bridleway'). Follow the signposted bridleway across the moor which is wet and rough in places.

Go through the gate, bear left across the moor and through another gate. Continue ahead with the fence on your left. Straight ahead through Woolly Hill Farm (Ark on the Edge Wildlife Sanctuary). Turn left at the road. Turn left at the junction (signposted Hamsterley). Turn left after about a 1000m (signposted with a blue National Byway sign). Take care on the steep descent down to the Forest Drive. Finally, turn right onto the Forest Drive and return to the Grove car park.

Huddersfield and West Yorkshire

Distance: 18 miles (29km)
Big hills: lots of small ones
Challenge: ●●☆☆☆

Useful refreshment stops

Standedge Tunnel Visitor Centre and Café, Waters Road, Marsden HD7 6NQ. 01484 844298

Sands House Inn, Blackmoorfoot Road, Crosland Hill, Huddersfield HD4 7AE. 01484 654478 www.thesandshouse.com

Wills O'Nats, Blackmoorfoot Road, Meltham, Holmfirth HD9 5PS. 01484 850078 www.willsonats.com

Riverhead Brewery Tap, 2 Peel Street, Marsden HD7 6BR. 01484 841270

Bike shops

Velocity Cycles, 70 Acre St, Lindley, Huddersfield HD3 3EL. 01484 455300 www.velocitycycles.co.uk

Huddersfield and West Yorkshire's rolling open moorland with short, sharp climbs through Linthwaite near the beginning and up Lowestwood Lane at the end

This ride is not about long slogs up never-ending inclines but short, sharp ascents rewarded by sudden stunning glimpses of the surrounding moorland, followed by equally quick drops that reveal a different landscape below.

Begin at the Walkers Arms car park in Golcar, ride up to the main road, Leymoor Road, and turn right. At the T-junction turn left down Carr Top Lane and take a sharp right onto Brook Lane. Climb sharply and follow round to drop down Lowestwood Lane on the left. Follow over canals to join the A62 at some lights. Take the first left up Hoyle House Road.

At the T-junction turn left then right onto Church Lane, alongside the golf course. At the next T-junction turn left then right at Sands House Inn. Take the rough track on the right after the airfield. At the farm buildings turn left to reach a T-junction with a road and turn right. Take the second left, Reservoir Side Road, to turn right alongside the reservoir. Turn right at another T-junction then first left, over the first crossroads then, at the next, turn right onto the B6107.

Straight over the crossroads, past the Whitehouse pub, keep straight ahead to the junction with Manchester Road A62.

Turn left and follow the road out of town to take a sharp right (signed 'unsuitable for motor vehicles').

Drop down to Tunnel End. Join the towpath towards Marsden and follow it all the way back to Titanic Mill. Turn left up Lowestwood Lane, right at the T-junction at the top and retrace your steps to the Walkers Arms car park.

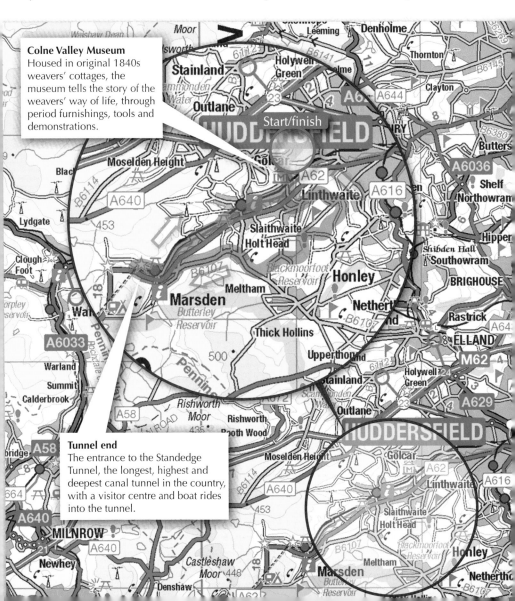

Colne Valley Museum
Housed in original 1840s weavers' cottages, the museum tells the story of the weavers' way of life, through period furnishings, tools and demonstrations.

Tunnel end
The entrance to the Standedge Tunnel, the longest, highest and deepest canal tunnel in the country, with a visitor centre and boat rides into the tunnel.

The Yorkshire Wolds

Distance: 23 miles (37km)
Big hills: 1
Challenge: ●●☆☆☆

A leisurely spin through the pretty villages and open countryside of the Yorkshire Wolds

Once upon a time you could travel by rail from Market Weighton in four directions. The railways had all closed by 1965 and the Beverley line is now one of two great cycle routes into town.

Leave Market Weighton to the north via Londesborough Road. Take the first right

Useful refreshment stops
The Goodmanham Arms, Main St, Goodmanham, YO43 3JA. 01430 873849 www.goodmanhamarms.co.uk
The Wellington Inn, 19 The Green, Lund, YO25 9TE. 01377 217294 www.thewellingtoninn.co.uk
The Pipe and Glass Inn, South Dalton, Beverley HU17 7PN. 01430 810246 www.pipeandglass.co.uk
The Light Dragoon, Etton, HU17 7PQ, 01430 810282
– Plus lots of choice in Market Weighton

Bike shops
Minster Cycles, 5–7 Norwood, Beverley HU17 9ET. 01482 867950 www.minstercycles.co.uk

signed to Goodmanham. Pass through the village and continue ahead for three miles. At T-junction beside a little green turn left signed to Middleton and then almost immediately right signed to Lund. Continue ahead at crossroads into the village centre. In front of the Wellington Arms turn right signed to Lockington.

Turn right at T-junction then soon left into Lockington. Pass along the main street then, beside the Rockingham, turn right and over a brick bridge. At T-junction with B1248 turn right then immediately left signed to Holme on the Wolds. Pass through the village and follow the road as it bears left towards and through South Dalton (for the Pipe and Glass and a view of Dalton Hall turn right after the church).

Pass over a crossroads then turn left at a T-junction into Etton. Turn right at the Light Dragoon. After 500m cross the former railway bridge then immediately turn right to leave the road and follow a track that leads down to the Hudson Way cycle path, which leads all the way back to Market Weighton.

The Way ends in an open, grassed area. Where the path splits fork left and continue ahead onto Hall Road briefly to reach the Londesborough Road. Turn left back to the car park. The Hudson Way crosses roads and farm tracks, so take care if you have children with you. It is also well used by walkers and narrow in places so a bell comes in useful.

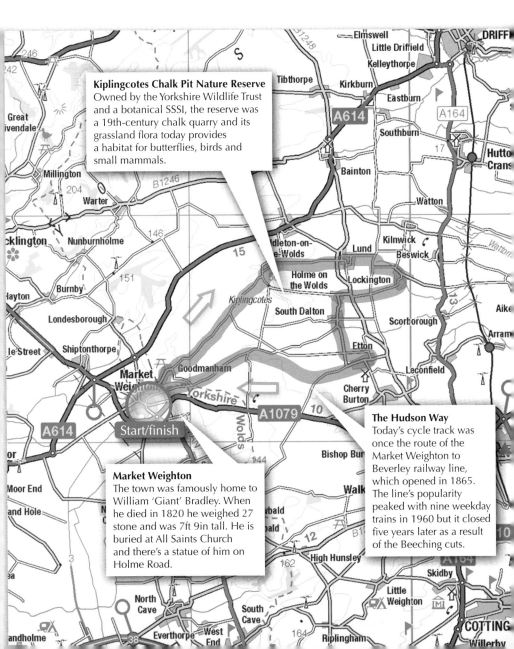

Kiplingcotes Chalk Pit Nature Reserve
Owned by the Yorkshire Wildlife Trust and a botanical SSSI, the reserve was a 19th-century chalk quarry and its grassland flora today provides a habitat for butterflies, birds and small mammals.

The Hudson Way
Today's cycle track was once the route of the Market Weighton to Beverley railway line, which opened in 1865. The line's popularity peaked with nine weekday trains in 1960 but it closed five years later as a result of the Beeching cuts.

Market Weighton
The town was famously home to William 'Giant' Bradley. When he died in 1820 he weighed 27 stone and was 7ft 9in tall. He is buried at All Saints Church and there's a statue of him on Holme Road.

Start/finish

East of Leeds

Distance: 22.5 miles (36km)
Big hills: none
Challenge: ❶❶❶☆☆

A day ride through pretty country villages east of Leeds, jam packed with historical gems

Leave Aberford centre via Cattle Lane (signed 'Barwick 2'). Turn right after the church in Barwick (signed 'Potterton 1'). At the T-junction turn right towards a dead-end. Turn left along the A64 (on cycle track) then soon right up a broad, unsurfaced track signed as the West Yorkshire cycle route. Turn left at the road to pass to and through Thorner.

At the A64, turn left then soon right signed 'Scholes 1'. Pass through the village and at a small green with a tree in the middle, turn right signed to Leeds. Cross over the road in front and straight down the bridleway (Leeds Country Way).

At a metal barrier turn left to pass Shippen House Farm. Turn right in front of derelict outbuilding and pass through a fieldgate to follow the bridleway under the M1 and over a railway line (via gate). Push your bike down the hedged footpath then turn left at the end towards Garforth.

Take the first left signed 'Barwick 1¼'. Just after Laverack Cottage turn right down a two and a half-mile track to Aberford.

Useful refreshment stops

The Black Swan, Barwick-in-Elmet LS15 4JP. 0113 281 3065

Orlando's at The Buffers, Rakehill Rd, Scholes LS15 4AL. 0113 262 0627

The Mexborough Arms, Main St, Thorner LS14 3DX. 0113 289 2316

The Crooked Billet Inn, Wakefield Rd, Saxton LS24 9QN. 01937 557389

The Greyhound Inn, Main St, Saxton LS24 9PY. 01937 557202

Bike shops

Wetherby Bike Shack (hire available), 9 Horsefair, Wetherby LS22 6JG. 0845 291 6014
www.wetherbybikeshack.co.uk

Turn right in the village, past almshouses then left at a crossroads to Lotherton Hall. After visiting the Hall, turn right signed 'Sherburn in Elmet 3½' then first left (unsigned) to Saxton. In the village bear left on Main Street to pass the church, then turn left down Dam Lane. At the T-junction with the B1217 turn left (church of St Mary is opposite the Crooked Billet pub). Turn right to Aberford. To visit the Triumphal Arch follow the signed permissive tarmac path that begins at Beech View off Cattle Lane in Aberford at the start of the ride. Return the same way to resume the circuit.

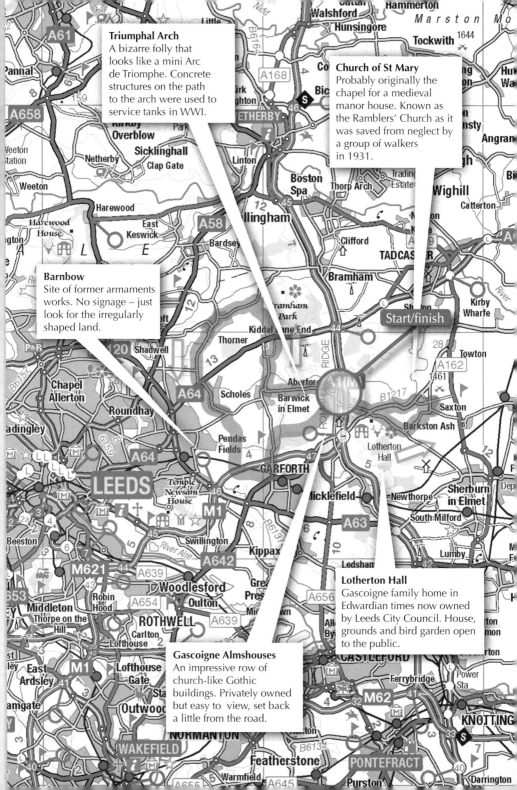

Triumphal Arch
A bizarre folly that looks like a mini Arc de Triomphe. Concrete structures on the path to the arch were used to service tanks in WWI.

Church of St Mary
Probably originally the chapel for a medieval manor house. Known as the Ramblers' Church as it was saved from neglect by a group of walkers in 1931.

Barnbow
Site of former armaments works. No signage – just look for the irregularly shaped land.

Start/finish

Lotherton Hall
Gascoigne family home in Edwardian times now owned by Leeds City Council. House, grounds and bird garden open to the public.

Gascoigne Almshouses
An impressive row of church-like Gothic buildings. Privately owned but easy to view, set back a little from the road.

Baldersdale

Distance: 11.4 miles (18.4km)
Big hills: 1
Challenge: ❂❂☆☆☆

An off-road ride taking in woodland, moorland and waterside trails through the remote Baldersdale in the North Pennines

Useful refreshment stops
The Fox and Hounds, Cotherstone, Barnard Castle, Co. Durham. DL12 9PF. 01833 650241 www.cotherstonefox.co.uk

The Red Lion, Cotherstone, Barnard Castle, County Durham, DL12 9QE. 01833 650236

Bike shops
Spitfire Cycles, 44 Galgate, Barnard Castle, County Durham DL12 8BH. 01833 690640 www.spitfirecycles.co.uk

Reservoirs, hay meadows, sandstone plateaus and moors are some of the interesting sights in this remote ride of special scientific interest. Tucked away out of sight from visitors to Teesdale is Baldersdale, whose river is a tributary of the Tees. A ride on these unexplored trails will take you into a place that is the epitome of tranquillity. Despite its remoteness this is an area of great interest since a rich variety of species inhabits the moorland, blanket bog and nearby hay meadows.

Start at the car park on south side of Hury Reservoir (Northumbrian Water car park). Turn right onto the road. Go straight ahead on the Northumbrian Water track, signposted Blackton Reservoir. Bear right through the gate, follow the track down, cross the footbridge and small dam. Turn left along the reservoir. Go through the gate beside Blackton Reservoir dam.

Join the stone track and continue ahead with the reservoir on your left.

After a short distance the stone track turns into a grassy track. Cross the little stone bridge and continue straight ahead. Go through the gate, signposted Blackton Reservoir Nature Reserve.

Continue straight ahead. Go through the gate near the bird hide, turn left onto the grassy track and then follow the Pennine Way left across the bridge.

Bear left at the fork, taking the lower track. Cross the bridge, straight ahead through the gate and follow the track up the hill to Clove Lodge.

Follow the track through the farm and go straight ahead on the road for around a mile. Turn right onto the Pennine Way, signposted Levy Pool and continue across the moor, skirting to the right of and below the large rock outcrop that is Goldsborough.

Cross the bridge over Yawd Sike. Continue ahead bearing left. At the post bear right. (There's a short cut here: bear left at How Beck Head, marked by a post. Go left of the Danger Area wall and follow this bridleway on the right side of How Beck for about 1.5 miles until you reach the road. Turn left to rejoin the main route.)

Go through the gate. Straight ahead keeping the fence/old wall on your left. At the cross track turn left through the field gate. Pass on the right of Battle Hill Farm. Turn left onto the road. Continue straight ahead on the road for another 1000m. At the Butter Stone (opposite Scots pine shelterbelt) turn left onto the bridleway (signposted) across the moor. Join the road and continue straight ahead.

Cross the cattle grid and at a T-junction turn left. Finally turn left at the T-junction signposted Hury and Blackton Reservoirs.

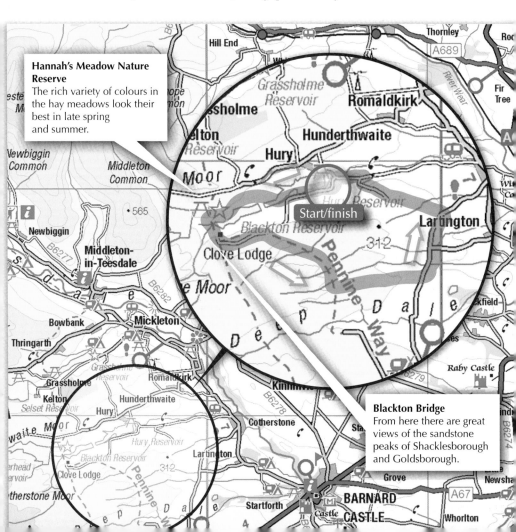

Hannah's Meadow Nature Reserve
The rich variety of colours in the hay meadows look their best in late spring and summer.

Start/finish

Blackton Bridge
From here there are great views of the sandstone peaks of Shacklesborough and Goldsborough.

East Yorkshire and the Humber Bridge

Distance: 20.5 miles (33km)
Big hills: 1
Challenge: ✪✪✪☆☆

A road ride with off-road sections through delightful East Yorkshire country in the shadow of the Humber Bridge

Humber Bridge, the world's fifth largest single span suspension bridge, is a mainstay of the East Yorkshire skyline and can be seen from the various villages in the undulating county. Impressive views can be had of the countryside across the other side of the water when riding along the shores of the Humber Estuary. Once into the hinterland, the sights of various pretty, affluent villages can be appreciated as the ride meanders through quiet country lanes.

From Hessle Foreshore car park follow Cliff Road west passing under Humber Bridge. Go through the hotel car park and pick up the Trans Pennine Trail (National Cycle Route 65). Follow the off-road trail to North Ferriby. Go along the High Street, following the signs for the Trans Pennine Trail. Just outside the village join the cycle path on the left and ride along the cycle lane on the A63. Cross the A63 via the zig-zag bridge to reach Melton. Turn left from the bridge and go straight on through

Useful refreshment stops

Country Park Inn Cliff Road, Hessle
Foreshore, Hessle, Hull HU13 0HB.
01482 640526
www.countryparkinn.co.uk

Millers Tea Room and Farm Shop, Raywell
Lodge Park, Riplingham Road, Raywell
HU16 5YL. 01482 631702
www.millerstearoomandfarmshop.co.uk

Sails Café, Skidby Mill, Beverly Rd, Skidby
HU16 5TF. 01482 847831
www.sailscafe.com

Duke of Cumberland High Street,
North Ferriby, Hull HU14 3JP.
01482 631592
www.dukeofcumberlandpub.co.uk

Green Dragon Inn Cowgate, Welton
HU15 1NB. 01482 666700

Bike shops

Cottingham Cycle Centre, 1 Station Road,
Cottingham, East Yorkshire HU16 4LL.
01482 845372
www.cottinghamcyclecentre.co.uk

Starbikes 204 Willerby Road, Hull
HU5 5JW. 01482 564673
www.starbikes.net

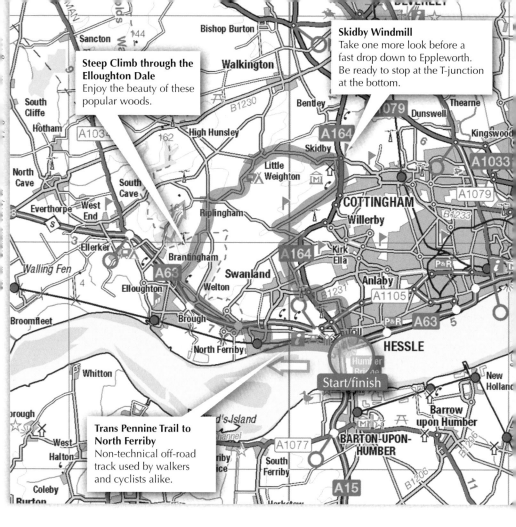

Steep Climb through the Elloughton Dale
Enjoy the beauty of these popular woods.

Skidby Windmill
Take one more look before a fast drop down to Eppleworth. Be ready to stop at the T-junction at the bottom.

Trans Pennine Trail to North Ferriby
Non-technical off-road track used by walkers and cyclists alike.

Melton to arrive in Welton. Follow the one-way system and pass the church and pond. Turn left onto Kidd Lane and go uphill to Elloughton.

After the descent turn right and climb Elloughton Dale. At the T-junction turn left to Riplingham. Turn right at the crossroads and take the first left at Manor Farm. At the sharp left-hand bend continue straight on to pick up the bridleway and follow it to the end then turn right to Skidby.

On the hill, just before the roundabout turn right and pass the windmill. At the bottom of the hill turn right to Eppleworth, then turn sharp left up the hill at the T-junction. Go downhill and turn right at the crossroads and then first left into Occupation Lane.

Continue straight on to Tranby Lane Farm. At the T-junction turn left and go straight on at the roundabout. Take the first right into Jenny Brough Lane. Follow the bendy road to Hessle. Go over the railway line and the A63 to Hessle Foreshore.

Nidderdale

Distance: 21 miles (34km)
Big hills: 1
Challenge: ●●☆☆☆

A tour of North Yorkshire's finest stately homes and quaint villages

Nidderdale in the Yorkshire Dales is home to the spa town of Harrogate and a World Heritage Site in Fountains Abbey. The route is very much a beginner-friendly one, starting and finishing in Knaresborough, a very pretty, historic market town, filled with classic Georgian architecture.

From Waterside (Riverside Walk) in Knaresborough, turn right onto the Harrogate-to-Knaresborough road, (A59), towards Knaresborough centre, then turn left at the traffic lights onto Boroughbridge Road (the A6055). Continue along the A6055 to turn left on Farnham Lane. At the T-junction in Farnham, turn right (Farnham Lane) and left on Copgrove Lane.

Bear right on to Occaney Lane, then left on Wath Lane before Staveley. Continue along Wath Lane to Copgrove, to turn left on to Apron Lane to Burton Leonard. Bear left in Burton Leonard on Station lane to Wormald Green. Left on Ripon Road (A61), then right, signposted Markington.

Continue into Markington and take the right turn right up Westerns Lane and right onto Howhills Road. Continue on Howhills Road, which turns into Fountains Lane. Turn right on to Church Walk to Fountains Abbey / Studley Royal visitor centre.

Return on Fountains Lane and How Hill Road to join Watergate Road. Continue to the T-junction, turn left, then next left up to Bishop Thornton.

Take the left turn in Bishop Thornton, through Shaw Mills. Continue on Pye

Lane to the junction with the B6165. Turn right through Burnt Yates and drop down a long descent before a left turn on to Hartwith Mill Private Toll Road.

Cross the bridge over the River Nidd and turn left into Birstwith. Straight through Birstwith on Elton Lane to Hampsthwaite. Turn right in Hampsthwaite, then left on to Hollins Lane, which turns into Lund Lane before turning left on Otley Road to Killinghall.

Turn left on the A61 at Killinghall, to the Ripley roundabout, take the first left to Ripley. Leaving Ripley, cross the roundabout at the Northern end of Ripley onto the A61 towards Ripon. Take the first right on Nidd Lane, left at the T-junction onto Brearton Lane before a left turn onto the B6165 Ripley Road. Follow the B6165 back into Knaresborough, turn right at the traffic lights to finish back at Waterside, Knaresborough.

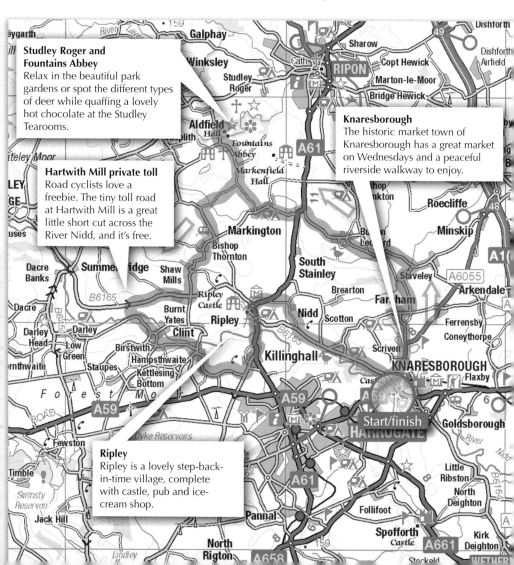

Studley Roger and Fountains Abbey
Relax in the beautiful park gardens or spot the different types of deer while quaffing a lovely hot chocolate at the Studley Tearooms.

Knaresborough
The historic market town of Knaresborough has a great market on Wednesdays and a peaceful riverside walkway to enjoy.

Hartwith Mill private toll
Road cyclists love a freebie. The tiny toll road at Hartwith Mill is a great little short cut across the River Nidd, and it's free.

Ripley
Ripley is a lovely step-back-in-time village, complete with castle, pub and ice-cream shop.

Castle Howard

Distance: 11.5 miles (18.5km)
Big hills: none – but lots of undulations
Challenge: ⊙⊙☆☆☆

An easy ride through North Yorkshire taking in Castle Howard

Everyone knows the Yorkshire Dales and North Yorks Moors but there are lots of other, smaller scenic bits dotted around the county including the Howardian Hills which stretch across a swathe of countryside about 10 miles north of York. A designated Area of Outstanding Natural Beauty, they take their name from the Howard family which owned – and still owns – Castle Howard.

Leave Terrington past the church and heading east. Fork right signed to Ganthorpe. Pass through the village. At a T-junction turn right if you want to visit Bulmer then return to the junction and continue ahead and over a crossroads to visit Welburn. Return to the crossroads and turn right up The Stray. Pass through Carrmire Gate and by the entrance to Castle Howard and keep going until a crossroads. Turn right

for a visit to Coneysthorpe, turning left in the village to circuit the green.

Return to the crossroads and continue ahead through a forest. Follow the road as it bears sharp left and, soon after, turn right to return to Terrington (repeating the start of the outgoing route).

Useful refreshment stops

Pattacakes Shop and Tea Room, Main St, Welburn YO60 7DX. 01653 618352 www.pattacakes.biz

The Arboretum Café, Castle Howard, YO60 7DA. 01653 648767 www.kewatch.co.uk/cafe.html

The Backotheshop Art Café (at the rear of Terrington village store) Terrington YO60 6QB. 01653 648530 www.backoftheshop.co.uk

Bike shops

Yates Cycles, Railway St, Malton YO17 7NS. 01653 605400 www.yatescycles.co.uk

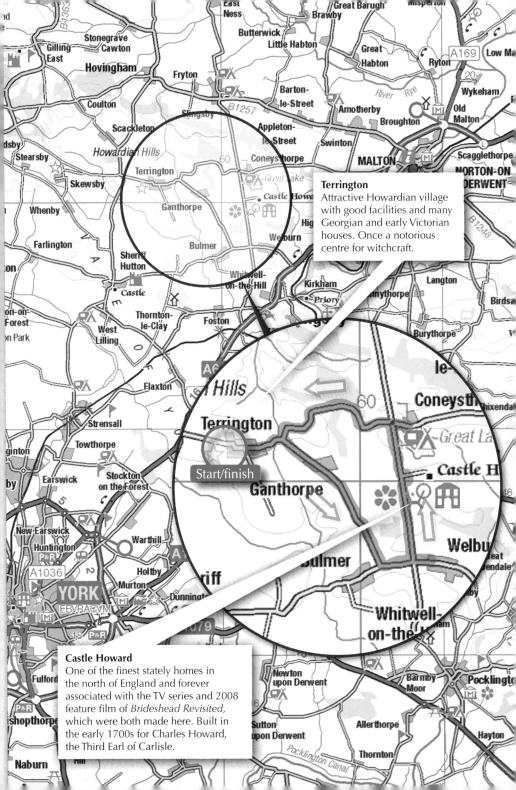

Terrington
Attractive Howardian village with good facilities and many Georgian and early Victorian houses. Once a notorious centre for witchcraft.

Castle Howard
One of the finest stately homes in the north of England and forever associated with the TV series and 2008 feature film of *Brideshead Revisited*, which were both made here. Built in the early 1700s for Charles Howard, the Third Earl of Carlisle.

Start/finish

The North Pennines

Distance: 13 miles (21km)
Big hills: 1
Challenge: ✪✪✪☆☆

A half-day off-road ride around the Packhorse Trails in the North Pennines

Situated between the Yorkshire Dales and Hadrian's Wall is the North Pennines Area of Outstanding Natural Beauty, the second largest such area in the UK and home to the Packhorse Trails. These off-road tracks, developed by the North Pennines Trust, are based on ancient thoroughfares that were used to transport lead and other goods to several towns.

Riding these trails takes you through a host of stunning settings amid a diverse landscape. Open heather moors and peatlands intersperse woodland and rivers. Passing different historical monuments also gives an indication of a celebrated industrial epoch.

Start at Bay Bridge car park in Blanchland, turn left out of the car park and take the third left up a steep hill (signposted 'no through road'). Bear right and continue uphill on the road. Go straight through the gate and left immediately after the pumping station (signposted 'bridleway'). Turn right through the gate and follow the bridleway, with the wall on your left.

Go through the gate, bear right and continue on the track across Birkside Fell. Turn right onto Carriers Way. Through the gate, continue straight on ('bridleway') and straight ahead at the crossroads. Turn left through the bridlegate ('byway').

Towards the bottom of the stony track turn right up a short climb. At Embley Farm turn left through the farmyard. Go straight ahead on the track, following the bridleway signs. At the ford go straight on to the road. At the S-bend bear right and uphill onto the road. At the sharp right-hand bend go straight through the gate ('bridleway').

After 200m, bear right. Go straight, passing Steel Hall on your left. Continue past Dukesfield Hall and right at the road.

Useful refreshment stops
White Monk Tearoom, Blanchland, Consett, County Durham DH8 9ST. 01434 675044

The Lord Crewe Arms Hotel, Blanchland, Northumberland DH8 9SP. 01434 675251 www.lordcrewehotel.co.uk

Bike shops
The Bike Place (hire available), 1 King Street, Bellingham NE48 2AX. 01434 220210 www.thebikeplace.co.uk

At the crossroads turn right ('Ladycross'). At the entrance to Ladycross Quarry continue on the track ('byway') and straight ahead at the next two junctions, then through the gate onto the moor.

After around 75m, continue ahead at the fork. Go through the gate and down the track. At the bottom of the hill, bear right. Go through the ford and continue on the track.

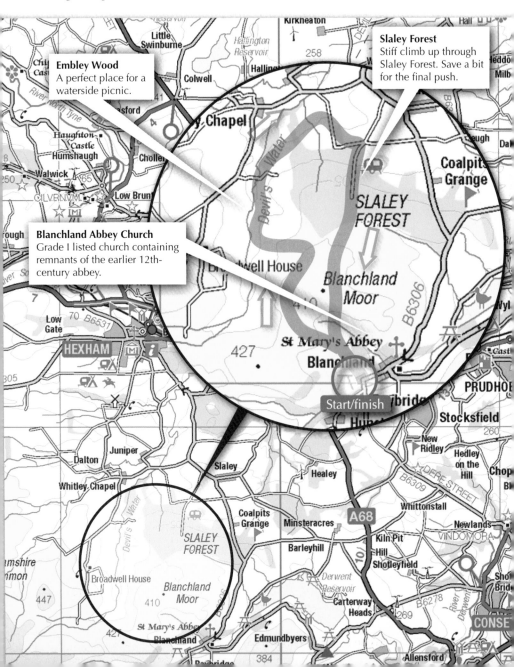

Embley Wood
A perfect place for a waterside picnic.

Slaley Forest
Stiff climb up through Slaley Forest. Save a bit for the final push.

Blanchland Abbey Church
Grade I listed church containing remnants of the earlier 12th-century abbey.

Start/finish

Big skies of the High Wolds

Distance: 15 miles (24.5m)
Big hills: 2
Challenge: ✪✪✪☆☆

A quick undulating tour of the Sledmere Estate and the High Wolds of Yorkshire, the area that artist David Hockney referred to as the 'big sky'

Perched on the High Wolds of Yorkshire is Sledmere House. This Georgian grade one listed stately home with its scenic gardens designed by Capability Brown makes for a great starting point for exploring the quiet countryside in the rolling hills. The house is open to the public from April to October when people can have the pleasure of admiring the family art collection and antique furniture as well as attending concerts in the gardens.

From Sledmere House turn left onto the B1253 (Kirby Lane). Follow the road to Kirby Grindalythe. Turn left towards Duggleby. Just before the village take the left fork down a lane to go into Duggleby village. In the village turn right to go down the High Street. Climb out of the village and go up Cupid's Alley and Broad Balk, following the road towards Settrington.

Turn right at the T-junction and follow the road to West Lutton. Pass through West Lutton and follow the road to East Lutton. Once outside the village, and just before the Helperthorpe village sign, turn right into Croome Dale Lane. Go straight on all the way back to Sledmere. Turn right to reach the start point at Sledmere House.

Useful refreshment stops

The Terrace Café, Sledmere House, Driffield, East Yorkshire YO25 3XG. 01377 236637 www.sledmerehouse.com

The Triton Inn, Sledmere, Driffield, Yorkshire YO25 3XQ. 01377 236078 www.thetritoninn.co.uk

Three Tuns Inn, Main Street, West Lutton, Malton YO17 8TA. 01944 738200

Bike shops

Yates Cycles, Railway Street, Malton, North Yorkshire YO17 7NS. 01653 605400. www.yatescycles.co.uk

Bell's Cycles, Unit One, The Spencer Centre, Westgate, Driffield YO25 6TJ. 01377 253070 www.bellscycles.t83.net

Eastgate Cycles, 70A Eastgate North, Driffield, YO25 6EB. 01377 253274 www.eastgatecycles.com

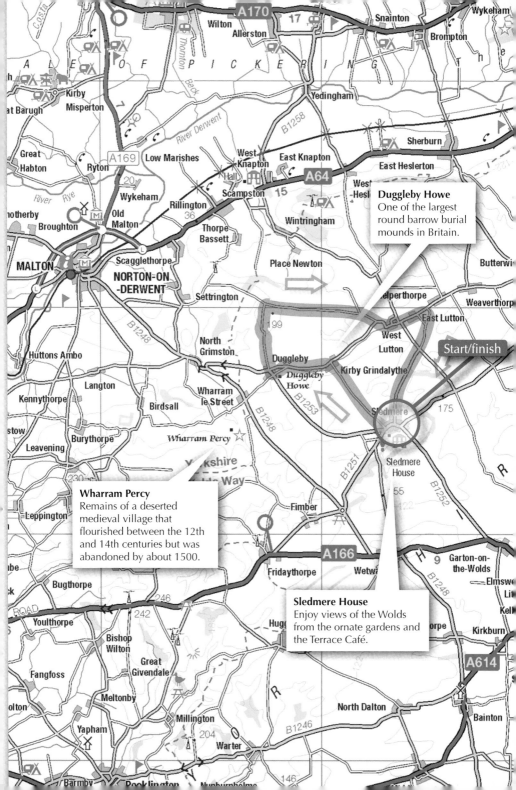

Duggleby Howe
One of the largest round barrow burial mounds in Britain.

Start/finish

Wharram Percy
Remains of a deserted medieval village that flourished between the 12th and 14th centuries but was abandoned by about 1500.

Sledmere House
Enjoy views of the Wolds from the ornate gardens and the Terrace Café.

Hadrian's Wall

Distance: 18 miles (30km)
Big hills: 4
Challenge: ❶❶❶❶☆

A hilly road ride that weaves around one of Britain's most important Roman remains

For a historical ride, what better example can you choose than a jaunt along Hadrian's Wall, the most famous Roman remain in England. From garrisoned soldiers to walkers and day-trippers, this 73-mile-long landmark has played host to millions of people since AD122.

The ride starts in the old town of Bardon Mill, where we follow National Cycle Network route 72 to Haltwhistle. From Bardon Mill railway station join the NCN 72 and head West towards Melkridge. Continue along the same road to Haltwhistle. Turn right and follow the B6233 into Haltwhistle centre.

Do a circuit of the town via Lanty's Lonnen, Main Street and Aesica Road. Turn right onto Fair Hill. At the end of Castle Hill, take a sharp left up Shield Hill. Climb the hill and cross the A6318 military road to reach Northumberland National Park. Follow the narrow road to Whiteside, then loop round to High Edges Green and finally, back towards Melkridge.

At the bottom of the hill take a sharp left and climb up Sook Hill. Follow the road round and go downhill to Steel Rigg car park. Descend the hill and cross the military road at the Once Brewed Youth Hostel. Take the first left to Vindolanda Roman Fort which will be busy with

Useful refreshment stops

Pillar Box Café, Westbourne House, Main Street, Haltwhistle, Northumberland NE49 0AZ. 01434 321 780

The Fort Tea Room, Aesica Road, Haltwhistle, Northumberland NE49 9DE. 01434 322037

Herding Hill Farm Shop & Bistro Café, Shield Hill, Haltwhistle, Northumberland NE49 9NW. 01434 320175

The Twice Brewed Inn, Bardon Mill, Hexham, Northumberland NE47 7AN. 01434 344534 www.twicebrewedinn.co.uk

Bike shops

The Bike Shop (hire available), 16–17 St Marys Chare, Hexham, Northumberland NE46 1NQ. 01434 601032 www.thebikeshophexham.com

Activcycles, 17 Watling Street, Corbridge, Northumberland NE45 5AH. 01434 632950 www.activ-cycles.co.uk

tourists. Follow this fairly narrow lane and climb up to Chesterholm.

At the T-junction turn right to go to Bardon Mill. Ride down the steep hill. At Westwood Cottages take a sharp left and follow the road to Bardon Mill.

Cross the busy A69 trunk road. At the next T-junction, turn right onto the National Cycle Network (Route 72) to reach the railway station again.

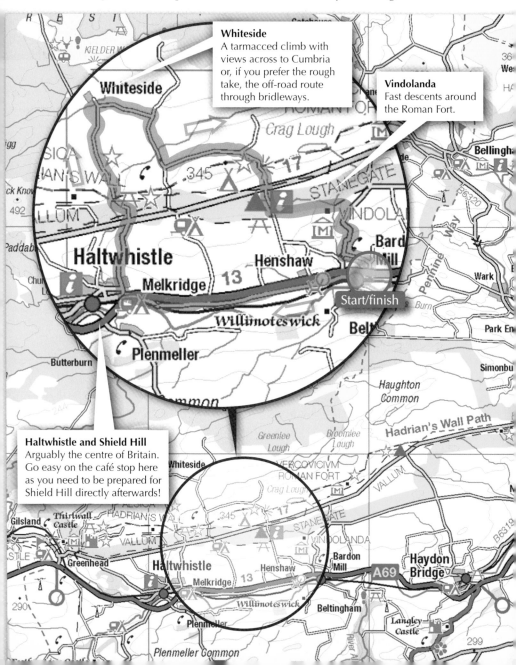

Whiteside
A tarmacced climb with views across to Cumbria or, if you prefer the rough take, the off-road route through bridleways.

Vindolanda
Fast descents around the Roman Fort.

Haltwhistle and Shield Hill
Arguably the centre of Britain. Go easy on the café stop here as you need to be prepared for Shield Hill directly afterwards!

The Ribblehead Viaduct

Distance: 23.5 miles (38km)
Big hills: rolling
Challenge: ⭐⭐⭐☆☆

A taste of the wilderness on a short hilly loop through the Yorkshire Dales

Starting out from the main car park in Ingleton (also a starting point for walkers taking on the Three Peaks walk – 26 miles, taking in Whernside, Ingleborough and Pen-y-ghent), the route begins up a short climb on the B6255 road towards Hawes before taking a right turn and heading down the Clapham Old Road.

Take a slight right at Cross Haw Lane, onto B6480. Turn right at The Green, B6480, continue on to the A65, left on the A65, next left (to Austwick) and continue through Main Street Austwick.

In Wharfe, turn right and continue on Austwick Road to Helwith Bridge. Turn left onto the B6479 at Helwith Bridge and continue through Horton in Ribblesdale and Selside.

The B6479, follows the route of the Settle to Carlisle railway and begins to get more remote and dramatic before giving a glimpse of one of the stunning architectural wonders of the north: the 400-metre Ribblehead Viaduct.

Turn left at the junction with the B6255 and head back on the B6255, Low Sleights Lane (Ribblehead) passing the Old Hill Inn. Turn right towards Chapel-le-Dale along Oddies Lane.

Once through Chapel-le-Dale, passing St Leonard's Church, this stretch of road is one of those that never disappoints – a very relaxing valley road, virtually car free, with big hills to the left and right (Ingleborough and Whernside). Continue along Oddies Lane into Ingleton, turn left towards the Rake, sharp left on Main Street, and continue to the high street.

Useful refreshment stops

Pen-y-ghent Café, Horton in Ribblesdale, North Yorkshire BD24 0HE.
01729 860333

The Old Hill Inn, Chapel Le Dale, Ingleton LA6 3AR. 01524 241256
www.oldhillinn.co.uk

Game Cock Inn, The Green, Austwick, Lancaster LA2 8BB. 01524 251226

Bike shops

3 Peaks Cycles (hire available), Market Place, Settle BD24 9EJ. 01729 824232

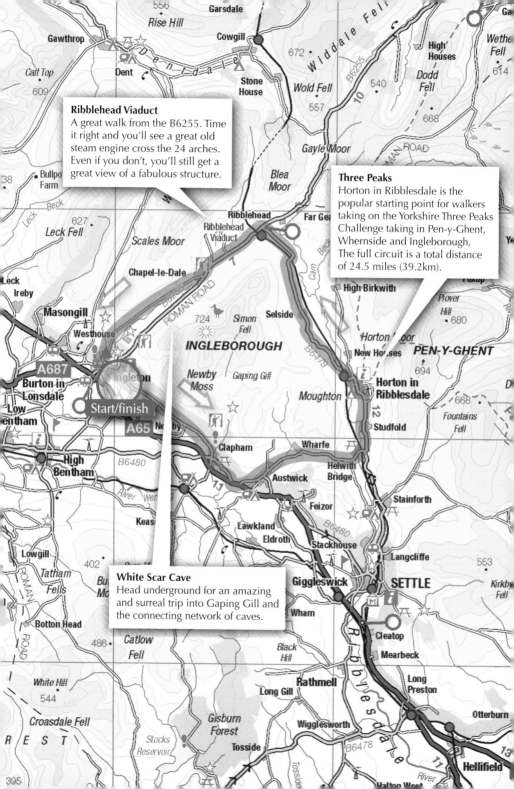

Ribblehead Viaduct
A great walk from the B6255. Time it right and you'll see a great old steam engine cross the 24 arches. Even if you don't, you'll still get a great view of a fabulous structure.

Three Peaks
Horton in Ribblesdale is the popular starting point for walkers taking on the Yorkshire Three Peaks Challenge taking in Pen-y-Ghent, Whernside and Ingleborough, The full circuit is a total distance of 24.5 miles (39.2km).

White Scar Cave
Head underground for an amazing and surreal trip into Gaping Gill and the connecting network of caves.

Start/finish

South Manchester

Distance: 12.5 miles (20km)
Big hills: none
Challenge: ●☆☆☆☆

An easy spin along the Fallowfield Loop – a former railway line running across suburban south Manchester

The Fallowfield Loop was formerly part of the Manchester Central Station Railway, built during the 1880s but closed down in 1988. The tracks were ripped up and the space left was either taken over for development or became derelict. In the late 1990s a group of local cyclists campaigned to convert what remained of the line into a traffic-free greenway across south Manchester. They joined forces with other local groups to form the Friends of Fallowfield Loop and with help from Sustrans, which now owns the trail, Manchester City Council, Sainsbury's and other benefactors, they created an off-road path for cyclists, pedestrians and horse riders that stretches over 6 miles (10km) from industrial Debdale in the east, to leafy Chorlton in the west.

This ride starts at Fairfield Station on Boothby Road, which is on the A635 just west of junction 24 of the M60. There is no specific car park at this end, but street parking is available. Heading south west, the path soon joins the disused railway

Useful refreshment stops
Reddish Vale Farm Tearoom, Reddish Vale Road, Reddish, Stockport SK5 7HE.
0161 480 1645
www.reddishvalefarm.co.uk
Plus lots in Chorlton or Fallowfield where the route crosses Wilmslow Road

Bike shops
Will's Wheels, 482 Manchester Road, Heaton Chapel SK4 5DL.
0161 432 4936
Ken Foster's Cycle Logic (hire available), 374-376 Barlow Moor Road, Chorlton-Cum-Hardy M21 8AZ. 0161 881 7160
www.kenfosterscyclelogic.co.uk

trackbed and is easily followed all the way to Chorlton. There is access at regular intervals along its length and there's good signage so you can leave or join it wherever it intersects with suburban streets. There's more information about the route available from The Friends of Fallowfield Loop at fallowfieldloop.org

Turn around at Chorlton to retrace your tracks to Fairfield Station or plan a different route back – the Fallowfield Loop links up Sustrans National Cycle Network routes 6, 60 and 85, so you can join this stretch up with a number of longer rides. The City Council website has more details: www.manchester.gov.uk/cycling.

M602 **MANCHESTER** **STALYBRI**

SALFORD

Trafford Centre

Trafford Park

STRETFORD A5103 Rusholme DROYLSDEN

Audenshaw M67 Mottram in Longdendale

Gorton Levenshulme DENTON HYDE A560 Broadbott

Chorlton-cum-Hardy Withington A34 Burnage Reddish Haughton Green Gee Cross ROMILEY Compstall

Heaton Moor A6 STOCKPORT Bredbury MARPLE

Didsbury M60 Offerton Green HAZEL GROVE NEW MILL

SALE Wythenshawe Hall CHEADLE High Lane

ALTRINCHAM HALE Baguley Hall GATLEY Heald Green CHEADLE HULME BRAMHALL Poynton Middlewood Sta Disley

M56 Manchester Airport Styal Handforth Higher Poynton Lyme Park

New Mills Morley Green WILMSLOW Start/finish

Mobberley

KNUTSFORD Knolls Green MANCHESTER

Whalley Range
This area became one of Manchester's first suburbs, when local businessman Samuel Brooks created an estate of homes for what he described as 'gentlemen and their families'. Brooks was born in Whalley, Lancashire, hence the name.

Burnage
This is where Liam and Noel Gallagher come from. They attended school at St Bernard's Primary and Barlow RC High School in Didsbury.

Blackden Heath

Goostrey

Holmes Chapel A54

Brereton

Forest of Bowland, Lancashire

Distance: 27 miles (43.5km)
Big hills: many
Challenge: ●●●☆

A spectacular tour through Lancashire's wild Forest of Bowland taking in plenty of flora and fauna in this Area of Outstanding Natural Beauty

This is a circular route, starting and finishing in the pretty village of Slaidburn, which is in the north-east of Lancashire. It's a roller-coaster ride with challenging climbs and swift descents right from the start and all the way to the finish, but you will be rewarded with the most amazing views and a great sense of achievement. I wouldn't advise doing this route when there is snow on the fells as it can get icy.

The route takes you through the Forest of Bowland – an Area of Outstanding Natural Beauty. The Forest of Bowland isn't all forest, the name also refers to the adjacent valleys and moorland areas. The area is known for wildlife, the hen harrier regularly breeds here and the number of peregrine falcons is increasing.

Start at Slaidburn village pay and display car park. Turn left out of the car park and ride over the bridge on the B6478. Be sure to select your hill-climbing gear now as this road climbs abruptly

with a tight bend. Stay on this road for about three miles until you reach a crossroads where you leave the B6478 and turn left onto the Quiet Lane following the sign for Gisburn Forest.

Follow this road past Stocks Reservoir where there is a picnic site on the left. Bear right here and continue past Dale House and across Clapham Common. When you reach a crossroads at Keasdon, with a signpost for Bentham and Settle, turn left and stay on this lane until you reach another crossroads then follow the sign to Slaidburn. This takes you back onto the Quiet Lane. Stay on this road all the way back to the village car park.

Useful refreshment stops
Riverbank Tea Rooms, 23 Chapel St, Slaidburn, Clitheroe BB7 3ES. 01200 446398 www.riverbanktearooms.co.uk

The Hark to Bounty Inn, Slaidburn, Clitheroe BB7 3EB. 01200 446246 www.harktobounty.co.uk

Bike shops
Pedal Power (hire available), Waddington Road, Clitheroe, Lancashire BB7 2HJ. 01200 422066 www.pedalpowerclitheroe.co.uk

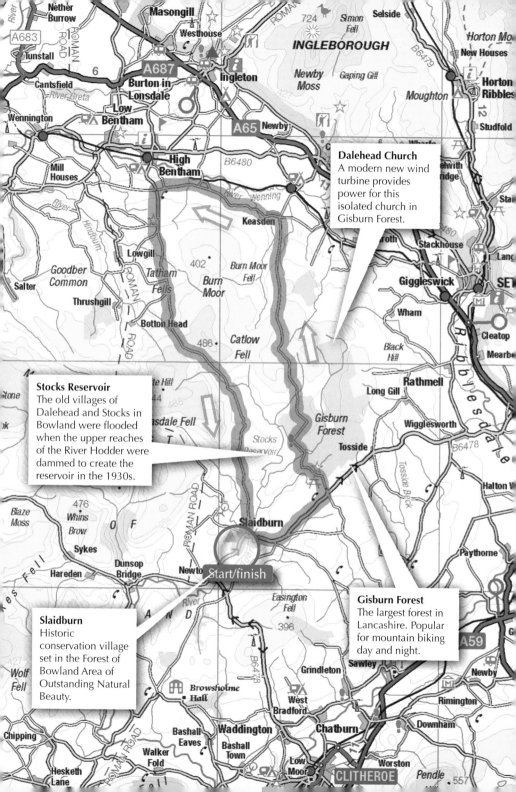

Dalehead Church
A modern new wind turbine provides power for this isolated church in Gisburn Forest.

Stocks Reservoir
The old villages of Dalehead and Stocks in Bowland were flooded when the upper reaches of the River Hodder were dammed to create the reservoir in the 1930s.

Gisburn Forest
The largest forest in Lancashire. Popular for mountain biking day and night.

Slaidburn
Historic conservation village set in the Forest of Bowland Area of Outstanding Natural Beauty.

Start/finish

Pendle

Distance: 27 miles (43.5km)
Big hills: lots and lots
Challenge: ✪✪✪✪☆

Allow a full day for this hilly ride and expect to have a good workout

Bridleways, moorland tracks, canal towpaths, country lanes and a particularly long ford... few routes take in such a rich and sometimes challenging variety of terrain as this whistlestop tour of the Pendle district.

Start at either Colne railway station or the car park of the adjacent leisure centre. Cross the main road (A56) and proceed up Bridge Street signed to Coldwell Activity Centre. At a crossroads at the top of the hill, continue ahead and down to pass the centre and then go around the first reservoir.

Turn left to leave the road and join the Pennine Bridleway. Just after a farmhouse, the track is surfaced for a few hundred metres. Where this road bears sharp left to Trawden (signed); continue ahead on the bridleway. Keep following the signs for Wycoller which takes you over a bridge and finally, via a left turn and Smithy Clough, to Wycoller.

Leave the village by the only road. Turn right at a T-junction in front of a football pitch then right again soon after,

Useful refreshment stops
Coldwell Activity Centre Tea Room, (located beside Coldwell Reservoirs). Back Lane, Southfield, Burnley BB10 3RD. 01282 601819 www.coldwell.org.uk

Wycoller Craft Centre & Tearooms, Wycoller Rd, Wycoller, Colne BB8 8SY. 01282 868395 www.wycollercraftcentre.co.uk.

The Alma Inn, Emmott Lane, Laneshawbridge, Colne BB8 7EG. 01282 857030 www.thealmainn.com

The Anchor, Salterforth, Barnoldswick BB18 5TT. 01282 813186.

Café Cargo, Foulridge Wharf BB8 7PP. 01282 865069 www.cafecargo.com.

Bike shops
Fox's Cycles, 20–22 Dockray St, Colne BB8 9HT. 01282 863017 www.foxscycles.com

signed for National Cycle Network Route 91. At the end of the descent in Laneshawbridge, turn left over an old stone bridge and briefly uphill to meet the A6068.

Cross over and continue almost ahead to the left of the Emmott Arms signed 'Lancashire Cycleway'. At the top of the hill bear left towards and past The

Alma Inn. Turn left (off the Skipton Old Road) just before a 'Caution – concealed entrance' sign. Almost immediately, and as the road bears left, continue ahead at the sign: 'Ford ½ mile. Road unsuitable for motors'.

Take the first left into Foulridge, reaching the main road at the Hare and Hounds pub. Turn right then second left in front of the war memorial down Lowther Lane. At the bottom, turn left onto Barnoldswick Road to leave Foulridge. Where the road bears sharp right continue ahead (signed 'Blacko 2') keeping the reservoir embankment to your right. About 300 metres after the Whitemoor Riding Centre turn right signed to a dead end. Don't worry. It isn't.

About 100 metres after Peel House Farm turn right through a gate onto a signed public bridleway. At the end turn left then immediately right up Hodge Lane signed 'Private Road. Public bridleway only'. This brings you out onto the B6383. Turn right and, after 300 metres at a bridge, go down steps to the canal towpath (NCN Route 68).

Immediately after Foulridge Wharf follow the road (Warehouse Lane) uphill, turn right at the crossroads, then left down Reedymore Lane to again pick up signs for Route 68 to Colne. After the Lake Burwain sailing club, follow the route as it forks right and off-road. At the end of the track turn right at the road, then left (don't cross the bridge) to continue in the same direction. Rejoin the canal towpath, go under the motorway then turn left to leave the canal. Follow signs for Route 68 to the start.

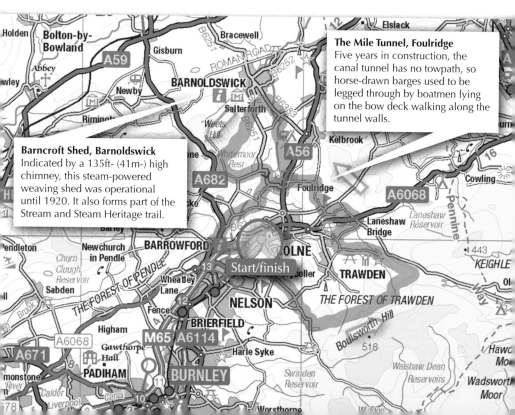

The Mile Tunnel, Foulridge
Five years in construction, the canal tunnel has no towpath, so horse-drawn barges used to be legged through by boatmen lying on the bow deck walking along the tunnel walls.

Barncroft Shed, Barnoldswick
Indicated by a 135ft- (41m-) high chimney, this steam-powered weaving shed was operational until 1920. It also forms part of the Stream and Steam Heritage trail.

Fylde country lanes

Distance: 22 miles (35km)
Big hills: nothing too tricky
Challenge: ✪✪☆☆☆

A gentle ride through the lanes on the beautiful Fylde coast

This ride is a 22-mile circular course starting and finishing at Wrea Green, travelling through the country lanes of the Fylde coast area.

The journey starts outside The Grapes pub overlooking the green. Take the B5259 (Ribby Road) east towards Kirkham, then at the roundabout, turn right onto the A583 (Preston New Road) then left onto the B5259 into Kirkham. Follow the road up onto Carr Lane, just off the B5192 (Preston Street), then take a sharp right onto Kirkham Road.

Turn left onto Church Road and continue for about two miles, turning left onto Roseacre Road. Stay on Roseacre until the B5269 in Elswick.

Cross onto Ash Road and follow it to Bonds Lane. Follow Copp Lane until turning left onto Leckonby Street in Great Eccleston. Turn left again at the T-junction onto High Street. Follow the road onto the A586 then turn left then right onto Blackpool Old Road. Follow the road around until the right turn onto Cartford Lane. Go straight down the road crossing Cartford bridge.

Turn left onto Rawcliffe Road and remain on that road, which changes its name as you enter Hambleton to Whin Lane. Keep on the same road, bearing right onto Mill Lane. At the end of Mill Lane turn left onto Bull Park Lane. At the roundabout, take the first exit, and head towards Shard Bridge on the A588.

At the traffic lights after the bridge turn left onto the A585 (Mains Lane). At the next set of traffic lights take the third road,

Useful refreshment stops

The Grapes, Station Rd, Wrea Green, Preston PR4 2PH. 01772 682927

The Derby Arms, Treales, Nr Kirkham, Preston PR4 3SH. 01772 683705
www.derbyarms-treales.co.uk

Cartford Inn, Little Eccleston, Nr Preston PR3 0YP. 01995 670166
www.thecartfordinn.co.uk

Bonds of Elswick ice cream bar, Bonds Lane, Elswick, Preston PR4 3ZE. 01995 670295
www.bondsofelswick.com

Bike shops

Apple Bikes, 8 Orchard Rd, St Annes-on-Sea FY8 1RY. 01253 725349

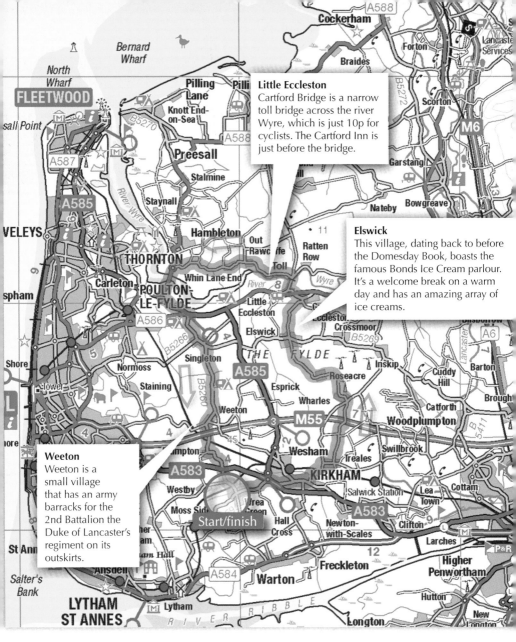

Little Eccleston

Cartford Bridge is a narrow toll bridge across the river Wyre, which is just 10p for cyclists. The Cartford Inn is just before the bridge.

Elswick

This village, dating back to before the Domesday Book, boasts the famous Bonds Ice Cream parlour. It's a welcome break on a warm day and has an amazing array of ice creams.

Weeton

Weeton is a small village that has an army barracks for the 2nd Battalion the Duke of Lancaster's regiment on its outskirts.

B5260 (Lodge Lane). Take the first exit at the mini-roundabout onto the B5260 (Station Road).

Stay on the same road as it becomes Weeton Road then Singleton Road. Turn right onto the B5260 (Church Road) and keep on that road. Turn left at the end, still on the B5260, cross the A583 (Preston New Road) and follow the road back into Wrea Green.

Chorley lanes

Distance: 31 miles (50km)
Big hills: none – but one long grind!
Challenge: ❶❷☆☆☆

A surprising variety of quiet lanes from Chorley provide an appealing loop out through the Lancashire countryside to the coast and back

Leave Buckshaw Village and head south through Euxton on the A49. Take the first right, Back Lane, to Ecclestone – the road is narrow so be prepared to stop for vehicles at some points.

At Ecclestone turn right, then first left and keep going until you pick up the National Cycle Network Route 91 towards Mawdesley. The road gradually rises all the way to High Moor and then drops quickly to Bispham. Go left, then right to Rufford, where the road gets a bit busier.

In Rufford go right, then left for Southport. At Mere Brow turn right for Preston and pick up the NCN 91 again.

The road narrows to single lane and goes through a floodplain – the road surface is uneven but OK to ride. Cross the main road for more of the same for several miles.

Turn right and right again for Croston (road surface bad here). Go through Croston and head for Ecclestone. After three-quarters of a mile take a left, then right back onto NCN 91 and follow signs back to Euxton and then Buckshaw Village.

Useful refreshment stops

Thowd Boatman's Cabin Coffee Shop, Fettlers Wharf Marina, Station Road, Rufford L40 1TB. 01704 822888

The Rigbye Arms, 2 Whittle Lane, Wrightington, Wigan WN6 9QB. 01257 462354 www.rigbyarms.com

The High Moor Restaurant, High Moor Lane, Wrightington WN6 9QA. 01257 252364 www.highmoorrestaurantwigan.co.uk

Bike shops

Merlin Cycles, A1 Buckshaw Link, Ordnance Road, Buckshaw Village, Chorley PR7 7EL. 01772 432431

Leisure Lakes Bikes, Mere Brow, Tarleton, Preston PR4 6JX. 01772 814990

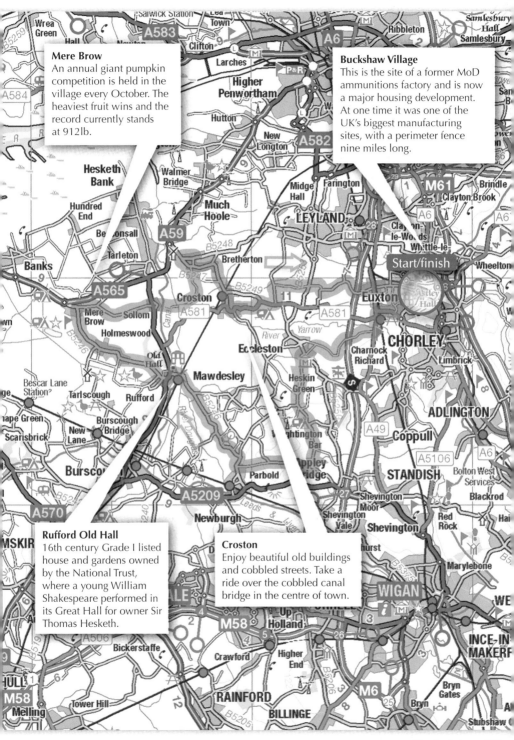

Mere Brow
An annual giant pumpkin competition is held in the village every October. The heaviest fruit wins and the record currently stands at 912lb.

Buckshaw Village
This is the site of a former MoD ammunitions factory and is now a major housing development. At one time it was one of the UK's biggest manufacturing sites, with a perimeter fence nine miles long.

Rufford Old Hall
16th century Grade I listed house and gardens owned by the National Trust, where a young William Shakespeare performed in its Great Hall for owner Sir Thomas Hesketh.

Croston
Enjoy beautiful old buildings and cobbled streets. Take a ride over the cobbled canal bridge in the centre of town.

Start/finish

Cobbled climbs around Burnley

Distance: 50.1 miles (80km)
Big hills: up and down the whole way round
Challenge: ✪✪✪✪✪

A challenging ride over cobbles, tracks and roads, through pretty villages

This 50-mile route stays within about 15 miles of Burnley and takes in some fantastic open scenery as you cross the Pennines as well as some winding, tree covered, tunnel-like climbs and descents. In true Belgian cycle race style, the route takes in several cobbled climbs. Lots of changes of road so plan the route carefully and take a map!

Leave the Pendle Heritage Centre, over the bridge and onto the A682 Gisburn Road. Turn right at Pasture Lane. Left to stay on Pasture Lane then left at Blacko Bar Road and right at Ridge Lane. Left at Jinny Lane, left again at Spenbrook Road,

right at Noggarth Road and right again up Hoarstones. Continue round to the right and turn left at Haddings Lane. Left at Guide Lane, then right at Barrowford Road / A6068. Right onto Higham Road then right onto Sabden Road, follow onto Back Lane and the left at the T-junction to follow Back Lane.

Follow for three miles, over two crossroads then turn left at Old Roman Road. Follow left to Whins Lane then over the crossroads at Trapp Lane. Turn right at the A6068 and then left at Slade Lane. Left at Burnley Road / A671 and then immediately right at Mill Street (cobbles).

Straight on at the top, right at Double Row (more cobbles), left at West Street, left at Arbory Drive, and straight over Whalley Rd (A671) onto Abories Avenue. Straight down Arbories Avenue and then right at Blackburn Road (A678). Turn left at Whalley Road / A680 followed by another left at Whinney Hill Road. Right to stay on Whinney Hill Road with a slight left at Station Road. Right at Lower Gate Road, left at Burnley Lane and follow onto Mill Hill Lane.

Right at Manchester Road then left at Accrington Road / A679. Right at Rossendale Road traffic lights, go straight across Manchester Road, right then left

Useful refreshment stops

Pendle Heritage Centre Tearoom, Park Hill, Barrowford, Nelson BB9 6JQ. 01282 677150 www.htnw.co.uk/phc

Plus lots of cafés, pubs and restaurants in Hebden Bridge

Bike shops

Blazing Saddles, 35 West End, Hebden Bridge HX7 8UQ. 01422 844435 www.blazingsaddles.co.uk

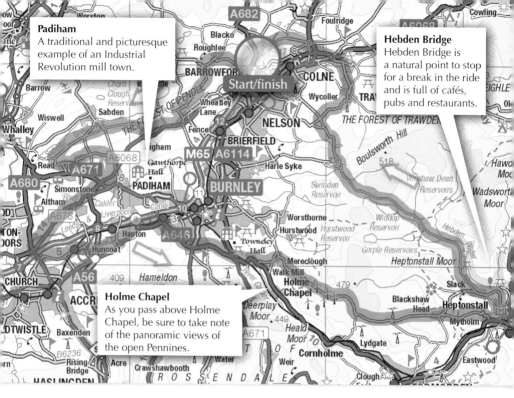

Padiham
A traditional and picturesque example of an Industrial Revolution mill town.

Hebden Bridge
Hebden Bridge is a natural point to stop for a break in the ride and is full of cafés, pubs and restaurants.

Holme Chapel
As you pass above Holme Chapel, be sure to take note of the panoramic views of the open Pennines.

down Burnley Road toward Todmorden and left at Park Road.

Right at Mount Lane then left at Red Lees Road. A slight right at Greencliffe Lane then right toward The Long Causeway. A slight right at The Long Causeway and round another slight right at Kebs Road – then in two miles, right at Badger Lane.

Turn left into Rawtenstall Bank, which turns left and becomes Glen View Road. Right to stay on Bank Terrace and follow the slight left at Church Lane. Left at the A646 and follow the slight left at Old Gate. Follow over the cobbles up and left.

Left at the top, sharp right at Heptonstall Road which then turns slightly right and becomes Town Gate, over cobbles. Turn left onto Slack Road then right at Widdop Road. A slight right to stay on Halifax Road, then right at the

bottom to stay on Halifax Road.

Turn right at Back Lane going straight over and continuing on Back Lane. Right turn at Lenches Road and left at Mill Green and follow to Shaw Street and look for a gap in the wall and cobbles, up right.

At the top, turn right at Doughty Street onto the cobbles. Left at Exchange Street, left at Boundary Street and right at Chapel Street onto some steep cobbles.

Right onto Albert Road. Left at Windy Bank and right at North Valley Road (A6068), immediately left on Dickson Street for more cobbles, then right at Temple Street. Then left up Townley Street, left at Montague Street onto cobbles. Right at Langroyd Road, first exit at the roundabout onto Red Lane and the turn left at Barnoldswick Road. Turn left onto the A682 Gisburn Road and left again at Colne Road (B6247) and home.

Morecambe Bay, Arnside and Silverdale

Distance: 10 miles (16km)
Big hills: 1
Challenge: ★☆☆☆☆

A short rolling route around Arnside and Silverdale, offering plenty of wildlife and stunning views

An easy going ride, taking in, coast, quiet roads and beautiful lakeland vistas.

Start at Arnside, where on-street parking is available. To begin the ride, head north with the bay on your left and the shops on the right. Follow Station Road onto Black Dyke Road, cross the railway line and the road now turns into a quiet country lane. This is a lovely undulating road with nothing very steep to worry about.

Continue as the road becomes Cold Well Lane and then turn left into Brackenthwaite Road. Keep riding past Keepers Cottage (Brackenthwaite Farm).

Bear right up a steepish incline onto Thrang Brow Lane, then it's downhill before you turn right onto Storrs Lane. (Take care on the downhill as it meets the junction.)

Follow Storrs Lane past Leighton Moss then turn left after the railway line onto Slackwood Lane, then take the second left onto Hollins Lane towards Jenny Brown's Point where there's a café which you'll see on the right.

Jenny Brown's Point is left down a narrow road. Here you have the option of riding down as a detour to look at the view across the bay, but to get back to Arnside you need to head in the opposite direction, back the way you came onto Lindeth Road, which turns into Stankelt Road as you continue along.

Turn off left onto Emesgate Lane and bear left at the fork in the road onto Cove Road, then bear right at Stone Bower. Go past Holgate's Caravan Parks and keep on this road until it turns into Silverdale Road and takes you along the coast on the B5282 into Arnside. (Watch out for the steep downhill slope.)

Useful refreshment stops

The RSPB Leighton Moss Tearoom, Carnforth LA5 0SW. 01524 701 601

The Wolfhouse Café, Lindeth Road, Silverdale LA5 0TX. 01524 701 405 www.wolfhousegallery.co.uk

The Big Chip Café, The Promenade, Arnside, Carnforth LA5 0HF. 01524 761874 www.arnsidechipshop.co.uk

Bike shops

Dyno Start, 1–3 Scotland Road, Carnforth LA5 9JY. 01524 732089 www.dynostart.com

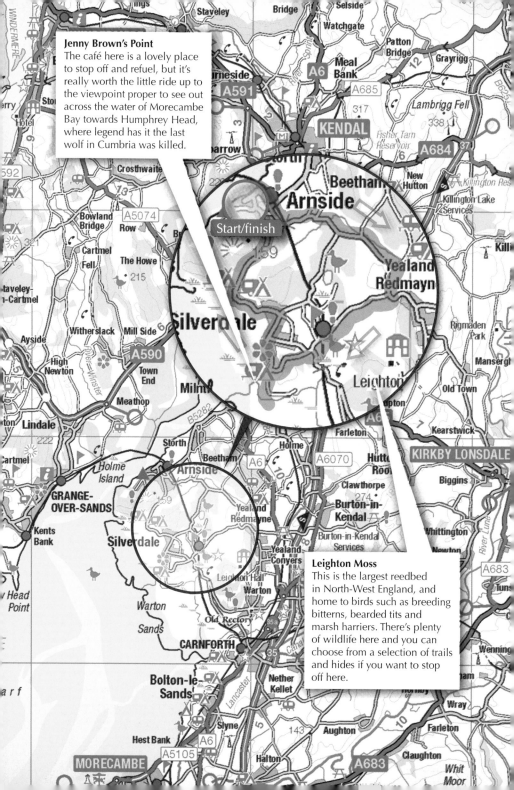

Jenny Brown's Point
The café here is a lovely place to stop off and refuel, but it's really worth the little ride up to the viewpoint proper to see out across the water of Morecambe Bay towards Humphrey Head, where legend has it the last wolf in Cumbria was killed.

Start/finish

Leighton Moss
This is the largest reedbed in North-West England, and home to birds such as breeding bitterns, bearded tits and marsh harriers. There's plenty of wildlife here and you can choose from a selection of trails and hides if you want to stop off here.

Lytham St Annes

Distance: 18 miles (29km)
Big hills: none
Challenge: ❶☆☆☆☆

A superb loop taking in scenic villages and breathtaking beaches

This route starts a little inland at the picturesque Wrea Green.

Leave Wrea Green signed 'Lytham 4' on the B5259. Pass over the level crossing at Moss Side. After 3.5 miles, as you enter Lytham and just before a roundabout turn right down Green Drive.

From this point start following the blue signs towards St Anne's on National Cycle Network Route 62. At the end of the drive turn immediately left down Park View Road. Just after a school and opposite the junction of Wykeham Road turn right to follow a short cycle track past a playground and BMX track and over a footbridge to emerge on Balham Road.

Turn left then right down South Park and, at the end, left onto Forest Drive. At a T-junction with the Blackpool Road, turn right briefly (Route 62 unsigned here) then first left after the church. Keep following the signs (which reappear at this point) past the golf club and over two crossroads staying on St Patrick's Road.

At the end turn left onto St Leonard's Road, go over the railway then turn first right down Caryl Road. At the end turn left down Highbury Road. At the junction with the A584 turn left then, just after the North Beach car park, turn right down Todmorden Road. Keep following the promenade past the pier and miniature golf course. After the Lawrence House

Useful refreshment stops

The Hole in One pub, Forest Drive, Lytham FY8 4QF. 01253 730598

Beach Terrace Café, South Promenade, Lytham St Annes FY8 1NW. 01253 711167

Salters Wharf Toby Carvery, South Promenade, Lytham St Annes FY8 1LS. 01253 713365

Fairhaven Lakeside Café, Inner Promenade, Lytham St Annes, FY8 1BD. 01253 734527

The Birley Arms, Bryning Lane, Warton, Preston PR4 1TN. 01772 679988 www.thebirleyarms.co.uk

The Grapes (Chef & Brewer), Station Road, Wrea Green PR4 2PH. 01772 682927

Bike shops

Apple Bikes (hire available), 8 Orchard Rd, St Annes-on-Sea FY8 1RY, 01253 725349 www.applebikes.co.uk

sports ground turn right into St Paul's car park.

Proceed to the end towards a brazier then pick up a traffic-free path around the lake. Stay on the path to pass the windmill. Eventually, you reach the A584

again. Turn right and proceed for about a mile then turn left down Lodge Lane following signs for Route 62 to Kirkham.

At a T-junction in Kellamurgh turn left to follow the Lancashire Cycleway sign back to Wrea Green.

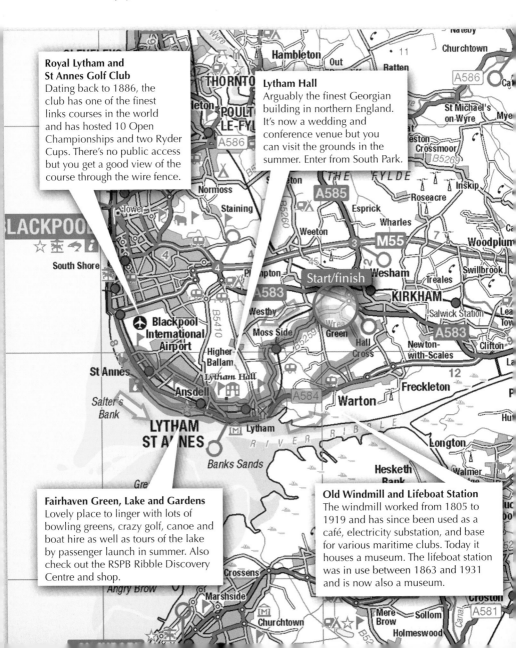

Royal Lytham and St Annes Golf Club
Dating back to 1886, the club has one of the finest links courses in the world and has hosted 10 Open Championships and two Ryder Cups. There's no public access but you get a good view of the course through the wire fence.

Lytham Hall
Arguably the finest Georgian building in northern England. It's now a wedding and conference venue but you can visit the grounds in the summer. Enter from South Park.

Fairhaven Green, Lake and Gardens
Lovely place to linger with lots of bowling greens, crazy golf, canoe and boat hire as well as tours of the lake by passenger launch in summer. Also check out the RSPB Ribble Discovery Centre and shop.

Old Windmill and Lifeboat Station
The windmill worked from 1805 to 1919 and has since been used as a café, electricity substation, and base for various maritime clubs. Today it houses a museum. The lifeboat station was in use between 1863 and 1931 and is now also a museum.

Hawkshead

Distance: 10 miles (16km)
Big hills: 3
Challenge: ★★☆☆☆

A short but hilly grind around Grizedale Forest, passing by the home of Beatrix Potter

With cafés galore and some fantastic visitor centres along the way, Grizedale Forest, and the surrounding Cumbrian area, is the perfect setting for a ride by mountain, hybrid or road bike. The southern Lake District has no shortage of hills with hefty gradients but you're always safe in the knowledge that there's a Cumberland sausage pie and a good brew awaiting at the end of the ride, to reward your efforts.

Head south out of the central visitor car park, at Hawkshead, and take a right. Then bear left until you get to the fork in the road, at which point take the road to the left. From this point onwards, you can't go far wrong – this is a really straightforward loop with very few points where you have to turn off.

Follow the road, passing Esthwaite Water on your left, and keep going until you meet the next fork in the road at Newby Bridge, after 1.5 miles, where you need to keep to the right.

Prepare for a hard climb as you turn to the right. It's over quickly but it's a steep

> **Useful refreshment stops**
> Grandy Nook Coffee Shop, Vicarage Lane, Ambleside LA22 0PB. 01539 436404
> Sun Cottage Café, Main Street, Hawkshead Ambleside LA22 0NT. 01539 436123
> Café at Visitor Centre, Grizedale Forest Park. 01229 860455
> The Kings Arms, Hawkshead, Ambleside LA22 0NZ. 01539 436372 www.kingsarmshawkshead.co.uk
> The Sun Inn, Main Street, Hawkshead, Ambleside LA22 0NT. 01539 436236 www.suninn.co.uk
>
> **Bike shops**
> Grizedale Visitor Centre (hire available), Grizedale Forest Park. 01229 860369

one. You can relax for a bit, staying on the same road for another 2–3 miles until the quarry, where you will need to take the road to the right.

A little over half a mile later, take the right turn, signposted to Satterthwaite and Grizedale. Keep heading towards Grizedale, on the same road, and you'll pass a car park on your right before heading up a climb to the main visitor centre.

Follow the same road out of Grizedale and keep going until you eventually descend back into Hawkshead, then take a left back into the visitor car park.

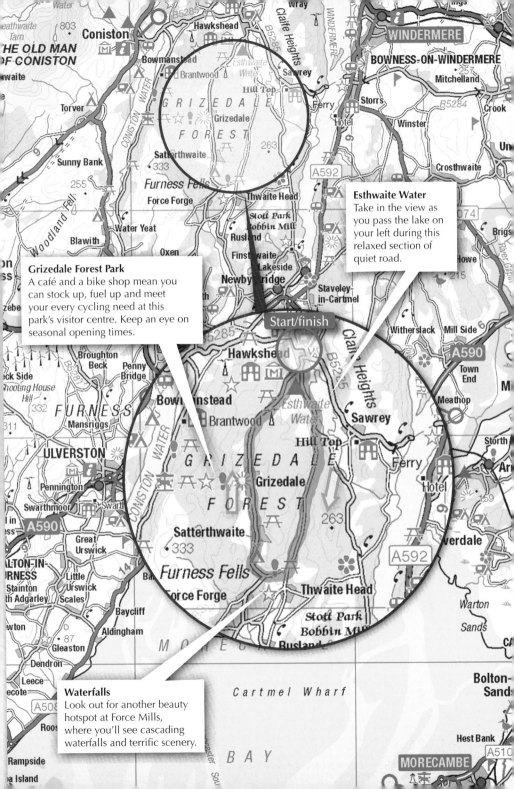

Grizedale Forest Park
A café and a bike shop mean you can stock up, fuel up and meet your every cycling need at this park's visitor centre. Keep an eye on seasonal opening times.

Esthwaite Water
Take in the view as you pass the lake on your left during this relaxed section of quiet road.

Waterfalls
Look out for another beauty hotspot at Force Mills, where you'll see cascading waterfalls and terrific scenery.

Start/finish

Cheshire cobbles

Distance: 35 miles (56km)
Big hills: none
Challenge: ❶❷☆☆☆

With more cobbled sections than your average ride, the flat, quiet back roads of North Cheshire have some real hidden gems for cyclists

This is a 35-mile loop around flat lanes punctuated by cobbled sections, taking 2-3 hours – a chance to ride the cobbles and taste a little of what the professional racers go through.

The route begins in the picturesque village of Grappenhall. Leave Grappenhall and head for Appleton Thorn. Here take a left for Antrobus and pick up signs for Arley Hall. From here head south through Polelane Ends and onto the A50 to Great Budworth. Turn sharp left at the Cock O'Budworth pub for Great Budworth (with caution as the road narrows at the left turn at the centre of the village).

Head to Pickmere then Lower Peover (take care using the A556 as this is a dual carriageway). Go left to Knutsford via the A50. In Knutsford go right then left for 'King Street and shopping'.

Exit here and take the side road parallel to Tatton Park towards Bucklow Hill.

Picking up the A5034 take care, the road is wide but busy. From here go to High Legh then drop down on to the A50 (fast road) for three-quarters of a mile then take a left on to Swine Yard Lane to Appleton Thorn. From here it's the same route back to Grappenhall.

Useful refreshment stops

Penny Farthing Museum (The Courtyard) – rear of 92 King Street, Knutsford WA16 6EQ. 01565 653974

The George and Dragon, High Street, Great Budworth, Northwich CW9 6HF www.georgeanddragonatgreatbudworth. co.uk

Bear's Paw Country Inn & Restaurant, Warrington Road, High Legh WA16 0RT. 01925 752573 www.thebearspawinn.co.uk

Bells of Peover, The Cobbles, Lower Peover, Knutsford WA16 9PZ. 01565 722269 www.thebellsofpeover.com

Bike shops

Ron Spencer Cycles, 186 Orford Lane, Warrington WA2 7BE. 01925 632668 www.ronspencercycles.co.uk

Dave Hinde, 227 Manchester Road, Northwich CW9 7NB. 01606 48608 www.davehinde.com

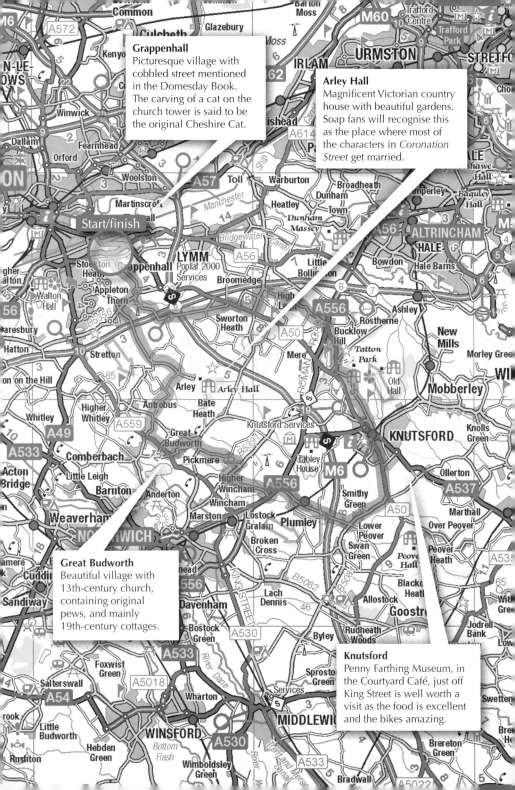

Grappenhall
Picturesque village with cobbled street mentioned in the Domesday Book. The carving of a cat on the church tower is said to be the original Cheshire Cat.

Arley Hall
Magnificent Victorian country house with beautiful gardens. Soap fans will recognise this as the place where most of the characters in *Coronation Street* get married.

Great Budworth
Beautiful village with 13th-century church, containing original pews, and mainly 19th-century cottages.

Knutsford
Penny Farthing Museum, in the Courtyard Café, just off King Street is well worth a visit as the food is excellent and the bikes amazing.

Start/finish

Blackpool seafront

Distance: 19 miles (30km)
Big hills: none
Challenge: ★☆☆☆☆

A flat, coastal spin from the bright lights of Blackpool, up the coast to Fleetwood and back again

The sea is never more than a few metres away on this easy coastal route, suitable for all the family. The route follows the National Cycle Network path that takes you along the coast, off-road, all the way to Fleetwood.

Start on the promenade in front of the tower. Join the signed National Cycle Network Route 62 and head north beside the road for 400 metres and then, just after the North Pier, down a slope and away from the road. Keep the sea to your left and you can't go wrong.

The trail ends when it leads up to the Esplanade in Fleetwood. Turn left and follow the coastal road (which becomes Queen Street and Dock Street) past the lighthouse, ferry terminal and museum. Around the corner as you approach a large Asda, go ahead at the first roundabout and ahead again at the second roundabout immediately outside the supermarket.

Pick up a cycleway starting to your left and keep in the same direction towards Freeport. Turn right at the next roundabout (or use the cycle crossing) down Denham Way then left into Copse Road to pass the Fishermen's Friend factory.

Just after the turn to Kilbane Street, cross the road towards the right and pass through a gap into Larkholme Lane. At the end at the junction with the A587, turn left onto a cycle path. At the traffic lights, turn right down West Way, which takes you back to the coastal cycle path. Turn left to return to Blackpool.

Useful refreshment stops
There are lots of pubs, cafés, takeaways and restaurants in Blackpool, Cleveleys and Fleetwood, with a few along the route itself (mainly at the Blackpool end)

Bike shops
The Bike Shop, 104 Red Bank Rd, Blackpool FY2 9DZ. 01253 351870
www.the-bikeshop.com

Boden's Cycles, 14 Station Terrace, Blackpool FY4 1HT. 01253 341449
www.bodencycles.com

Sam Taylor Bikes, 5–21 Vicarage Rd, Blackpool FY4 4EF. 01253 763442
www.samtaylorbikes.co.uk

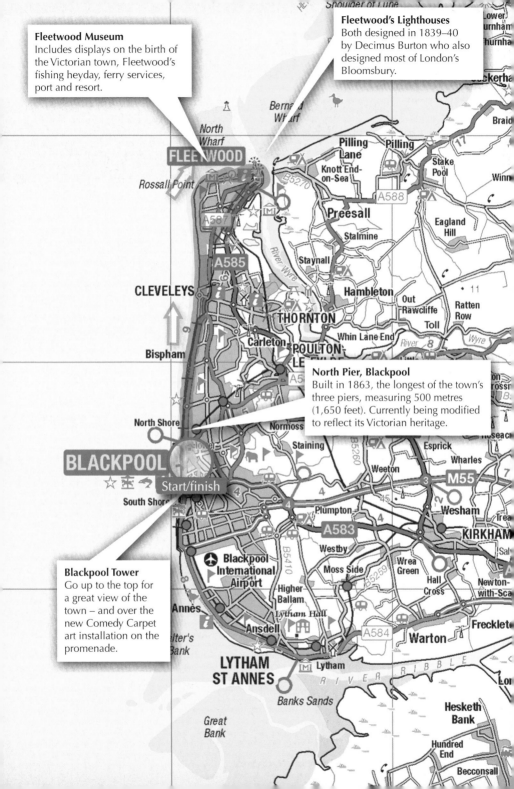

Fleetwood Museum
Includes displays on the birth of the Victorian town, Fleetwood's fishing heyday, ferry services, port and resort.

Fleetwood's Lighthouses
Both designed in 1839–40 by Decimus Burton who also designed most of London's Bloomsbury.

North Pier, Blackpool
Built in 1863, the longest of the town's three piers, measuring 500 metres (1,650 feet). Currently being modified to reflect its Victorian heritage.

Blackpool Tower
Go up to the top for a great view of the town – and over the new Comedy Carpet art installation on the promenade.

Start/finish

FLEETWOOD
CLEVELEYS
Bispham
North Shore
BLACKPOOL
South Shore
Anne's
LYTHAM ST ANNES

North Wharf
Rossall Point
Bernard Wharf
Pilling Lane
Pilling
Knott End-on-Sea
Stake Pool
Winn
Preesall
Eagland Hill
Stalmine
Staynall
Hambleton
Out Rawcliffe
Ratten Row
THORNTON
Toll
Carleton
Whin Lane End
POULTON-LE-FYLDE
Normoss
Staining
Esprick
Wharles
Weeton
Wesham
Plumpton
KIRKHAM
Blackpool International Airport
Westby
Wrea Green
Hall Cross
Newton-with-Sca
Moss Side
Higher Ballam
Freckle
Lytham Hall
Warton
Ansdell
Lytham
Banks Sands
Great Bank
Hesketh Bank
Hundred End
Becconsall

Shoulder of Lune
Braid
Preesall
Stalmine
Knott End-on-Sea
Rossall Point
North Wharf
Carleton

Lake District – the Jennings Rivers Ride route

Distance: 35 miles (56km)
Big hills: 1
Challenge: ✪✪☆☆☆

A lovely road ride through the Lake District on one of the three routes of the Jennings Rivers Ride

The Jennings Rivers Ride (named after the brewery based in Cockermouth) is held to raise money for the charitable work of the Cumbria Community Foundation which makes grants to local charities and people in need. It's a series of three bike rides which start and finish in Keswick and called the Rivers Ride because sections of the routes follow river courses and criss-cross over many of the bridges that were either destroyed and replaced, or were badly damaged during the floods of 2009.

The ride starts in the Lakeland town of Keswick, which is the second biggest town in the Lake District after Windermere. Leaving from Keswick Museum, follow Brundholme Road to the junction with the A5271, turn right to cross the A66 roundabout onto the A591. Follow the A591, turn left onto the B5291 over a bridge and turn right onto an unclassified road. Turn right again and follow the unclassified road, which becomes Isel Road.

Useful refreshment stops
Lakeland Pedlar Cafe, Bell Close, Keswick, Cumbria CA12 5JD. 01768 774492

Casa Bella, 24 Station Street, Keswick, Cumbria CA12 5HJ. 01768 775575
www.casabellakeswick.co.uk

Dog and Gun, 2 Lake Road, Keswick, Cumbria CA12 5BT. 01768 773463

Bike shops
Keswick Bikes, 133 Main St, Keswick, Cumbria, CA12 5NJ. 01768 773355
www.keswickmountainbikes.co.uk

Continue into Cockermouth then turn right onto Castlegate Drive, left onto Station Road, left onto Victoria Road (B5292) and continue out of Cockermouth on the B5292 towards Lorton.

Turn right towards Southwaite, left at Green Trees, follow the road to Low Lorton, turn right on the B5269 and then left onto an unclassified road through Scales. Turn right onto an unclassified road which leads onto Winlatter Pass.

Continue into Braithwaite, take an unclassified road signposted 'Coledale Beck' to Newlands Beck, passing Derwent Water, and into Grange. Go over the bridge and left at the T-junction onto the B5289 back into Keswick.

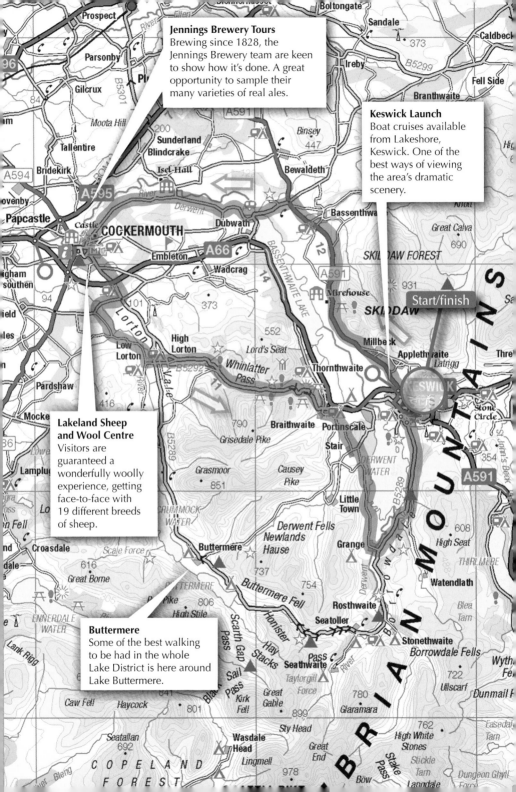

Jennings Brewery Tours
Brewing since 1828, the Jennings Brewery team are keen to show how it's done. A great opportunity to sample their many varieties of real ales.

Keswick Launch
Boat cruises available from Lakeshore, Keswick. One of the best ways of viewing the area's dramatic scenery.

Lakeland Sheep and Wool Centre
Visitors are guaranteed a wonderfully woolly experience, getting face-to-face with 19 different breeds of sheep.

Buttermere
Some of the best walking to be had in the whole Lake District is here around Lake Buttermere.

Start/finish

Cumbrian countryside

Distance: 27.5 miles (44km)
Big hills: 2
Challenge: ✪✪✪☆☆

A scenic ride taking in some of the landscapes that inspired Turner

This ride meanders through the beautiful Cumbrian countryside and into the Yorkshire Dales National Park. It's a route that really has it all – quiet lanes, rolling hills, beautiful fells, picturesque villages and numerous pubs and cafés. It starts in Kirkby Lonsdale, which is a historic market town in an Area of Outstanding Natural Beauty.

Start at the Devil's Bridge in Kirkby Lonsdale. Ride east over the bridge and turn left onto the A683 towards Casterton. Ride through Casterton and follow this road until you reach a right turn signposted for Barbon. Ignore all other signs for Barbon until this turning, which has a stone sign just before a bridge.

Continue through Barbon past the inn on the right and the church on the left. Ride up a short, sharp hill. Continue over a cattle grid and onto the quiet road through Barbondale. Follow this road. You will come to a fairly steep downhill section (one-in-seven in places) to meet a T-junction. Turn right and go downhill to the next T-junction and turn right

again. Follow this road into Dent. If you ride over the cobbles, you will pass two tea rooms and reach the Sun Inn. Return back the way you came through Dent.

Stay on this road to Sedbergh, bearing left over the river. Follow Finkle Street into the town for cafés and pubs. Leave Sedbergh by Main Street and follow until you see a road sign for Kirkby Lonsdale

Useful refreshment stops
Emily's Tea Shop 1 Market Square, Kirkby Lonsdale, LA6 2AN. 01524 272772 www.emilysteashop.com

Meadowside Café Bar, The Laning, Dent, LA10 5QJ. 01539 625329

Stone Close Tea Room, Main Street, Dent, LA10 5QL. 01539 625231

The Sun Inn, Main Street, Dent, LA10 5QL. 01539 625208

Duo Cafe Bar and Bistro, 32 Main Street, Sedbergh, Cumbria LA10 5BL. 015396 20552. www.duo-sedbergh.co.uk

Bike shops
Escape Bike Shop, Kirkstead Farm, Westhouse, Ingleton LA6 3NJ. 015242 41226 www.escapebikeshop.com

(A683). Go past the garage and take the next turning left. Follow this road to a sign for the M6; take the next right (on a bend, so take care). The house on the corner as you turn is Four Lane Ends Farm.

Continue until you reach Killington New Bridge. Ride over the bridge and take the next left signposted Killington and Old Hutton. Follow this lane alongside the River Lune. Pass Lune View on the right, Dry Beck Farm on the left. Climb a hill to the crossroads. With a 'no through road' sign on the right, take the left turn alongside drystone walls going south.

Descend through woodland and follow this lane for a descent through farmland, past Nether Hall, past a sign for Underley Schools on the left. Pass the signpost for Ruskin's View on the right and go into Kirkby Lonsdale. Stay on this road in the one-way system into Market Street. Follow this road to the give-way sign, then go straight on past Market Square on the left. At the end of this road, turn left, signposted Skipton. Take the next turning on the left back to the car park.

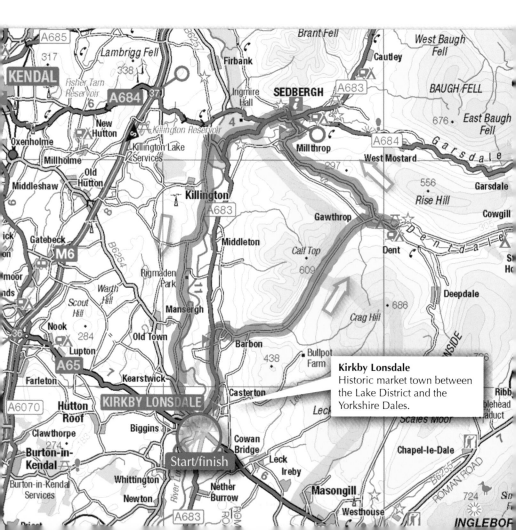

Kirkby Lonsdale
Historic market town between the Lake District and the Yorkshire Dales.

Coed-y-Brenin Trail Centre

Distance: 10.8 miles (17.4km)
Big hills: 2
Challenge: ✪✪✪☆☆

A challenge for your fitness on the Cyflym Coch trail at Coed-y-Brenin – the first trail centre to be developed in the United Kingdom

The Cyflym Coch trail at the Coed-y-Brenin trail centre is described as difficult on the map and the trickiest section comes in a rocky stretch at the start. After that it eases off to a combination of singletrack and gravel roads.

Head out of the front of the visitor centre under the huge mountain bike forks and onto the Pinderosa trail. The Afon Eden river will be on your right. Continue along the rocky section until you cross an asphalt river and rejoin the forest on the Dream Time trail. Always follow the red fox Cyflym Coch signs to avoid getting lost or accidentally disorientated. Come out to the Pont car park and cross the bridge over the river.

Turn left and follow the river until you hit the second fire road on your right. Head up this until you see the red fox signs on your right that lead down the Uncle Fester trail.

Once out of the trees turn sharp left, be in a low gear, and head up the forest road. The signs will direct you right down the last section of singletrack, the Pink Heifer.

At the bottom, rejoin the forest road by the river. Turn right and head back to the bridge and the Pont car park. The river will now be on your left. Once over the bridge, follow the gentle gradient fire road back to the visitor centre. Afon Eden will be on your left the whole time. A bike wash is available at the end of the route if you prefer to get all the gunk off your bike before you try another trail or head home.

Useful refreshment stops

Visitor Centre Café, Forest Park, Coed-y-Brenin, Dolgefeiliau, Dolgellau LL40 2HZ. 01341 440 747
www.forestry.gov.uk/wales

Mawddach Restaurant and Bar, Llanelltyd, Dolgellau LL40 2TA. 01341 424 020
www.mawddach.com

Bike shops

Beics Brenin, Coed-y-Brenin Visitor Centre, Dolgellau LL40 2HZ.
01341 440 728 www.beicsbrenin.co.uk

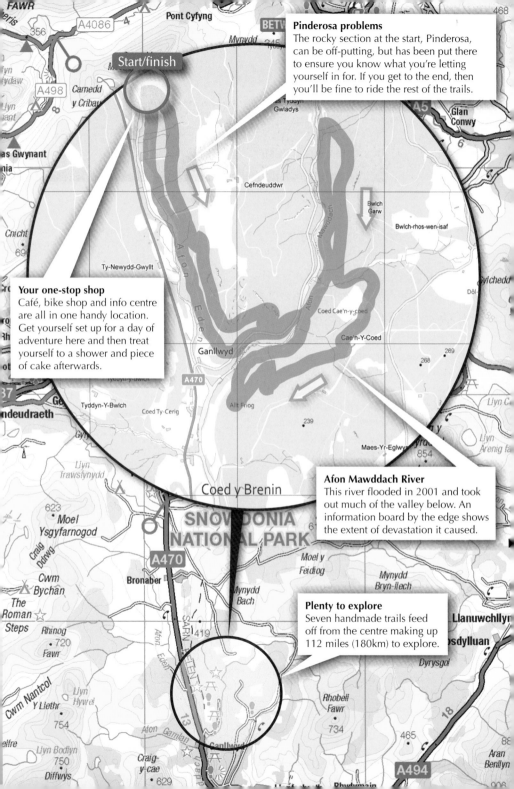

Pinderosa problems
The rocky section at the start, Pinderosa, can be off-putting, but has been put there to ensure you know what you're letting yourself in for. If you get to the end, then you'll be fine to ride the rest of the trails.

Start/finish

Your one-stop shop
Café, bike shop and info centre are all in one handy location. Get yourself set up for a day of adventure here and then treat yourself to a shower and piece of cake afterwards.

Afon Mawddach River
This river flooded in 2001 and took out much of the valley below. An information board by the edge shows the extent of devastation it caused.

Plenty to explore
Seven handmade trails feed off from the centre making up 112 miles (180km) to explore.

Welsh lakes

Distance: 32 miles (52km)
Big hills: 2
Challenge: ✪✪✪✪☆

A challenging loop that hurdles spectacular mountains between two of Wales' most scenic lakes

Bala Lake, or Llyn Tegid to give it its Welsh name, is best known as Wales's largest natural lake, although in truth it's not totally natural; the original waterway was actually flooded by Thomas Telford to help feed the ill-fated Ellesmere Canal. Natural or not, though, it's still a very scenic waterway, tucked beneath lofty mountains on the eastern fringes of the Snowdonia National Park.

A few miles to the south of Bala lies another equally stunning body of water, Lake Vrynwy, which makes no claims of natural heritage. Vrynwy was originally constructed in the late 1800s to provide water to Liverpool and Birmingham.

The two lakes are separated by some lofty hills and hurdled by a couple of mountain roads that are just perfect for a half-day outing. It's basically two big climbs followed by two lengthy descents and easy lakeside sections in between. The Lake Vyrnwy Visitor Centre is perfectly placed for mid-ride refreshment.

Useful refreshment stops
Artisans Coffee Shop, The Old Sawmill, Lake Vyrnwy SY10 0NA. 01691 870317 www.artisans-lakevyrnwy.co.uk

Old Barn Cafe, Unit 1, Lake Vyrnwy, Llanwyddyn SY10 0LZ. 01691 870377 www.oldbarncafe.com

Tavern Bar, Lake Vyrnwy Hotel, Llanwyddyn SY10 0LY. 01691 870692

The Eagles Inn, Llanuwchllyn, Bala LL23 7UB. 01678 540278 www.yr-eagles.co.uk

White Lion Hotel, High St, Bala LL23 7AE. 01678 520314 www.thewhitelionbala.com

Bike shops
Artisans Coffee Shop (hire available) – see above

Old Barn Café (hire available) – see above

Take the B4403 from Bala town south through Llangower towards Llanuwchllyn. Immediately ahead of the village sign, bear left towards Dinas Mawddwy (single track road). Stay with this past a hamlet and junction at Tallard and climb to Bwlch-y-Groes. Keep ahead for 500m and turn left at a low brick wall. Now follow this down to a T-junction on the shores of Lake Vyrnwy.

Turn right to the dam and keep ahead to the visitor centre and café. Then cross the dam and turn left to continue up the east shore. At the far end, turn right (signed Rhos-y-Gwaliau, Bala) and climb to the pass then drop into Cwm Hirnant. Stay on the main road to Rhos-y-Gwaliau and climb away, always on the main road. Drop to meet the B4431 and turn left to follow this back to Bala.

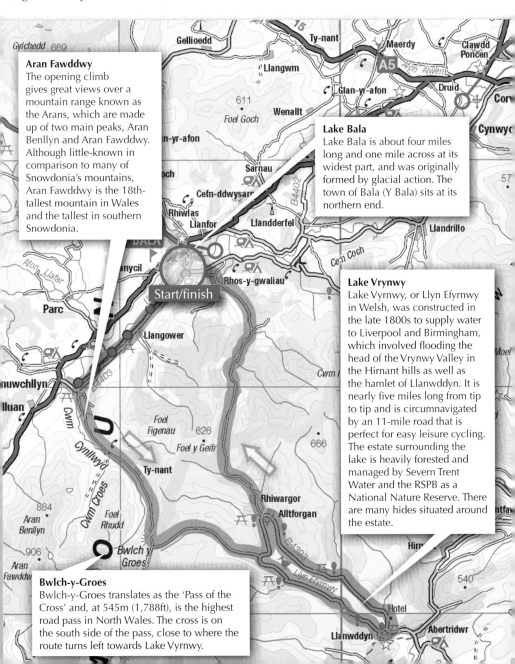

Aran Fawddwy
The opening climb gives great views over a mountain range known as the Arans, which are made up of two main peaks, Aran Benllyn and Aran Fawddwy. Although little-known in comparison to many of Snowdonia's mountains, Aran Fawddwy is the 18th-tallest mountain in Wales and the tallest in southern Snowdonia.

Lake Bala
Lake Bala is about four miles long and one mile across at its widest part, and was originally formed by glacial action. The town of Bala (Y Bala) sits at its northern end.

Lake Vrynwy
Lake Vrynwy, or Llyn Efyrnwy in Welsh, was constructed in the late 1800s to supply water to Liverpool and Birmingham, which involved flooding the head of the Vrynwy Valley in the Hirnant hills as well as the hamlet of Llanwddyn. It is nearly five miles long from tip to tip and is circumnavigated by an 11-mile road that is perfect for easy leisure cycling. The estate surrounding the lake is heavily forested and managed by Severn Trent Water and the RSPB as a National Nature Reserve. There are many hides situated around the estate.

Bwlch-y-Groes
Bwlch-y-Groes translates as the 'Pass of the Cross' and, at 545m (1,788ft), is the highest road pass in North Wales. The cross is on the south side of the pass, close to where the route turns left towards Lake Vyrnwy.

Start/finish

Cardiff on the Taff Trail

Distance: 20 miles (32km)
Big hills: 1 (the Bwlch y Cwm)
Challenge: ❷❷☆☆☆

A pleasant ride at the Cardiff city end of the Taff Trail

The Taff Trail is a 55-mile walking and cycling path from Cardiff Bay into the Brecon Beacons. On Summer Sundays the Brecon Bike Bus will run you and your bike to the trailhead, and you can ride back to Cardiff. This ride though is a quick trip the other way, just for 10 miles – enough to get out of the city and visit a country landmark.

The destination landmark is Castell Coch, a Victorian folly standing just outside Cardiff on a beautiful wooded hill above the village of Tongwynlais. The building is a gothic fantasy created by the third Marquess of Bute in 1871 and built on the site of a genuine medieval castle.

Start the ride from outside the Welsh Assembly building next to Roath Dock, head west and you soon see Taff Trail signs. Then it's just a matter of sticking to them. There are a couple of road crossings near the Millennium Stadium, but after that it's plain cycling. The only complication comes when the route leaves the trail for the spur to Castell Coch. Look for a right turn just a few metres north of the M4, which you ride under, then follow the signs to arrive at Tongwynlais.

Useful refreshment stops
Pedal Power Café (see bike shops below)

The Waterguard, Harbour Drive, Cardiff Bay CF10 4PA. 029 2049 9034

The Bosphorus, Mermaid Quay, 31 Mermaid Quay, Cardiff Bay CF10 5BZ. 029 2048 7477 www.bosphorus.co.uk

Bike shops
Pedal Power Bike Hire (hire available) Pontcanna Caravan Park CF11 9XR. 029 2039 0713 www.cardiffpedalpower.org

Bike Shed Wales, 243–245 Cathedral Road, Pontcanna, Cardiff CF11 9PP. 029 2066 8772 www.bikeshedwales.com

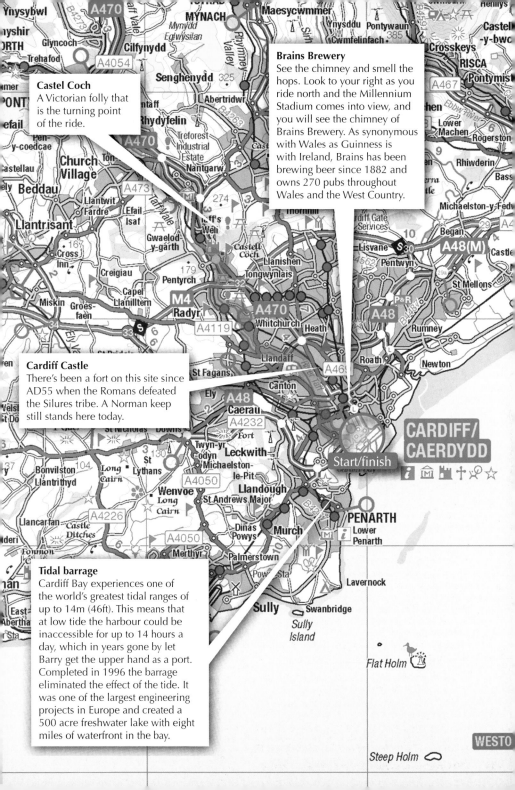

Castel Coch
A Victorian folly that is the turning point of the ride.

Brains Brewery
See the chimney and smell the hops. Look to your right as you ride north and the Millennium Stadium comes into view, and you will see the chimney of Brains Brewery. As synonymous with Wales as Guinness is with Ireland, Brains has been brewing beer since 1882 and owns 270 pubs throughout Wales and the West Country.

Cardiff Castle
There's been a fort on this site since AD55 when the Romans defeated the Silures tribe. A Norman keep still stands here today.

Tidal barrage
Cardiff Bay experiences one of the world's greatest tidal ranges of up to 14m (46ft). This means that at low tide the harbour could be inaccessible for up to 14 hours a day, which in years gone by let Barry get the upper hand as a port. Completed in 1996 the barrage eliminated the effect of the tide. It was one of the largest engineering projects in Europe and created a 500 acre freshwater lake with eight miles of waterfront in the bay.

Start/finish

CARDIFF/
CAERDYDD

Snowdonia spectacular

Distance: 31.4 miles (50.5km)
Big hills: 4
Challenge: ✪✪✪✪☆

Hairpin bends, mountain climbs and an assault on Pen-y-Pass: this Snowdonia spectacular has all the drama of an Alpine epic

Clocking in at around 30 miles in the stunning scenery of Snowdonia, and full of challenging hills and breathtaking descents, there is something here to suit every taste.

Starting in the town of Llanberis on Llanberis High Street, go north-west until you hit the A4086. Follow this past the lake, then take the turning on the right, signed to Bangor and the A5. Take the first right on the smaller road, and quickly left and right past the lakeside, then another right up the narrow road that follows the shoreline. Follow this up the climb.

At the top turn left and follow this road down through the village. Go on past the fair-sized church with spire, then turn right up the road signed Bethesda and Tregarth. Take a right at the next junction, then a left signed Mynydd Llandygai.

Follow this road until a junction with the B4409, with a white house opposite. Take a right along the B4409 and follow until the junction with the A5, at

which point turn right again, signed Betws-y-Coed.

Follow the A5 a short way until the old A5 junction. This is easy to miss; as the valley opens up there is what looks like a tiny country road on the right, with a brown footpath and bike sign. This is the old A5, turn right onto it. Follow this road – couple of sharp hills and cattle grids – until it rejoins the current A5 at the car park. Take a right, towards the lake and Tryfan. Follow the A5 around the mountain until you reach Capel Curig.

Useful refreshment stops
Pinnacle Café, Capel Curig, Conwy
LL24 0EN. 01690 720201

Pete's Eats, 40 High Street, Llanberis
LL55 4EU. 01286 870117
www.petes-eats.co.uk

Y Gwynedd Inn, High Street, Llanberis
LL55 4SU. 01286 870203

Bike shops
Nearest are in Caernarfon and Bangor:

Beics Menai Cycles (hire available),
1 Slate Quay, Caernarfon LL55 2PB.
01286 676804

Evolution Bikes, 141 High Street, Bangor,
LL57 1NT. 01248 355770

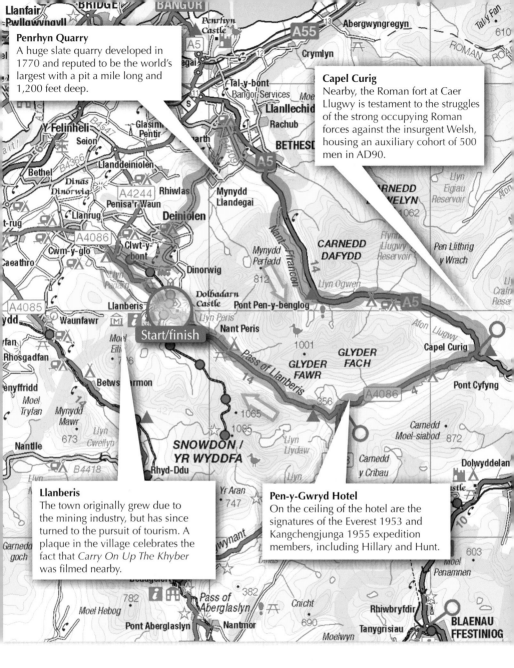

Penrhyn Quarry
A huge slate quarry developed in 1770 and reputed to be the world's largest with a pit a mile long and 1,200 feet deep.

Capel Curig
Nearby, the Roman fort at Caer Llugwy is testament to the struggles of the strong occupying Roman forces against the insurgent Welsh, housing an auxiliary cohort of 500 men in AD90.

Llanberis
The town originally grew due to the mining industry, but has since turned to the pursuit of tourism. A plaque in the village celebrates the fact that *Carry On Up The Khyber* was filmed nearby.

Pen-y-Gwryd Hotel
On the ceiling of the hotel are the signatures of the Everest 1953 and Kangchengjunga 1955 expedition members, including Hillary and Hunt.

Start/finish

Here take a right at the stores, signed Llanberis, and follow the road (A4086).

At the hotel take the right turn which goes towards Snowdon. Follow the road through Pen-y-Pass and down the other side. Follow this road into Llanberis, and take a left after the pedestrian traffic lights to find yourself back on the High Street.

Pembrokeshire

Distance: 11 miles (18km)
Big hills: none
Challenge: ●●☆☆☆

Pembrokeshire is the perfect spot for an amble by bike, thanks to hundreds of miles of empty roads and some of the most beautiful scenery in Wales

The Pembrokeshire Coast National Park is 386 square miles (621km²) with 260 miles (418km) of coastline, the largest such area in the UK. Developed in 1952, the park attracts 7.2 million visitors a year, yet there is always a little corner you can find and keep to yourself.

Start this ride at the Bluestone Resort in Canaston Wood and turn left towards Blackpool. After around 500m, turn left onto a minor road then right to Blackpool Mill and follow the road along the bridge across the river. Shortly after crossing the river, turn right and continue along until the road joins the A40.

Turn right, onto the A40, then take the first left through the cutting at Canaston Bridge. Continue along this road for a mile, before taking the right fork at Whiteleys. Head straight on to Llawhaden. Arriving at the village green, turn right immediately onto the bridleway.

The bridleway will join a road, at

> **Useful refreshment stops**
> Bluestone Resort (238 lodges in 500 acres of natural habitat. The complex has a no-car policy, a variety of shops, three restaurants, a wine bar, a pub and a wellness centre.) The Grange, Canaston Wood, Narberth SA67 8DE. 01834 887971 www.bluestonewales.com
>
> Ultracomida (delicatessen and restaurant) 7 High Street, Narberth, Wales, SA67 7AR. 01834 861491 narberth@ultracomida.co.uk
>
> **Bike shops**
> Pembrokeshire Bikes (hire available), 1 Rushacre Enterprise Park, Redstone Rd, Narberth, Dyfed SA67 7ET. 01834 862755

which point continue ahead and follow the road around a left bend. Turn right to cross the river, then take the first right at the T-junction immediately afterwards. Continue straight on, up a short incline, and after arriving in Robeston Wathen take the first left towards the A40.

Turn left onto the A40 and then immediately right onto the B4314 towards Narberth. Continue on the B4314 into Narberth, taking a right turn just before reaching the junction with the A478. Continue through the car park onto a bridleway, then follow it downhill and

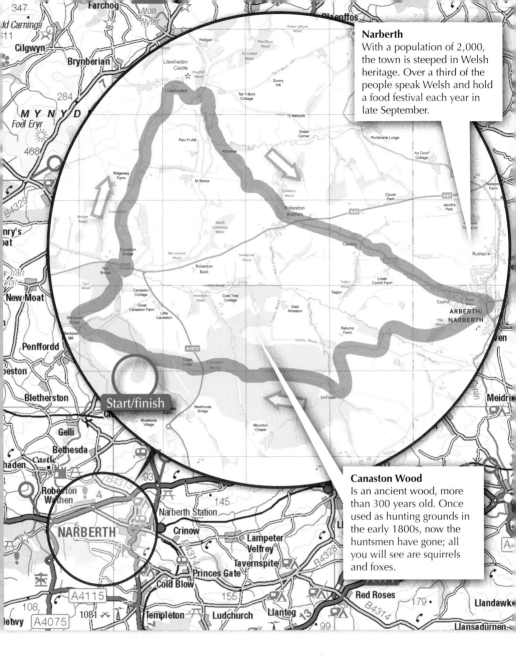

Narberth
With a population of 2,000, the town is steeped in Welsh heritage. Over a third of the people speak Welsh and hold a food festival each year in late September.

Canaston Wood
Is an ancient wood, more than 300 years old. Once used as hunting grounds in the early 1800s, now the huntsmen have gone; all you will see are squirrels and foxes.

through some woods before turning left onto a road after around one mile. Follow this road for 200m, then turn right onto Valley Road. Take the first left onto Back Lane, skirting alongside Canaston Wood. Then take the first right through Canaston Wood. Continue along this road, cross the A4075, then return to the starting point on the left after about a mile-and-a-half.

Cambrian classic

Distance: 31 miles (50km)
Big hills: 2
Challenge: ✪✪✪☆

A tough tour of the mountains that lie between the Bwlch Nant yr Arian and the village of Tal-y-bont on two roads that were just built for cycling

The Cambrian Mountains stretch across the whole of Mid Wales; from the Dyfi Estuary, near Machynlleth, in the north, all the way to the Afon Twyi, near Llandovery, in the south. Heavily forested, and with few main roads running through them, they form a wild and windswept backbone to the principality. The highest and most spectacular of these mountains are in the north of the range, where the 752m Pen Pumlumon Fawr presides over the expansive waters of the Nant y Moch Reservoir. The foothills of this giant are as lonely as any in the country yet they are traversed by two roads that, joined together, make up the majority of this classic tour.

Bwlch Nant yr Arian is best known as a mountain bike centre, but it has plenty of parking and a café so is a good place to start despite adding a bit to the distance and a climb at the end.

From here, head back out onto the A44 and turn left to Ponterwyd. Pass the garage and then take the first left into a narrow lane. Follow this up and then down, keeping left (high) at a fork after around 2000m. Cross the ford and now follow the road all the way to a cattle grid next to some standing stones at the back end of Bwlch Nant yr Arian.

Keep ahead at a junction with a forest track (hybrids can join here) and turn left at the fork on the shores of Llyn Blaenmelindwr. Continue around to another junction where you keep straight

Useful refreshment stops
Bwlch Nant yr Arian Visitor Centre,
  2 miles west of Ponterwyd SY23 3AD.
  01970 890453

Black Lion Hotel, Aberystwyth SY24 5ER.
  01970 832555

The Druid Inn, Goginan, Aberystwyth
  SY23 3NT. 01970 880650

Bike shops
Cyclemart (hire available), Cilcennin,
  Lampeter, Ceredigion SA48 8RS. 01570
  470079 www.cyclemart.co.uk

Summit Cycles, Aberystwyth,
  65 North Parade, Aberystwyth SY23 2JN.
  01970 626061 www.summitcycles.co.uk

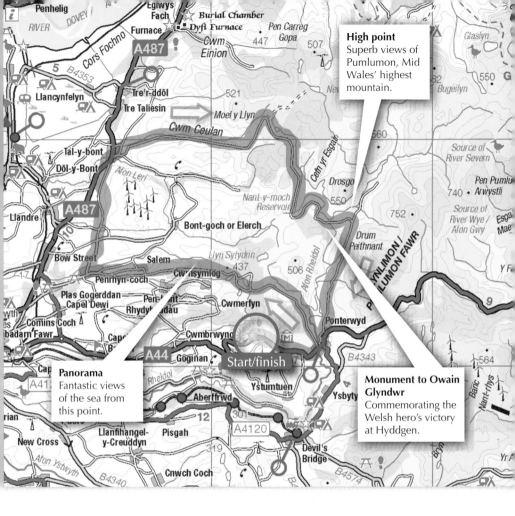

High point
Superb views of Pumlumon, Mid Wales' highest mountain.

Panorama
Fantastic views of the sea from this point.

Monument to Owain Glyndwr
Commemorating the Welsh hero's victory at Hyddgen.

Start/finish

ahead with a car park to your right and a bank to your left. Climb to the top and then keep ahead to drop all the way into Penrhyn-coch. At the main junction turn right (signed Bontgoch). Follow this, ignoring a few turnings on both sides, to a crossroads on top of a hill. Keep straight ahead here, signed Tal-y-bont, and now stay with this all the way to the A487.

Turn right into Tal-y-bont and then at a triangle of grass, with the Black Lion and White Lion directly ahead, fork right onto a lane. Carry up past the Black Lion

and ignore a left fork at the top of the hill. Continue up to another left fork and take this (signed Nant-y-moch).

Now stay on this lane all the way up to the pass at the very top and then down to the shores of the reservoir. Continue around the reservoir to the dam and cross it to then climb to a T-junction, where you keep straight ahead. Now follow this all the way to a right fork on the edge of Ponterwyd. Take this and drop down to the A44, where you turn right to climb back up to Bwlch Nant yr Arian.

Mold, Denbigh and Ruthin

Distance: 48.5 miles (78km)
Big hills: many
Challenge: ✪✪✪☆☆

A ride through a part of Mold in north-east Wales that's heaving with heritage and crammed with castles

Mold is in the county of Flintshire, in north-east Wales, and is the starting point for this testing ride with some challenging climbs. The market town of Mold has quite a history, and there is evidence to suggest there has been a settlement on or around the site since the Bronze Age.

There are fabulous views across the Clwyd valley, the castle ruins and old town walls in Denbigh, waterfalls and weirs along the River Clywedog and the sights of Ruthin with its clock tower, distinctive black-and-white wood-framed buildings and Red Castle, dating back to the 13th century, and so called because it is made from the distinctive local red sandstone.

Start on Mold High Street by St Mary's Church. Turn left above the church and continue to Gwernaffield-y-Waun then turn left at the church there and continue to the junction of the A494 to turn right and continue through Loggerheads to take the right up through Moel Famau country park, and descend to Llanbedr-Dyffryn-Clwyd.

Take a right past St Peter's Church to Llangwyfan, bearing left on the roundabout to Denbigh. Coming out of Denbigh, pick up the B4501 and continue to the crossroads with the B5435 to turn left to Saron and climb over to Cyffylliog and Bontuchel.

Carry on to Ruthin and take the minor road off the square to pass the castle and pick up the A494 briefly. Turn left to Dyffryn Clywd, crossing the A525 to continue to the B5429 and turn right. Continue through Graig-fechan and Pentre-celyn and turn left on to the A525 and up the Nant-y-Garth pass.

At Pen-y-Stryt, turn left on to the A5104 and continue through Rhydtalog. Bear left then left again to pick up the lanes back into Mold to finish.

Useful refreshment stops
Caffi Florence, Loggerheads Country Park, Ruthin Road, Loggerheads CH7 5LH. 01352 810397 www.caffiflorence.co.uk

Y Pantri, 39–41 High Street, Denbigh LL16 3HY. 01745 814276

Ruthin Craft Centre, Park Road, Ruthin LL15 1BB. 01824 704774

Bike shops
The Bike Factory, 153–161 Broughton, Chester, CH3 5BH. 01244 317893

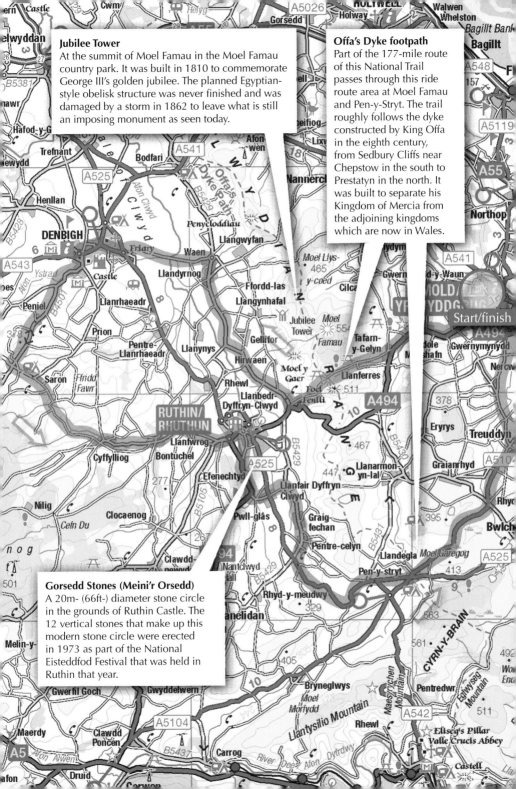

Jubilee Tower
At the summit of Moel Famau in the Moel Famau country park. It was built in 1810 to commemorate George III's golden jubilee. The planned Egyptian-style obelisk structure was never finished and was damaged by a storm in 1862 to leave what is still an imposing monument as seen today.

Offa's Dyke footpath
Part of the 177-mile route of this National Trail passes through this ride route area at Moel Famau and Pen-y-Stryt. The trail roughly follows the dyke constructed by King Offa in the eighth century, from Sedbury Cliffs near Chepstow in the south to Prestatyn in the north. It was built to separate his Kingdom of Mercia from the adjoining kingdoms which are now in Wales.

Gorsedd Stones (Meini'r Orsedd)
A 20m- (66ft-) diameter stone circle in the grounds of Ruthin Castle. The 12 vertical stones that make up this modern stone circle were erected in 1973 as part of the National Eisteddfod Festival that was held in Ruthin that year.

Start/finish

Tayside

Distance: 23 miles (37km)
Big hills: none
Challenge: ●●☆☆☆

A pleasant ride in Tayside, taking in a famous battlefield

Head north from Letham main square, out of the village. At the T-junction, turn left towards Dunnichen. Pass the church on the left and at the T-junction turn left towards Bowriefauld. Take the next left and keep straight ahead to drop down over a bridge to a T-junction.

Turn right, away from the Plash Mill, then left up a short climb to a crossroads. Turn left, signed Guthrie, Friockheim.

Turn right at the T-junction and continue past a sign for West Mains of Gardyne to Conosyth. At the junction with the B961 turn right and continue climbing to Redford. At Redford, pass a left turn and take the first right. Pass the turning to the old quarries on right and take the first left towards Carmyllie.

At the T-junction turn left then right to drop down past Carmyllie Church on the right. At a T-junction turn left, to meet the B961 again. Stop at Milton Haugh Farm Shop to the left, or turn right to continue.

At the crossroads, turn right on to B9128, then first left to East and West Skichen. Continue over the B978 to a T-junction at Holemill to turn right to Whigstreet.

Cross over the B9127 to a T-junction, to turn right and over the old railway line. Follow to a T-junction and turn right toward Craichie. In Craichie turn left towards Bowriefauld, then in Bowriefauld turn left, signed Letham, then immediately right to arrive back in the main square.

Useful refreshment stops

The Hamelt Tearoom, The Square, Letham. 01307 818286

Letham Craft Shop and Tearoom, Auldbar Rd, Letham DD8 2PD. 01307 818448

The Corn Kist Coffee Shop at Milton, Haugh Farm Shop, Carmyllie, Arbroath DD11 2QS. 01241 860579

The Letham Hotel, The Square, Letham DD8 2PZ. 01307 818218 www.letham-hotel.com

The Commercial Inn, The Square, Letham DD8 2PZ. 01307 818245

Bike shops

The Outdoor Store (hire available), 97 East High Street, Forfar DD8 2EQ. 01307 465471

Cycle World, Millfield Feus, Arbroath DD1 2QJ. 01241 876034 www.cycle-world.co.uk

Angus Bike Chain, 29 Commercial St, Arbroath DD11 1NA. 01241 875510

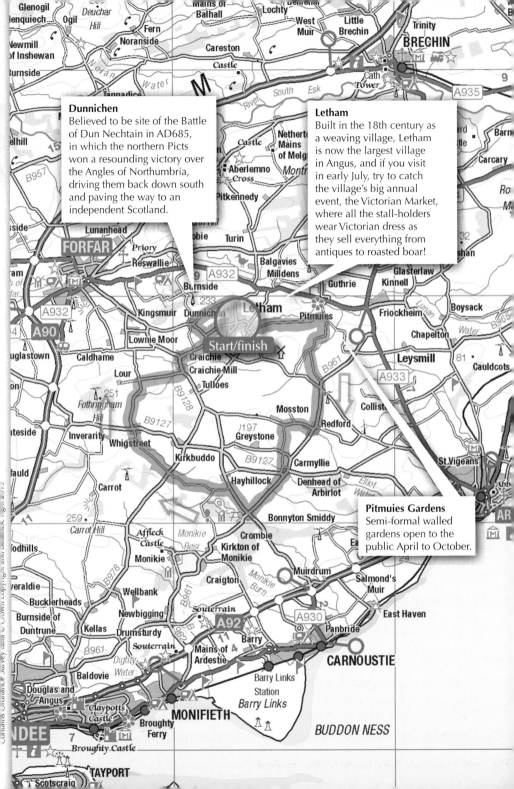

Dunnichen
Believed to be site of the Battle of Dun Nechtain in AD685, in which the northern Picts won a resounding victory over the Angles of Northumbria, driving them back down south and paving the way to an independent Scotland.

Letham
Built in the 18th century as a weaving village, Letham is now the largest village in Angus, and if you visit in early July, try to catch the village's big annual event, the Victorian Market, where all the stall-holders wear Victorian dress as they sell everything from antiques to roasted boar!

Pitmuies Gardens
Semi-formal walled gardens open to the public April to October.

Start/finish

Galloway Forest trails

Distances: Big Country route: 36 miles (58km);
Palgowan trail: 8.7 miles (14km);
The Glen: 3.7 miles (6km); Green Torr: 5.6 miles (9k
Big Hills: 3 **Challenge:** ✪✪✪✪☆

A day-long off-road ride, hidden away in the middle of Galloway Forest

Glentrool is one of the Seven Stanes trail centres ('stane' is Celtic for stone). It's one of the more remote but also the most family-orientated. Four trails guide you round this breathtaking scenery: the Big Country Route is all on fire road or minor roads; the Palgowan trail, green-graded and featuring some 10 per cent singletrack; The Glen, 35 per cent of which is singletrack; and the more technically demanding Green Torr blue trail, with 65 per cent singletrack. The Big Country loop featured here heads south from the visitor centre, contouring round the side of the mammoth hills of Craignaw and Larg Hill, both more than 500m at the summit.

It's gentle going on the Big Country loop and entering the Wood of Cree, the forest (an RSPB nature reserve) closes in around you. The trail turns a corner when it reaches the village of Minnigaff, at the edge of Newton Stewart, crossing the Penkiln Burn river and heading north, climbing through a valley with The Old Edinburgh Road tracing the ridge line to your right and Glenshalloch Hill rising on

Useful refreshment stops
Glentrool Visitor Centre, Glentrool Forest, Nr Newton Stewart, Wigtownshire DG8 6SZ. 01671 840302
www.7stanes.gov.uk
(The café and a visitor centre at the trailhead are closed over winter. Visit the nearby town of Newton Stewart out of season)

Bike shops
The Break Pad (hire available), Kirroughtree, Palnure, Newton Stewart DG8 7BE. 01671 401303
www.thebreakpad.com

your left. It's here that Glentrool overlaps with another of the 7Stanes trail centres – Kirroughtree, the black-graded route meeting the fire road on the Edinburgh Road. While Glentrool is designated a family-orientated centre, Kirroughtree is strictly for experienced mountain bikers – there are rocky trails, jumps and big drops to get the adrenaline flowing.

Look right at point 33 (the trail has constant reference points so you won't get lost) and you'll see Murray's Monument on the hillside. The stone obelisk was erected in honour of Alexander Murray (1775 to 1813), the son of a shepherd, who learnt to read and write by studying the Bible, and eventually went on to become

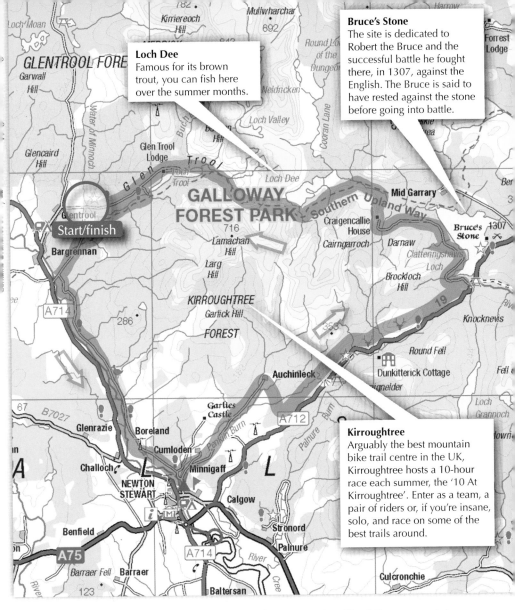

Loch Dee
Famous for its brown trout, you can fish here over the summer months.

Bruce's Stone
The site is dedicated to Robert the Bruce and the successful battle he fought there, in 1307, against the English. The Bruce is said to have rested against the stone before going into battle.

Kirroughtree
Arguably the best mountain bike trail centre in the UK, Kirroughtree hosts a 10-hour race each summer, the '10 At Kirroughtree'. Enter as a team, a pair of riders or, if you're insane, solo, and race on some of the best trails around.

Start/finish

professor of Oriental Languages at Edinburgh University.

The Axe Head Stane Skirting Black Loch is next – a tough climb, up round Poultriebouie Hill and Munwhul. It's well worth the effort, though, since the payoff is a fast descent on the road. Passing Loch Dee on your right, you'll soon come across

the Giant's Axe Head Stane, a vast stone sculpture shaped like a stone-age axe.

Finally, it's back to the trail centre, skirting Loch Trool, after which the centre is named. If that's not enough and you're interested in a gentle introduction to mountain biking, the green trails are well worth a look.

Dumfriesshire

Distance: 26.5 miles (42.6km)
Big hills: 1
Challenge: ⚫⚫☆☆☆

A fine ride around the Dumfriesshire countryside visiting the magnificent Sweetheart Abbey

Beginning in Dumfries, facing the river Nith, beside the Devorgilla Bridge on Whitesands, turn right and follow the road to traffic lights. Turn left on to Galloway Street, go straight through the traffic lights, on to Laurieknowe.

Continue to a fork and bear left onto the A711, follow to a roundabout, taking the first exit and continue to a second roundabout. Take the second exit, cross the A711 on to the No. 7 Cycletrack, bearing right away from the road, to reach a gate.

Turn right on to an old military road, which, after a stiff climb, undulates for approximately three miles through Lochfoot then for another four miles to the hamlet of Milton. Once through Milton, turn left onto a single-track road signposted for Kirkgunzeon.

Follow this for two miles, turn left on to a narrow road and continue to Drumcoltran Tower. The road then undulates through countryside to a junction. Turn right, and continue to the A711 just before Beeswing. Turn left on to the A711, then immediately right on to a minor road signposted New Abbey. The road passes by Loch Arthur Creamery and Loch Arthur and continues for five miles to reach New Abbey at the A710.

Turn right into the village, following the main street to Sweetheart Abbey. After visiting Sweetheart Abbey, return along the A710 through New Abbey, passing Shambellie Wood. The road climbs steeply, then descends, down past Mabie Forest and through the hamlet of Islesteps, the road turning sharp right.

Useful refreshment stops
The Globe Inn, 56 High Street, Dumfries DG1 2JA. 01387 252335 www.globeinndumfries.co.uk

Abbey Cottage Tearoom, Main Street, New Abbey, Dumfries DG2 8BY. 01387 850377 www.abbeycottagetearoom.com

Bike shops
Kirkpatrick Cycles, 13–15 Queen Street, Dumfries DG1 2JG. 01387 254011 www.kirkpatrickcycles.com

The Cycle Centre (hire available), 10–12 Academy Street, Dumfries DG1 1BY. 01387 259483 www.cycle-centre.com

The Shed (hire available), The Steading, Mabie Forest, Dumfries DG2 8HB. 01387 270275 www.cycle-centre.com

Continue along the A710 into Dumfries, turning right into the Pleasance Way, signposted for the A75 Carlisle. Follow this over Troqueer Road on to St Michael's Bridge Road, and descend to a set of traffic lights; turn left on to Whitesands.

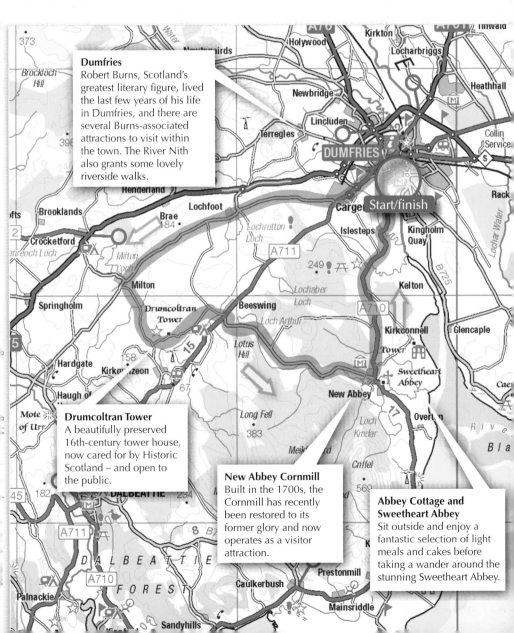

Dumfries
Robert Burns, Scotland's greatest literary figure, lived the last few years of his life in Dumfries, and there are several Burns-associated attractions to visit within the town. The River Nith also grants some lovely riverside walks.

Drumcoltran Tower
A beautifully preserved 16th-century tower house, now cared for by Historic Scotland – and open to the public.

New Abbey Cornmill
Built in the 1700s, the Cornmill has recently been restored to its former glory and now operates as a visitor attraction.

Abbey Cottage and Sweetheart Abbey
Sit outside and enjoy a fantastic selection of light meals and cakes before taking a wander around the stunning Sweetheart Abbey.

Edinburgh and the Forth Bridge

Distance: 25 miles (40km)
Climbs: gentle gradients but no significant climbs
Challenge: ⭐⭐☆☆☆

The Scottish capital is surrounded by great riding. This route heads out on roads and trails to the Forth Rail Bridge

This route follows National Cycle Network routes 1 and 76, which are very clearly signposted all the way to South Queensferry, with excellent maps and further information available at www. sustrans.org.uk.

Starting at Haymarket railway station, turn left out of the station and take the first left down Haymarket Yards to join National Cycle Network 1.

Follow signs to join the traffic-free cycle path. At the junction with Silverknowes Road, cross over onto Silverknowes Drive, then take the first left. Cut through to Cramond Road South and go straight over.

At the T-junction with Barnton Avenue turn right. Keep straight on, past the golf course, to rejoin Barnton Avenue West. At the crossroads go straight on to reach Cramond Old Bridge.

Climb up to the main road, leaving NCN 1 to turn right along NCN 76. Follow the rough road through a gate. Take the second left then right at the crossroads, following route 76 signs all the way up to Dalmeny House then turning right to follow the path round to the front of the house.

Continue straight on, along the coastal path, to South Queensferry. Retrace the route to return to Edinburgh.

Useful refreshment stops
The Rail Bridge Bistro, 4 Newhalls Road, South Queensferry EH30 9TA. 0131 331 1996 www.therailbridgebistro.com
Plus lots of choice in Edinburgh

Bike shops
The Bike Chain, 30 Rodney Street, Edinburgh EH7 4EA. 0131 557 2801 www.thebikechain.co.uk

Edinburgh Bicycle Co-op, 8 Alvanley Terrace, Edinburgh EH9 1DU. 0131 228 3565 www.edinburghbicycle.com

Leith Cycles (hire available), 276 Leith Walk, Edinburgh EH6 5BX. 0131 467 7775 www.leithcycleco.com

Bike Station, 250 Causewayside, Newington, Edinburgh EH9 1UU. 0131 668 1967

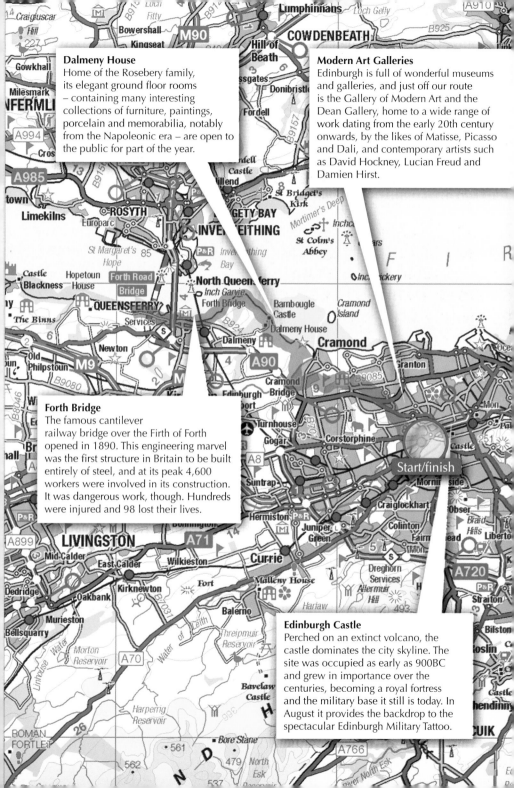

Dalmeny House
Home of the Rosebery family, its elegant ground floor rooms – containing many interesting collections of furniture, paintings, porcelain and memorabilia, notably from the Napoleonic era – are open to the public for part of the year.

Modern Art Galleries
Edinburgh is full of wonderful museums and galleries, and just off our route is the Gallery of Modern Art and the Dean Gallery, home to a wide range of work dating from the early 20th century onwards, by the likes of Matisse, Picasso and Dali, and contemporary artists such as David Hockney, Lucian Freud and Damien Hirst.

Forth Bridge
The famous cantilever railway bridge over the Firth of Forth opened in 1890. This engineering marvel was the first structure in Britain to be built entirely of steel, and at its peak 4,600 workers were involved in its construction. It was dangerous work, though. Hundreds were injured and 98 lost their lives.

Edinburgh Castle
Perched on an extinct volcano, the castle dominates the city skyline. The site was occupied as early as 900BC and grew in importance over the centuries, becoming a royal fortress and the military base it still is today. In August it provides the backdrop to the spectacular Edinburgh Military Tattoo.

Above Glasgow

Distance: 20 miles (32.4km)
Big hills: 1
Challenge: ●●☆☆☆

A fine route of almost entirely traffic-free riding above Glasgow

Beginning from the Stables pub, which overlooks the Forth and Clyde Canal, just outside Kirkintilloch, six miles north of central Glasgow, this is a virtually traffic-free route along towpaths, disused railway lines and the country lanes of East Dunbartonshire.

From The Stables, turn left along the towpath and under the bridge. Continue along the towpath, follow up and over the road at Kirkintilloch and down onto the towpath again on the other side.

At the signpost for Strathkelvin Railway Path and Milton of Campsie, turn left and follow the road to reach a roundabout. Follow signs off the roundabout, through a narrow path and across a road to join the Railway Path proper on the other side.

Follow the path, coming up and over a road briefly at Milton of Campsie, all the way to Strathblane. Leaving the path, turn left on Strathblane Road (A891) to reach the T-junction and turn left again onto Milgarvie Road (A81). Take the first right, Dumbrock Road, then first left up Old

Mugdock Road. At the T-junction turn left, then after 500m turn left again. Take care at the T-junction with the A81, turning right, then quickly left down Craigmaddie Road.

Turn left before the graveyard at Baldernock, right at the T-junction then first left followed by a second right to cross the A807 at Balmore, onto Old Balmore Road. Take the second right, onto a very straight track between fields, narrowing to a path. At the end of the field, curve left then right to cross a metal bridge and follow the path alongside the golf course. Join Cadder Road to reach the canal, then turn left onto the towpath to reach The Stables again.

Useful refreshment stops
The Stables, Glasgow Bridge, Kirkintilloch, Glasgow G66 1RH. 0141 777 6088

Willow Tearooms (the famous tearooms, designed by Charles Rennie Mackintosh, are a few miles away), 217 Sauchiehall Street, Glasgow G2 3EX. 0141 332 0521

Bike shops
Wheelcraft, Unit 4, Aldessan House, Campsie Glen, Glasgow G66 7AB. 01360 312709 www.wheelcraft.net

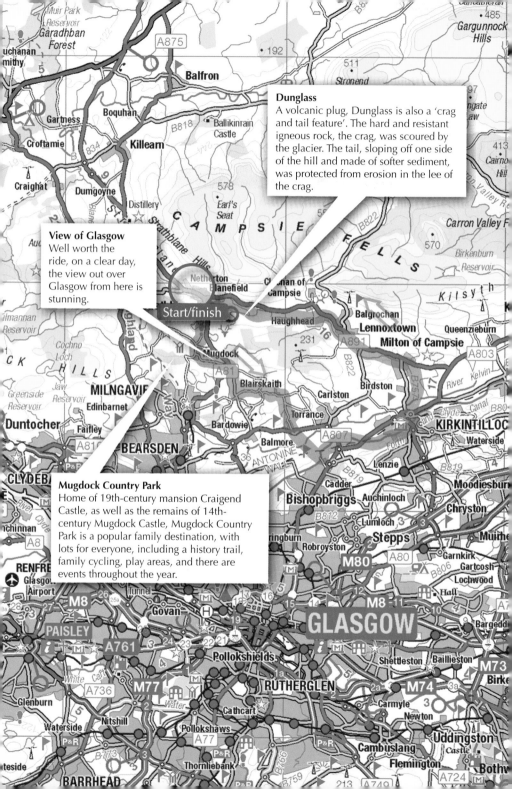

Dunglass
A volcanic plug, Dunglass is also a 'crag and tail feature'. The hard and resistant igneous rock, the crag, was scoured by the glacier. The tail, sloping off one side of the hill and made of softer sediment, was protected from erosion in the lee of the crag.

View of Glasgow
Well worth the ride, on a clear day, the view out over Glasgow from here is stunning.

Start/finish

Mugdock Country Park
Home of 19th-century mansion Craigend Castle, as well as the remains of 14th-century Mugdock Castle, Mugdock Country Park is a popular family destination, with lots for everyone, including a history trail, family cycling, play areas, and there are events throughout the year.

Loch Katrine

Distance: 13 miles (20km)
Big hills: 1
Challenge: ❂❂✩✩✩

A picturesque lochside ride with gently rolling hills in Rob Roy's former stamping ground

This ride involves catching the ferry from Trossachs Pier to the other end of the loch and then cycling the 13 miles back again. The ferry runs every day from April 1 to October 31 (check the website for times). Once you take to your bike from the Pier Café, the route is a very simple one, and a basic route map is available from the boat ticket office.

From the Pier Café follow the road out of the car park until you see some white gates to your right and a small sign indicating 'cycle route this way'. Turn in here and follow the road past houses and over a hill to drop down to the loch on the other side.

Follow straight ahead, cross a small bridge at the head of the loch and continue to follow the road as it now curves to the right, towards Glengyle House. Continue up behind the house and, keeping the loch on your right, follow the road all the way back to the pier.

You can detour down to the lochside at a turning just before a small bridge, where a path is signposted. This will eventually bring you back up onto the road again to continue as above.

Useful refreshment stops

Brenachoile Café, Trossachs Pier, Loch Katrine FK17 8HZ. 01877 376799 www.lochkatrine.com

The Pier Café, Stronachlachar by Loch Katrine, The Trossachs, Stirlingshire. 01877 386374 www.thepiercafe.com

The Forth Inn, Aberfoyle. 01877 382372 www.forthinn.com

Bike shops

Katrinewheelz (hire available), Trossachs Pier, Loch Katrine, By Callander, Stirling FK17 8HZ. 01877 376366 www.katrinewheelz.co.uk

For steamship and cruiser enquiries and general information go to www.lochkatrine.com

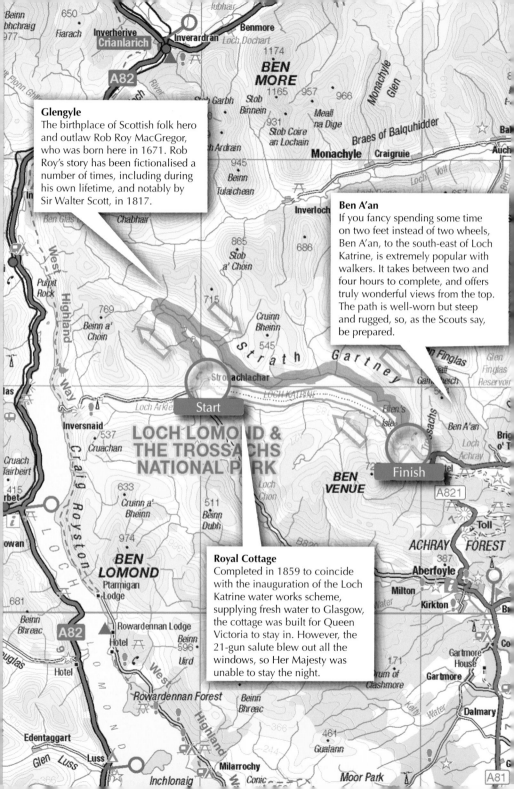

Glengyle
The birthplace of Scottish folk hero and outlaw Rob Roy MacGregor, who was born here in 1671. Rob Roy's story has been fictionalised a number of times, including during his own lifetime, and notably by Sir Walter Scott, in 1817.

Ben A'an
If you fancy spending some time on two feet instead of two wheels, Ben A'an, to the south-east of Loch Katrine, is extremely popular with walkers. It takes between two and four hours to complete, and offers truly wonderful views from the top. The path is well-worn but steep and rugged, so, as the Scouts say, be prepared.

Royal Cottage
Completed in 1859 to coincide with the inauguration of the Loch Katrine water works scheme, supplying fresh water to Glasgow, the cottage was built for Queen Victoria to stay in. However, the 21-gun salute blew out all the windows, so Her Majesty was unable to stay the night.

Start

Finish

LOCH LOMOND & THE TROSSACHS NATIONAL PARK

Great Cumbrae

Distance: 14 miles (23km)
Big hills: 1 (on the inner circuit)
Challenge: ❶☆☆☆☆

A gentle tap around Scotland's most family friendly island with a tougher inland excursion

Great Cumbrae is as easy to reach as it is to cycle around. Just an hour's drive from Glasgow and a 10-minute crossing on the ferry from Largs, the outer loop is a gentle ride and perfect for families and the inner loop offers a little more challenge if you're feeling energetic.

You can't really go wrong with the route as it follows the B-road that tightly hugs the coast throughout and there is only one junction, which you barely register. To all intents and purposes the coast road is a cycle track and, in parts, as rough as one (not that it matters) with the exception of the stretch between Millport and the ferry slip which is plied by the connecting bus service.

Start at Kames Bay just to the east of the centre of Millport, the only settlement on the island, and proceed anti-clockwise around the back of the beach. Follow the road round the bulky south-eastern headland and then head north past Lion Rock. Just across the sea to the south you can see Portencross

Castle and Goldenberry Hill and, next to them, Clydeport freight terminal and the Hunterston marine construction yard and power station, reminders that Great Cumbrae is anything but a far-flung Scottish island. There are lots of natural features and wildlife hereabouts too – including shag, cormorant, eider duck and grey seals.

Follow all the way around the coast road on the B896 and back to Millport, then for the inner loop, when back in

Useful refreshment stops

Shop at National Centre for watersports near the slipway. 01475 530757 www.nationalcentrecumbrae.org.uk

Fintry Bay tearooms in the middle of the west coast of the island. 01475 530426

Other options include The Royal George hotel, fish and chips, Chinese and Indian takeaways and several low-budget restaurants in Millport.

Bike shops

On Your Bike (hire available), Stuart St, Millport. 01475 530300 www.onyourbikemillport.com

Mapes (hire available), Guildford St, Millport. 01475 530444. www.mapesmillport.co.uk

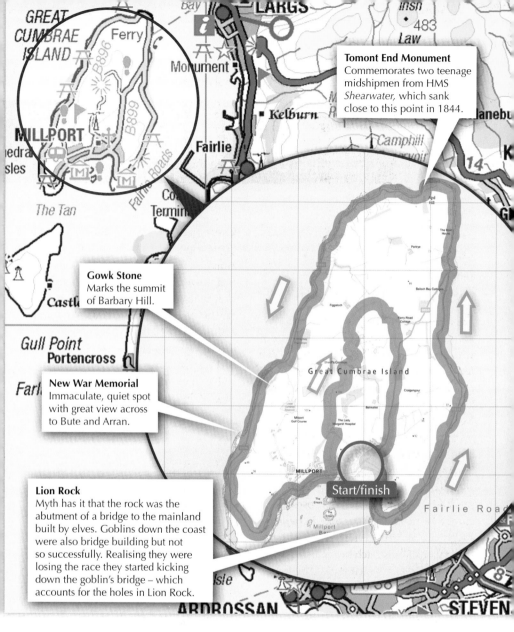

Tomont End Monument
Commemorates two teenage midshipmen from HMS *Shearwater,* which sank close to this point in 1844.

Gowk Stone
Marks the summit of Barbary Hill.

New War Memorial
Immaculate, quiet spot with great view across to Bute and Arran.

Lion Rock
Myth has it that the rock was the abutment of a bridge to the mainland built by elves. Goblins down the coast were also bridge building but not so successfully. Realising they were losing the race they started kicking down the goblin's bridge – which accounts for the holes in Lion Rock.

Start/finish

Millport, continue past the harbour and Garrison House then turn left signed to the cathedral. Once in open country follow the sign to the left indicating a parking spot and viewpoint a mile away. The road takes you up Barbary Hill, a steep little midget with a summit of just 127 metres, but which provides a panorama that is well worth the effort. After the viewpoint follow the road as it bears right at the top of the loop and then back to Kames Bay.

Acknowledgments

Thanks to all the contributors of the ride articles for *Cycling Active*: Aidan, Mike Breckon, David Bradford, Martin Burton, Anthony Butler, Chris Catchpole, Avril Charlton, Graham Charlton, Rebecca Charlton, Gary Coltman, Penny Comins, Bryony Costin, Janet Coulson, Jamie Darlow, Maria David, Derri Dunn, Luke Edwardes-Evans, Jonathan Emery, Keith Fergus, Rupert Fowler, Max Glaskin, Cath Harris, Aimee Hart, Aodan Higgins, Adam Holder, Tom Hutton, William Irwin, Andy Jones, Andy Kay, Paul Kirkwood, Andrew Knight, Matt Lamy, Matthew Levett, Andrew McCandlish, Andy McGrath, Brian McNea, Nick Rearden, Simon Richardson, Rick Robson, Sandy Sehmi, Kaj Scarsbrook, Simon Scarsbrook Phoebe Sneddon, James Shrubsall, Chris Sidwells, Simon Smythe, Ben Spurrier, Callum Tomsett, Patrick Trainor, Matthew Tugwell, Simon Warren, Andy Waterman.

The rides in the book were originally published in *Cycling Active* between September 2009 and November 2012. Every effort has been made to verify and update all information but it is strongly advised to plan ahead and check opening times of cafés and pubs and availability of bike hire.

Photography © Andy Jones except front cover (bottom) © cymru / Alamy

First published in March 2013

A catalogue record for this book is available from the British Library

ISBN 978 0 85733 358 2

Published by Haynes Publishing,
Sparkford, Yeovil, Somerset BA22 7JJ, UK
Tel: 01963 442030 Fax: 01963 440001
Int. tel: +44 1963 442030 Int. fax: +44 1963 440001
E-mail: sales@haynes.co.uk
Website: www.haynes.co.uk

Haynes North America Inc.,
861 Lawrence Drive, Newbury Park,
California 91320, USA

Designed and typeset by Neil Baber www.neilbaber.co.uk

Printed and bound in the USA by Odcombe Press LP,
1299 Bridgestone Parkway, La Vergne, TN 37086